T0301741

DIGITIZATION IN SUPPLY CHAIN MANAGEMENT
Trends, Challenges and Solutions

Trends, Challenges and Solutions in Contemporary Supply Chain Management

ISSN: 2737-5390

Series Editors: Steven Carnovale, *Florida Atlantic University, USA*
Sengun Yeniyurt, *Rutgers University, USA*

Published

Trends, Challenges and
Solutions in Contemporary
Supply Chain Management
Volume 2

DIGITIZATION IN SUPPLY CHAIN MANAGEMENT
Trends, Challenges and Solutions

editors

Sengun Yeniyurt
Rutgers Business School, USA

Steven Carnovale
Florida Atlantic University, USA

World Scientific

NEW JERSEY · LONDON · SINGAPORE · BEIJING · SHANGHAI · HONG KONG · TAIPEI · CHENNAI · TOKYO

Published by

World Scientific Publishing Co. Pte. Ltd.

5 Toh Tuck Link, Singapore 596224

USA office: 27 Warren Street, Suite 401-402, Hackensack, NJ 07601

UK office: 57 Shelton Street, Covent Garden, London WC2H 9HE

Library of Congress Cataloging-in-Publication Data

Names: Yeniyurt, Sengun, editor. | Carnovale, Steven, editor.

Title: Digitization in supply chain management : trends, challenges and solutions /
    editors, Sengun Yeniyurt, Rutgers Business School, USA,
    Steven Carnovale, Florida Atlantic University, USA.

Description: New Jersey : World scientific, [2024] | Series: Trends, challenges and
    solutions in contemporary supply chain management, 2737-5390 ; vol 2 |
    Includes bibliographical references and index.

Identifiers: LCCN 2023053670 | ISBN 9789811286629 (hardcover) |
    ISBN 9789811286636 (ebook) | ISBN 9789811286643 (ebook other)

Subjects: LCSH: Business logistics. | Industrial management--Technological innovations. |
    Information technology--Management.

Classification: LCC HD38.5 .D5454 2024 | DDC 658.5--dc23/eng/20231117

LC record available at https://lccn.loc.gov/2023053670

British Library Cataloguing-in-Publication Data

A catalogue record for this book is available from the British Library.

For any available supplementary material, please visit
https://www.worldscientific.com/worldscibooks/10.1142/13686#t=suppl

Desk Editors: Nimal Koliyat/Lum Pui Yee

Typeset by Stallion Press
Email: enquiries@stallionpress.com

Printed in Singapore

© 2024 World Scientific Publishing Company
https://doi.org/10.1142/9789811286636_fmatter

About the Editors

Sengun Yeniyurt, PhD, is a Professor and the Vice Dean for Academic Programs and Learning Assurance at Rutgers Business School. He is also the Co-Editor-in-Chief of Rutgers Business Review (RBR). Professor Shen Yeniyurt was the Chair of the Marketing Department from 2020 to 2022. He is the founding Co-Editor-in-Chief of Rutgers Business Review (founded 2016) and the founding Co-Director of the Center for Market Advantage (founded 2015). He served as the Vice-Chair of the Marketing Department from 2019 to 2020 and the Vice-Chair of the Supply Chain Management and Marketing Sciences Department from 2012 to 2013. He also served as the founding Academic Co-Director of the New Brunswick Undergraduate Program in Supply Chain and Marketing Sciences from 2008 to 2013. Shen has an outstanding interdisciplinary research record across multiple disciplines at RBS. He was the recipient of the Rutgers Business School Dean's Research Professorship in 2019 and was a Rutgers University Chancellor's Scholar (2016–2018). He was also the recipient of the Best Marketing Professor by the Rutgers Business Governing Association in 2011.

 **Steven Carnovale**, PhD, is an Associate Professor of Supply Chain Management at the College of Business at Florida Atlantic University and the Co-Editor-in-Chief of the *Journal of Purchasing and Supply Management*. Dr Carnovale is a supply chain strategist specializing in interfirm networks, risk management and global sourcing/production networks. He is an Associate Editor at the *Journal of Supply Chain Management*. His research has appeared in the *Journal of Supply Chain Management*, the *Journal of Business Logistics*, the *Journal of Purchasing and Supply Management*, the *Journal of International Business Studies*, the *International Journal of Production Economics*, the *European Journal of Operational Research* and *Annals of Operations Research* among others. Dr Carnovale earned his BS and PhD degrees at Rutgers University, specializing in Supply Chain Management and Marketing Sciences. Dr Carnovale is a frequent speaker at both academic and professional supply chain meetings on topics related to supply networks and analytics, with a specific focus on how firms can use these concepts to generate enhanced visibility and financial performance within their supply chains and extended enterprises.

Contents

https://doi.org/10.1142/9789811286636_0001

CHAPTER 1

Framing Digitalization and Supply Chain Management

Sengun Yeniyurt[*,‡] and Steven Carnovale[†,§]

Rutgers Business School, New Brunswick, NJ
†*Florida Atlantic University, College of Business, Boca Raton, FL*
‡*yeniyurt@business.rutgers.edu*
§*scarnovale@fau.edu*

In late 2022 and early 2023, Open AI unleashed their "ChatGPT" large language model, and in the six months since then and at the writing of this chapter, the development of its capabilities, power, and scope have grown truly exponentially. While this example is not explicitly related to supply chain management, the potential for generative AI, large language models, and other digitalization technology(ies) have immeasurable potential for supply chain management applications. In recent years, the Internet of Things (IoT), Industry 4.0 (I4.0), blockchain technology, increases in computing power, and a transition to cloud-based architecture combine to enable transitioning away from legacy data-sharing standards (e.g., electronic data interchange) and have opened up the ability for real-time sharing of bilateral data between supply chain partners, facilitating true real-time information sharing. The question then becomes, how do we navigate it? Questions such as these are not trivial when recent industry reports indicate that over 50% of companies surveyed do not yet have a plan or roadmap in place for their digital supply chain transformation,[1] with recent estimates indicating that

---

[1]https://www.gartner.com/en/supply-chain/topics/supply-chain-digital-transformation.

the size of the digital supply chain market, in 2020, was approximately $3.91 billion with forecasts indicating that it may exceed $13 billion by 2030.[2]

Compounding the issues relating to the scale, size, and overall expansiveness of the "digitized supply chain" is the scope of functional areas that supply chain management touches (e.g., sourcing and procurement, manufacturing and production, warehousing and outbound/return delivery of products and services), all of which is compounded by recent macroeconomic pressures as well as geopolitical tension (e.g., global conflicts, trade wars, sanctions and import tariffs/taxes, pandemics). The combination of these factors has led to the need for this book and likely much more work on this area. So, we offer the following compilation of material to explore the dynamics of digital supply chains from an academic perspective, highlighting various critical areas of applications and solutions to pressing challenges.

Each chapter provides a different perspective of how digital technologies can and are transforming the supply chain and operations management. The book discusses a variety of digital technologies, from the IoT to artificial intelligence, and from blockchain technologies to autonomous mobile robots, utilizing real work examples and in-depth discussions of their advantages as well as drawbacks.

The first chapter, after this introduction, focuses on the effect of digital transformation on supply chain relationships. The authors explain the changes that I4.0 technologies are bringing to the industry and specifically to supply chain management. The authors discuss both the advantages and disadvantages that such technologies provide for supply chain management and supply chain relationships. Further, the authors discuss the effect of information technologies on supply chain agility. This chapter provides a solid grounding of the key role that digitization will play in the high-tech supply chains of the future.

The second chapter focuses on supply chain risk management. The author explains the importance of supply chain mapping and visualization for risk management. He also discusses the IoT, big data analytics, artificial intelligence, and blockchain technologies. The chapter also provides an in-depth overview of the importance of risk monitoring. Now, more than ever, firms require visualization in order to appropriately manage their supply chains and to mitigate the potentially detrimental effects of disruptions. This

---

[2]https://www.helpnetsecurity.com/2022/03/04/digital-supply-chain-2030/.

is particularly poignant as recent industry estimates suggest that 85% of disruptions arise from Tier 2 and beyond.[3]

The third chapter focuses on blockchain, explaining the basics of the technology and how it is being used in supply chain management. The authors explain the distributed ledger technology, proof of work and mining, proof of stake, tokens, coins, gas, and hashing algorithms. They also discuss serialization and non-fungibility and provide a brief history of the evolution of blockchain technologies. Further, the chapter indicates various benefits that blockchain technologies provide for supply chain management, such as security, recalls, and counterfeit prevention. The utilization of blockchain technologies across different industries is also explained. This is a critical area for future exploration, and this chapter provides a solid grounding and context for future work.

Then, the fourth chapter continues the discussion of blockchain technologies by focusing on their utilization to improve supply chain resilience. Supply chain resiliency has significantly increased in importance over the last few years and companies are continuing to invest in methods and technologies that further increase the resiliency of their operations. This chapter first introduces the traditional supply chain management data structures and its effect on resiliency and then develops a new approach that is based on blockchain technologies. Further, the chapter discusses the effect of blockchain technologies on resiliency utilizing two real-world case studies. As geopolitical tensions rise alongside the natural disasters and other threats, this chapter provides a critical context and strategies for firms to employ to increase resilience.

The fifth chapter discusses the adoption of blockchain technologies by the African maritime industry. The authors provide an overview of the digitalization trends in the maritime industry by focusing on the benefits of digital technologies. Next, the authors reveal some recent challenges faced by the global maritime industry, such as the negative effects of COVID-19 on maritime tourism and shipping. The chapter also explains the current digital transformation trends in the global maritime industry and explain where the African maritime industry stands in this transformation. The authors also discuss the challenges and opportunities provided by blockchain technologies to the African maritime industry and provide some recommendations and highlight the advantages of the use of blockchain in this context.

[3]https://www.resilinc.com/solutions/multi-tier-mapping/.

The penultimate chapter covers the role of digital transformation in the healthcare industry by focusing on optimizing the supply chain operations in a hospital setting. The authors provide an in-depth case study of the digital transformation principles applied to the surgery processes at a private hospital in Switzerland and show how digital twins and artificial intelligence algorithms can be utilized to optimize hospital operations. As a result, the hospital improved its performance, minimizing costs and saving time. Time-invariant lessons, complimented with digital technology is at the heart of this chapter, and the book overall.

The final chapter explains how autonomous mobile robots can be utilized in warehousing and distribution. The chapter explains the growth trends in autonomous mobile robots, provides a literature review of the extant literature regarding this topic, and provides an overview of different theoretical perspectives that can be used to investigate this phenomenon. Next, the authors provide a detailed overview of the benefits of this technology as well as the barriers to its adoption. The chapter also provides several real-world examples of the adoption of this new technology.

Thematically, these chapters represent a modest attempt to start the exploration into the digitalization of the supply chain, but there is much more work to do. We encourage scholars to study these topics and continue to add their own brick to the wall of knowledge to which we, humbly, hope to contribute.

https://doi.org/10.1142/9789811286636_0002

CHAPTER 2

Digital Supply Chains: Industry 4.0 from a Supply Chain Relationship Perspective

Honey Zimmerman[*,¶], George A. Zsidisin[†,||],
and Florian Schupp[‡,§,**]

*College of Business and Technology, Western Illinois University,
Macomb, Illinois, USA
†Supply Chain Management, John W. Barriger III,
University of Missouri, St. Louis, Missouri, USA
‡School of Business, Social and Decision Sciences,
Constructor University, Bremen, Germany
§Schaeffler Automotive Bühl, Bühl, Germany
¶hm-zimmerman@wiu.edu
||gzsidisin@umsl.edu
**Florian.Schupp@schaeffler.com

Abstract

Supply chains cannot operate today without information technology (IT). Although IT is critical for effectively and efficiently managing supply chains, it is well-established that the crux of supply chain management concerns the relationships formed between and among firms that form the interorganizational structures which provide the products and services to the final consumer. Hence, we need to recognize how evolving technologies align with and support supply chain relationships. This chapter provides a high-level perspective of the role digitalization has in supply chain management and specifically with supply chain relationships.

Keywords: Industry 4.0 technology; I4.0; Digitalization; Buyer-supplier relationships; Supply chain agility; Supply chain integration.

Introduction

Supply chains today are heavily reliant on information technologies and information systems for greater competitiveness and success. Without information technology (IT), the level of supply chain integration and collaboration among businesses that exist today would not be possible (Arcidiacono *et al.*, 2019; Schupp & Wöhner, 2017). IT allows for complex and large amounts of data to be exchanged among supply chain partners. Additionally, it increases visibility throughout the entire supply chain with real-time sharing of information. The alignment of IT platforms across supply chain partners is critical to their responsiveness of the changing market environments (Kim *et al.*, 2013). IT, in general, has had a major influence on the development of supply chain management.

The purpose of this chapter is to provide a high-level perspective of the role IT has in supply chain management and specifically with supply chain relationships. Based on recent literature, we will first introduce IT in terms of its current state of Industry 4.0 (I4.0). We then provide an overview of buyer–supplier relationships, and how current technologies affect those relationships. As we have recently learned during COVID-19, supply chains need to be able to quickly adapt, and hence we introduce the concept of supply chain agility, and then unravel the intersection of I4.0 and supply chain agility.

Progression of Technology

Throughout history, the progression of technology created four major paradigm shifts in manufacturing. The first industrial revolution was the era of mechanical power marked by the discovery of steam power in the 18th century, and the second industrial revolution was characterized by the innovation of mass production and electrical power. The third industrial revolution dawned the era of computerization or the "digital revolution" around the 1970s. We are currently in the fourth industrial revolution, often referred to as I4.0, which is differentiated by the integration of information and industrial technologies (Ben-Daya *et al.*, 2019).

For decades, technology has enabled us to exchange information easier, both internally and externally among organizations. Barrett and Konsynski (1982) state, *the interchange of information, whether subtle or concrete, forms the basis of all organizational activity* (p. 93). The first *external* integration system was electronic data interchange (EDI) in the 1960s and 1970s. It significantly changed how organizations conducted business within the supply chain. Numerous studies focus on the phenomena surrounding this external integration (Schubert & Legner, 2011), which has continued to evolve over the years. The internet intensified electronic collaboration with the emergence of e-commerce and e-business applications. Buyers and suppliers worldwide began to share information and conduct transactions electronically. Additionally, stand-alone supplier relationship management (SRM) applications, as well as customer relationship management (CRM) applications, have further developed to provide higher levels of functionality to manage external relationships (Richey *et al.*, 2010). The evolution of technology is in a constant state of change.

I4.0 technologies such as artificial intelligence (AI), robotics, the Internet of Things (IoT), and data analytics are among the top reported technology trends in the supply chain and logistics industry (Arcidiacono *et al.*, 2019; Robinson, 2020). These technologies are among those that distinguish I4.0. More specifically, Stentoft *et al.* (2019) proposed 12 technologies that comprise I4.0: big data analytics, autonomous robots, simulation, horizontal, and vertical system integration, the IoT (including sensors), cyber security, the cloud, additive manufacturing, augmented reality, artificial intelligence (AI), mobile technologies, and radiofrequency identification (RFID) and real-time location systems (RTLS) technologies. However, Culot *et al.* (2020) note how there remains ongoing confusion between I4.0 and similar concepts such as digitalization.

Digitalization refers to the *many domains of social life [that] are restructured around digital communication and media infrastructures,* as opposed to *digitization*, which is the actual *process of converting analog streams of information into digital bits* (Brennen & Kreiss, 2016, p. 1). Furthermore, the "digital age" or "digital era" are more generic terms used to describe the world in which we live today. The digital age is often also called the information age, which started in the 1970s. The Cambridge Dictionary defines the digital age as, "the present time, when most information is in a digital form, especially when compared to the time when computers were not used" (Digital Age, 2019).

The aforementioned confusion noted by Culot *et al.* (2020) is, in part, due to a lack of consistency regarding the specific technologies and applications included in I4.0 research. Additionally, the list of technologies is continually growing. There is limited empirical research on these particular topics as they apply to the management of supply chains (Handfield, 2017), likely due to their novelty.

The basis of I4.0 is the adoption of these technologies to gather and analyze data in real time, which provides valuable information for decision-making (Frank *et al.*, 2019). According to Frank *et al.* (2019), I4.0 was first coined in 2011 in Germany as an initiative between their federal government, universities, and private companies to develop advanced production systems. There are four technologies that Frank *et al.* (2019) refer to as "base technologies" for I4.0 because they provide the underlying intelligence and connectivity for more advanced I4.0 technologies. These include big data, data analytics, the cloud, and IoT. The layer of base technologies *enable the I4.0 concept* (p. 16).

There are a few primary driving forces behind I4.0: the accelerating growth of data, the greater need for more advanced analysis of this data, the heightened prevalence of human-to-machine and machine-to-machine interactions, and the advancement of industrial technologies such as robotics and additive manufacturing (Sader *et al.*, 2019). There is still much to be learned about the benefits that I4.0 technologies have on firm performance, as well as the adoption and implementation of such technologies (Culot *et al.*, 2020) and potential negative effects that may occur.

Outcomes of I4.0 Technologies

I4.0 technologies facilitate greater connectivity and integration within the supply chain and accelerate collection and analysis of vast amounts of data for improved performance. These technologies enable firms to have flexible manufacturing, improve strategic and operational decision-making, increase productivity, improve efficiency and utilization of resources, and adapt more quickly to changes in the market (Dalenogare *et al.*, 2018). The advantages of I4.0 technologies are classified into three categories: horizontal integration, vertical integration, and end-to-end integration. In this context, horizontal integration refers to the *integration of firms within the supply chain* (e.g., suppliers and customers). Vertical integration is defined as the *integration within a firm* between the organization's different hierarchical levels, functional areas, and business units. End-to-end integration, also called end-to-end engineering, is the overall *integration through the complete value chain of a product*, from product design to post-sale (Sader *et al.*, 2019). In other words, a considerable advantage of I4.0 is the ability to facilitate integration between many echelons.

It is also important to recognize that there could be some negative consequences and risks to digitalization, and more specifically, I4.0 technology implementation. First, new technologies may pose a threat to established and current technologies and/or those that utilize such technologies. For example, the creation of new digital business models could be problematic for established organizations, depleting the relevance of old business models, disrupting the interactions between supply chain partners or within supply chain networks (Trittin-Ulbrich *et al.*, 2021). Additionally, digital inequalities exist in I4.0 technologies such as artificial intelligence and big data across cultures. Small to medium-sized enterprises and firms in emerging countries seem to face more significant barriers to implement the use of I4.0 and possess lower I4.0 readiness than large companies (Stentoft *et al.*, 2019).

Another potential downfall is the steep learning curve that often accompanies new technologies and technology acceptance (or lack thereof) by employees. Goodwin-Sak *et al.* (2019) suggest that employees must perceive that technology is necessary in order for successful adoption. In other words, the technology needs to solve a problem or address an issue that current technology cannot. The mentality of "if it isn't broke, don't fix it" creates resistance to accepting the new technology. Additionally, they found that organizational culture is an important influence on technology adoption, stating that an organization with (p. 14) is more likely to realize successful adoption by their workforce. Lastly, and most importantly, security is a major concern for companies seeking to implement I4.0 technologies, such as cloud services. The risk of intellectual property theft, data breaches, and system hacks are major concerns of organizations today (Gaudenzi *et al.*, 2018). Cyber security risks in supply chains are becoming more and more evident globally as attacks of this nature are not uncommon in today's digital environment unfortunately.

Alignment of IT platforms across supply chain partners is a critical factor in responsiveness to changing market environments (Kim *et al.*, 2013). Continuously advancing technology and information-sharing is enabling supply chains around the globe to thrive and become more sophisticated and responsive. Competition is no longer between individual firms, rather one supply chain against another, and IT is a major driving force that enables this to happen so efficiently and effectively.

Buyer–Supplier Relationships

Scholars have studied the relationship between buyers and suppliers in great depth, grounded in various theories. For example, researchers have studied buyer–supplier relationships (BSR) through the theoretical lens of relational exchange theory (Zaheer *et al.*, 1998), relational view (Whipple *et al.*, 2015), the resource-based view (Squire *et al.*, 2009), resource dependence (Schmitz *et al.*, 2016), and social capital (Villena *et al.*, 2011). However, the most common theoretical perspectives adopted in BSR research are based on the social exchange theory (Nyaga *et al.*, 2010) and transaction cost economics (Autry & Golicic, 2010).

Research also shows that collaborative BSR provide extensive benefits. Such benefits include a high level of commitment (Ring & Van de Ven, 1994), loyalty (Prahinski & Fan, 2007), greater integration and information-sharing (Wagner & Bode, 2014), market responsiveness (Narayanan *et al.*, 2015), operational performance (Delbufalo, 2012), agility (Narayanan *et al.*, 2015), innovation sharing (Wagner & Bode, 2014), synchronization of the supply chain, knowledge exchange (Vanpoucke *et al.*, 2014), positive financial performance (e.g., ROI, sales growth, cash flow) (Delbufalo, 2012), and product and service quality (Jack & Powers, 2015), many of which have been found to lead to greater competitive advantage (Monczka *et al.*, 1998). This list is not comprehensive, as there is significant research on the benefits of collaborative buyer–supplier relationships. Critical factors in promoting collaborative BSR include, but are not limited to, quality and frequency of communication (Paulraj *et al.*, 2008), common goals (Wilson, 1995), technological preparedness (Jack & Powers, 2015), and trust (Bachmann & Inkpen, 2011).

Information-exchange mode as a dimension of BSR refers to the interaction patterns of organizations (Hoque & Rana, 2020). Information-sharing has been shown to positively impact commitment and trust (Nyaga *et al.*, 2010), and perceived trustworthiness between organizations was correlated to greater information sharing in BSR (Cheng *et al.*, 2008). Many scholars agree that information exchange facilitates collaboration in BSR, and a collaborative BSR involves the sharing, exchange, or co-development of information, products, and technologies (Hoque & Rana, 2020). It is important to note that I4.0 technologies are also reported to enhance information exchange.

Effects of Advanced Technology on Relationships

Relationships within and across organizations of a supply chain facilitate knowledge sharing and integration, which in turn enhances the ability of supply chains to be responsive, agile, and resilient (Kim *et al.*, 2013). IT extends enterprises, promotes alliances, and directly connects buyer and supplier organizations throughout the supply chain network (Pagani & Pardo, 2017). An organization's technological capability can certainly have a positive effect on collaboration with external partners (Sanders & Premus, 2005).

Technological advancements enable greater collaboration across firms, but likewise buyer–supplier-specific relationships rely heavily on trust and cooperation (Zaheer *et al.*, 1998). Business relationships are ultimately based on interactions between people within the organizations (Gligor & Holcomb, 2013). Research streams about communication channels inspired the generation of the media richness theory (Daft & Lengel, 1983), the social presence theory (Short *et al.*, 1976), and the theory of media synchronicity (Dennis & Valacich, 1999).

An earlier study by Leek *et al.* (2003) investigated the assumption that moving away from face-to-face interactions, and even audio communication (e.g., telephone), to more email- and internet-based exchanges would result in more task-oriented transactions, less compromise, less personal interaction (e.g., e-commerce), and ultimately, less trust. In turn, it was expected that relationships would become more formal, detached, and challenging to manage. However, majority of the buyers and suppliers that participated in the study did not agree with the researchers' expectations. Instead, the participants felt the new technology allowed them to form new relationships, create more communication channels and more frequent interactions (albeit more IT-based), and enhance the speed and accuracy of the interactions with supply chain partners (Leek *et al.*, 2003). These findings are important since I4.0 technologies allow for increased machine-to-machine communication, reduce the need for human intervention, and lessen human-to-human interaction.

Previous studies have found that IT alignment is key to a successful strategic collaboration between the supply chain partners (Vanpoucke *et al.*, 2017). Suppliers are also more willing to invest in a relationship, including technology, with a customer firm when trust and communication are present in the BSR (Zhang *et al.*, 2015). Some studies have found that dedicated investments, which are those committed to a relationship with a specific buyer or supplier (Heide & John, 1990), lead to trust (Ganesan, 1994). While other studies found that investment does not significantly impact trust in the BSR, they also suggested that suppliers are more likely to commit to relationships with buyers who are engaged in a greater exchange of information (Nyaga *et al.*, 2010). Similarly, research indicates that effective use of technology is an essential criterion for a successful BSR collaboration (Ramanathan *et al.*, 2011).

Supply Chain Agility

Scholarly research on "organizational agility" dates back to the late 1990s within the context of manufacturing; however, studies regarding agility within supply chains did not start until around 2000 (Fayezi *et al.*, 2017). Although some researchers and practitioners use the terms flexibility and agility interchangeably, many scholars argue that supply chain flexibility and supply chain agility are discrete capabilities (Fayezi *et al.*, 2015; Gligor *et al.*, 2013; Swafford *et al.*, 2006).

Fayezi *et al.* (2015) define supply chain agility as a *strategic* ability to sense and respond to internal or external uncertainties, whereas supply chain flexibility is more of an *operational* capability to efficiently change in response to those uncertainties. Flexibility is generally related to internal aspects of an organization, whereas agility is related more toward its external aspects (Gligor *et al.*, 2013). Research indicates that supply chain flexibility directly and positively affects supply chain agility (Swafford *et al.*, 2008). Many scholars suggest that flexibility is an important antecedent of supply chain agility (Braunscheidel & Suresh, 2009). However, Gligor *et al.* (2013) concluded that flexibility is one of the *dimensions* of supply chain agility. Their multidisciplinary approach found five dimensions of firm supply chain agility (FSCA): alertness, accessibility, decisiveness, swiftness, and flexibility (Gligor *et al.*, 2013).

Alertness, defined as the ability to quickly detect changes, opportunities, and threats (Gligor *et al.*, 2013), was first posited as a distinct dimension of FSCA by Li *et al.* (2008). Alertness is displayed by the prompt recognition of changes in both the direct supply chain and the surrounding environment, while also discerning emergent market trends and anticipating disruptions (Li *et al.*, 2008). Once an organization is aware of a potential change, it must access relevant, real-time information to proceed with an agile response, which is the second dimension of FSCA, accessibility. The third dimension, decisiveness, is the ability to make decisions with resolve, which includes coming up with potential options, selecting the best option, and responding to the change accordingly. Gligor *et al.* (2013) posit these three dimensions as the cognitive part of FSCA, whereas the last two dimensions — swiftness and flexibility — are considered the physical dimensions of FSCA. Swiftness is defined as the ability to execute decisions *quickly*, whereas flexibility is the ability to adapt tactics and operations as needed. From their study, Gligor *et al.* (2013) formed a more comprehensive definition for FSCA:

> *A firm's supply chain agility is manifested through the firm's cognitive and physical capabilities that enable the firm to quickly detect changes, opportunities, and threats (alertness), access relevant data (accessibility), make resolute decisions on how to act (decisiveness), quickly implement decisions (swiftness), and modify its range of supply chain tactics and operations to the extent needed to implement the firm's strategy (flexibility).* (p. 102)

Prior research has found that agility is the central trait of the "best" supply chains (Lee, 2004). Furthermore, previous studies have found that IT integration affects supply chain flexibility, resulting in a higher supply chain agility, which suggests that investing in IT integration with supply chain partners builds agility (Swafford *et al.*, 2008).

I4.0 and Firm Supply Chain Agility

Large organizations, in particular, are implementing I4.0 technologies in the current global business environment because of the versatility of applications and the scope of benefits. Some large corporations, such as Coca-Cola, General Electric, Toyota, and Amazon, have been leveraging I4.0 technologies for several years now (Lee, 2015). Such sophisticated IT solutions exist to support daily operations, drive operational efficiency, and deliver greater value to the customer at a new level in today's fast-paced business environment (Gates & Bremicker, 2017). However, the problem revealed through anecdotal evidence suggests only a few companies have implemented I4.0 technologies enterprise wide. The most significant value of I4.0 will be achieved when an end-to-end I4.0 environment is realized. Much of the I4.0 technology adoption is "focused on solving a pain point … [in which] projects tend to be isolated, of limited scope, and driven through functional silos" (Gates & Bremicker, 2017, p. 5).

One likely reason why more companies have not adopted I4.0 technologies on a grander scale is that the return on investment is neither clear enough to quantify nor is it easy to justify its investment (Gates & Bremicker, 2017). It takes significant resources to implement a new technology — not just financial capital, but also human capital with the time and training required. It is essential to have a clear idea of the potential economic and non-financial returns of such an investment.

In addition to having potential financial implications, reported examples of non-financial benefits of I4.0 include better information, real-time data, improved decision-making, superior product or service quality, enhanced responsiveness, increased customer satisfaction, enhanced supplier relationships, and greater collaboration with supply chain partners (Gates & Bremicker, 2017).

Scholars have studied the relationship between IT and supply chain management, specifically buyer–supplier relationships (BSR), from many different perspectives (Pagani & Pardo, 2017). Scholars have also studied the importance of relationships among supply chain partners to firm performance across multiple disciplines, including marketing, management, information systems, operations management, and supply chain management (Swanson *et al.*, 2018). Most research on this topic has focused on how relational factors, such as trust, commitment, and communication, contribute to positive outcomes within interorganizational relationships, including market responsiveness, operational performance, and agility (Narayanan *et al.*, 2015).

With a specific focus on agility, Narayanan *et al.* (2015) found that collaboration is positively associated with agility performance in a BSR. The impact of collaboration on agility is mediated by trust. Additionally, they found that collaboration positively moderates the effect of trust on agility performance in a BSR. Therefore, we recognized there is a positive association between BSR and agility. However, it is not clear if or what influence I4.0 technology has on that association.

Conclusion

Understanding how technology affects business relationships and firm performance is an ongoing process as technology evolves. Companies seek to justify significant investments into capital-intensive technology, and stakeholders want to know that there is a return on investment for such technology. The productivity gains are not yet clear. The relative novelty of I4.0 means that scholarly research so far has minimally investigated these specific technologies and how they affect business relationships and supply chain agility. More research needs to investigate the alignment among strategy and digital technologies (Arcidiacono *et al.*, 2019), as well as the influence of organizational culture on technology adoption (Goodwin-Sak *et al.*, 2019). As technology continues to advance, the list of I4.0 technologies will keep growing; therefore, ongoing research will need to expand to include the latest and most advanced technologies.

During the COVID-19 pandemic, we were able to see first-hand how information technologies were able to support and sustain our societies — albeit with a few setbacks here and there. Technology only advances, and our current I4.0 systems will be considered antiquated in a century from today (and most likely much sooner). What remains constant is the need for firms to adapt to ever-changing environments to survive in the long term — to be agile in seizing new opportunities, as well as averting problems in their supply chains. However, individual firms cannot do it alone, not today nor in the future. Therefore, the key summative takeaway from this chapter is that we need to recognize how evolving technologies such as I4.0 align with and support supply chain relationships and likewise, how relationships can influence technology. We hope this chapter sets the tone for the remainder of this book and ultimately advances the discussion of the role of I4.0 in supply chain agility and relationships.

References

Arcidiacono, F., Ancarani, A., Di Mauro, C., & Schupp, F. (2019). Where the rubber meets the road. Industry 4.0 among SMEs in the automotive sector. *IEEE Engineering Management Review*, **47**(4), 86–93.

Autry, C. W., & Golicic, S. L. (2010). Evaluating buyer–supplier relationship–performance spirals: A longitudinal study. *Journal of Operations Management*, **28**(2), 87–100. https://doi.org/10.1016/j.jom.2009.07.003.

Bachmann, R., & Inkpen, A. C. (2011). Understanding institutional-based trust building processes in inter-organizational relationships. *Organization Studies*, **32**(2), 281–301. https://doi.org/10.1177/0170840610397477.

Barrett, S., & Konsynski, B. (1982). Inter-organization information sharing systems. [Special issue]. *MIS Quarterly*, **6**, 93–105. https://doi.org/10.2307/248993.

Ben-Daya, M., Hassini, E., & Bahroun, Z. (2019). Internet of things and supply chain management: A literature review. *International Journal of Production Research*, **57**(15–16), 4719–4742. https://doi.org/10.1080/00207543.2017. 1402140.

Braunscheidel, M., & Suresh, N. (2009). The organizational antecedents of a firm's supply chain agility for risk mitigation and response. *Journal of Operations Management*, **27**, 119–140. https://doi.org/10.1016/j.jom.2008.09.006.

Cheng, J. H., Yeh, C. H., & Tu, C. W. (2008). Trust and knowledge sharing in green supply chains. *Supply Chain Management: An International Journal*, **13**(4), 283–295. https://doi.org/10.1108/1398540810882170.

Culot, G., Nassimbeni, G., Orzes, G., & Sartor, M. (2020). Behind the definition of Industry 4.0: Analysis and open questions. *International Journal of Production Economics*, **226**(107617), 1–15. https://doi.org/10.1016/j.ijpe.2020.107617.

Daft, R. L., & Lengel, R. H. (1983). *Information Richness. A New Approach to Managerial Behavior and Organization Design* (Technical Report No. TR-ONR-DG-02). Retrieved from Texas A and M Univ College Station Coll of Business Administration, Defense Technical Information Center website https://apps.dtic.mil/sti/citations/ADA128980.

Dalenogare, L. S., Benitez, G. B., Ayala, N. F., & Frank, A. G. (2018). The expected contribution of industry 4.0 technologies for industrial performance. *International Journal of Production Economics*, **204**, 383–394. https://doi. org/10.1016/j.ijpe.2018.08.019.

Delbufalo, E. (2012). Outcomes of inter-organizational trust in supply chain relationships: A systematic literature review and a meta-analysis of the empirical evidence. *Supply Chain Management: An International Journal*, **17**(4), 377–402. https://doi.org/10.1108/13598541211246549.

Dennis, A. R., & Valacich, J. S. (1999). Rethinking media richness: Towards a theory of media synchronicity. *Proceedings of the 32nd Annual Hawaii International Conference on Systems Sciences* (pp. 1–10). https://doi.org/10.1109/HICSS. 1999.772701.

Fayezi, S., Zutshi, A., & O'Loughlin, A. (2015). How Australian manufacturing firms perceive and understand the concepts of agility and flexibility in the supply chain. *International Journal of Operations & Production Management*, **35**, 248–281. https://doi.org/10.1108/IJOPM-12-2012-0546.

Fayezi, S., Zutshi, A., & O'Loughlin, A. (2017). Understanding and development of supply chain agility and flexibility: A structured literature review. *International Journal of Management Review*, **19**, 379–407. https://doi.org/10.1111/ ijmr.12096.

Frank, A. G., Dalenogare, L. S., & Ayala, N. F. (2019). Industry 4.0 technologies: Implementation patterns in manufacturing companies. *International Journal of Production Economics*, **210**, 15–26. https://doi.org/10.1016/j.ijpe.2019.01.004.

Ganesan, S. (1994). Determinants of long-term orientation in buyer-seller relationships. *Journal of Marketing*, **58**(2), 1–19. https://doi.org/10.1177/002224299405800201.

Gates, D., & Bremicker, M. (2017). Beyond the hype: Separating ambition from reality in I4.0. KPMG International. Retrieved from https://home.kpmg.com/xx/en/home/insights/2017/05/beyond-the-hype-separating-ambition-from-reality.html.

Gaudenzi, B., Siciliano, G., & Zsidisin, G. A. (2018). Supply chain finance and cyber risk: An illustrative case study. In Wendy T., Lydia B., & Lisa M. E. (Eds.) *Supply Chain Finance: Solutions for Financial Sustainability, Risk Management and Resilience in the Supply Chain* (pp. 161–176). London, United Kingdom: Kogan Page Publishing.

Gligor, D. M., & Holcomb, M. (2013). The role of personal relationships in supply chains. The *International Journal of Logistics Management*, **24**(3), 328–355. https://doi.org/10.1108/IJLM-07-2012-0067.

Gligor, D., Holcomb, M., & Stank, T. (2013). A multidisciplinary approach to supply chain agility: Conceptualization and scale development. *Journal of Business Logistics*, **34**(2), 94–108. https://doi.org/10.1111/jbl.12012.

Goodwin-Sak, C., McClain-Mpofu, C., Wieck, M., Zimmerman, H., & Merritt, S. (2019). Courageous cultures embrace automation: A grounded theory investigation to determine individual willingness to adopt automation in the workplace. *Proceedings of the Ninth International Conference on Engaged Management Scholarship, Belgium, September 5, 2019*. https://doi.org/10.2139/ssrn.3454062.

Handfield, R. (2017). Preparing for the era of the digitally transparent supply chain: A call to research in a new kind of journal. *Logistics*, **1**(1), 2. https://doi.org/10.3390/logistics1010002.

Heide, J. B., & John, G. (1990). Alliances in industrial purchasing: The determinants of joint action in buyer-supplier relationships. *Journal of Marketing Research*, **27**(1), 24–36. https://doi.org/10.1177/002224379002700103.

Hoque, I., & Rana, M. B. (2020). Buyer-supplier relationships from the perspective of working environment and organizational performance: Review and research agenda. *Management Review Quarterly*, **70**(1), 1–50. https://doi.org/10.1007/s11301-019-00159-4.

Jack, E. P., & Powers, T. L. (2015). Managing strategic supplier relationships: antecedents and outcomes. *Journal of Business & Industrial Marketing*, **30**(2), 129–138. https://doi.org/10.1108/JBIM-08-2011-0101.

Kim, D., Cavusgil, S. T., & Cavusgil, E. (2013). Does IT alignment between supply chain partners enhance customer value creation? An empirical investigation. *Industrial Marketing Management*, **42**(6), 880–889. https://doi.org/10.1016/j.indmarman.2013.05.021.

Lee, H. L. (2004). The triple-A supply chain. *Harvard Business Review*, **82**(10), 102–112.

Lee, K. (2015, March). How the internet of things will change your world. *CSCMP's Supply Chain Quarterly*. Retrieved from https://www.supplychainquarterly.com/topics/Technology/20150331-how-the-internet-of-things-will-change-your-world/.

Leek, S., Turnbull, P. W., & Naude, P. (2003). How is information technology affecting business relationships? Results from a UK survey. *Industrial Marketing Management*, **32**(2), 119–126. https://doi.org/10.1016/S0019-8501(02)00226-2.

Li, X., Chung, C., Goldsby, T. J., & Holsapple, C. W. (2008). A unified model of supply chain agility: The work-design perspective. *International Journal of Logistics Management* **19**(3), 408–435. https://doi.org/10.1108/09574090810919224.

Monczka, R. M., Petersen, K. J., Handfield, R. B., & Ragatz, G. L. (1998). Success factors in strategic supplier alliances: The buying company perspective. *Decision Sciences*, **29**(3), 553–577. https://doi.org/10.1111/j.1540-5915.1998.tb01354.x.

Narayanan, S., Narasimhan, R., & Schoenherr, T. (2015). Assessing the contingent effects of collaboration on agility performance in buyer–supplier relationships. *Journal of Operations Management*, **33**, 140–154. https://doi.org/10.1016/j.jom.2014.11.004.

Nyaga, G. N., Whipple, J. M., & Lynch, D. F. (2010). Examining supply chain relationships: Do buyer and supplier perspectives on collaborative relationships differ? *Journal of Operations Management*, **28**(2), 101–114. https://doi.org/10.1016/j.jom.2009.07.005.

Pagani, M., & Pardo, C. (2017). The impact of digital technology on relationships in a business network. *Industrial Marketing Management*, **67**, 185–192. https://doi.org/10.1016/j.indmarman.2017.08.009.

Paulraj, A., Lado, A. A., & Chen, I. J. (2008). Inter-organizational communication as a relational competency: Antecedents and performance outcomes in collaborative buyer–supplier relationships. *Journal of Operations Management*, **26**(1), 45–64. https://doi.org/10.1016/j.jom.2007.04.001.

Prahinski, C., & Fan, Y. (2007). Supplier evaluations: The role of communication quality. *Journal of Supply Chain Management*, **43**(3), 16–28. https://doi.org/10.1111/j.1745-493X.2007.00032.x.

Ramanathan, U., Gunasekaran, A., & Subramanian, N. (2011). Supply chain collaboration performance metrics: A conceptual framework. *Benchmarking: An International Journal*, **18**(6), 856–872. https://doi.org/10.1108/14635771111180734.

Richey, R. G., Tokman, M., & Dalela, V. (2010). Examining collaborative supply chain service technologies: A study of intensity, relationships, and resources.

Journal of the Academy of Marketing Science, **38**(1), 71–89. https://doi.org/10.1007/s11747-009-0139-z.

Robinson, A. (2020, February). Top six supply chain technology trends for 2020. Retrieved from https://www.supplychain247.com/article/top_six_supply_chain_technology_trends_for_2020.

Sader, S., Husti, I., & Daroczi, M. (2019). Industry 4.0 as a key enabler toward successful implementation of total quality management practices. *Periodica Polytechnica Social and Management Sciences*, **27**(2), 131–140. https://doi.org/10.3311/PPso.12675.

Sanders, N. R., & Premus, R. (2005). Modeling the relationship between firm IT capability, collaboration, and performance. *Journal of Business Logistics*, **26**(1), 1–23. https://doi.org/10.1002/j.2158-1592.2005.tb00192.x.

Schmitz, T., Schweiger, B., & Daft, J. (2016). The emergence of dependence and lock-in effects in buyer–supplier relationships — A buyer perspective. *Industrial Marketing Management*, **55**, 22–34. https://doi.org/10.1016/j.indmarman.2016.02.010.

Schubert, P., & Legner, C. (2011). B2B integration in global supply chains: An identification of technical integration scenarios. *The Journal of Strategic Information Systems*, **20**(3), 250–267. https://doi.org/10.1016/j.jsis.2011.04.001.

Schupp, F., & Wöhner, H. (Eds.) (2017). *Digitalisierung im Einkauf*. Wiesbaden, Germany: Springer-Verlag.

Short, J., Williams, E., & Christie, B. (1976). *The Social Psychology of Telecommunications*. Toronto: Wiley.

Squire, B., Cousins, P. D., Lawson, B., & Brown, S. (2009). The effect of supplier manufacturing capabilities on buyer responsiveness. *International Journal of Operations & Production Management*, **29**(8), 766–788. https://doi.org/10.1108/01443570910977689.

Stentoft, J., Jensen, K. W., Philipsen, K., & Haug, A. (2019, January). Drivers and barriers for Industry 4.0 readiness and practice: A SME perspective with empirical evidence. *Proceedings of the 52nd Hawaii International Conference on System Sciences*, pp. 5155–5164. https://doi.org/10.24251/HICSS.2019.619.

Swafford, P. M., Ghosh, S., & Murthy, N. (2006). The antecedents of supply chain agility of a firm: Scale development and model testing. *Journal of Operations Management*, **24**(2), 170–188. https://doi.org/10.1016/j.jom.2005.05.002.

Swafford, P. M., Ghosh, S., & Murthy, N. (2008). Achieving supply chain agility through IT integration and flexibility. *International Journal of Production Economics*, **116**(2), 288–297. https://doi.org/10.1016/j.ijpe.2008.09.002.

Swanson, D., Goel, L., Francisco, K., & Stock, J. (2018). An analysis of supply chain management research by topic. *Supply Chain Management*, **23**(2), 100–116. https://doi.org/10.1108/SCM-05-2017-0166.

Thomas, E. (2013). Supplier integration in new product development: Computer mediated communication, knowledge exchange and buyer performance. *Industrial Marketing Management,* **42**(6), 890–899. https://doi.org/10.1016/j.indmarman.2013.05.018.

Trittin-Ulbrich, H., Scherer, A. G., Munro, I., & Whelan, G. (2021). Exploring the dark and unexpected sides of digitalization: Toward a critical agenda. *Organization,* **28**(1), 8–25.

Vanpoucke, E., Vereecke, A., & Boyer, K. K. (2014). Triggers and patterns of integration initiatives in successful buyer–supplier relationships. *Journal of Operations Management,* **32**(1–2), 15–33. https://doi.org/10.1016/j.jom.2013.11.002.

Vanpoucke, E., Vereecke, A., & Muylle, S. (2017). Leveraging the impact of supply chain integration through information technology. *International Journal of Operations & Production Management,* **37**(4), 510–530. https://doi.org/10.1108/IJOPM-07-2015-0441.

Villena, V. H., Revilla, E., & Choi, T. Y. (2011). The dark side of buyer–supplier relationships: A social capital perspective. *Journal of Operations Management,* **29**(6), 561–576. https://doi.org/10.1016/j.jom.2010.09.001.

Wagner, S. M., & Bode, C. (2014). Supplier relationship-specific investments and the role of safeguards for supplier innovation sharing. *Journal of Operations Management,* **32**(3), 65–78. https://doi.org/10.1016/j.jom.2013.11.001.

Whipple, J. M., Wiedmer, R., & Boyer, K. K. (2015). A dyadic investigation of collaborative competence, social capital, and performance in buyer-supplier relationships. *Journal of Supply Chain Management,* **51**(2), 3–21. https://doi.org/10.1111/jscm.12071.

Wilson, D. T. (1995). An integrated model of buyer-seller relationships. *Journal of the Academy of Marketing Science,* **23**(4), 335–345. https://doi.org/10.1177/009207039502300414.

Zaheer, A., McEvily, B., & Perrone, V. (1998). Does trust matter? Exploring the effects of interorganizational and interpersonal trust on performance. *Organization Science,* **9**(2), 141–159. https://doi.org/10.1287/orsc.9.2.141.

Zhang, C., Wu, F., & Henke Jr, J. W. (2015). Leveraging boundary spanning capabilities to encourage supplier investment: A comparative study. *Industrial Marketing Management,* **49**, 84–94. https://doi.org/10.1016/j.indmarman.2015.04.012.

CHAPTER 3

Digitization and Supply Chain Risk Management

Hakan Yildiz

Department of Global Supply Chain Management,
Mike Ilitch School of Business, Wayne State University,
Detroit, Michigan, USA
hakan@wayne.edu

Abstract

This chapter focuses on supply chain risk management and the use and impact of digitization in this domain. The COVID-19 pandemic, geopolitical risks, and natural disasters in recent years underscored the vulnerabilities in supply chains. During the same timeframe, the world also witnessed the emergence of various digital technologies that enable real-time information sharing, data-driven decision-making, and collaboration to enhance operational performance and resilience. In this context, this chapter reviews the transformative role of digital technologies, such as supply chain mapping, visualization tools, Internet of Things (IoT), big data analytics, Blockchain, Artificial Intelligence (AI), and early warning systems.

Keywords: COVID-19; Supply chain resilience; Supply chain disruption; Visualization; Digital twin; Supply chain mapping; Traceability; Early warning; Risk monitoring.

Introduction

As supply chains became more globalized and complex, they also have become more susceptible to various types of risks, ranging from low-impact recurring events to high-impact "black swan" type of very rare events. With the very visible disruptions that were induced by COVID-19, supply chain risk management has become a center-stage topic attracting the attention of not just academics, but also governments, media, and the general public. According to a report on supply chain resilience during the COVID-19 pandemic, firms that experienced supply chain disruptions in 2020 were five times higher than in 2019 (Elliott, 2021).

The causes of supply chain disruptions, their impact on firms, and the propagation of the disruptions through time and geographies are among the first set of topics that are of interest. Supply chain practitioners and scholars are also interested in investigating how to deal with these disruptions using various strategies and how to make supply chains more resilient. The value of timely and accurate information, its sharing among supply chain partners, making optimized decisions based on data, and collaboration has been widely studied and documented in extant supply chain management literature as a means to achieve better operational performance, agility, and resilience. The recent technological advancements in computing, data storage, sensors, and connectivity allow for many possibilities in tackling the supply chain disruptions in a time- and cost-effective way. By collecting data across their supply chains, firms can create a digital footprint of not just their immediate supply chain but also their extended supply chain that spans supply chain partners that do not have a direct relationship with the focal firm. Visualization tools allow supply chain managers to view such extended supply chains in a clear, intuitive way, allowing them to see potential problems, risks, bottlenecks, and solutions.

By integrating cyber and physical systems along supply chain processes through the use of Internet of Things (IoT) devices, firms can create the digital twin of their supply chains (Liao *et al.*, 2017; Minner *et al.*, 2017). This allows them to monitor the flow of goods and services (Goh *et al.*, 2013) and also can potentially allow them to better identify, assess, mitigate, and monitor risks (Schlüter *et al.*, 2017) through the utilization of big data analytics. Digitized supply chains can allow for a faster response to disruptions (Monostori *et al.*, 2010). It also makes coordination and collaboration among supply chain partners easier. New technologies like blockchain allow transparency across the supply chain securely. Furthermore, through the use of Artificial Intelligence (AI), firms can react to disruptions autonomously by learning from a large amount of historical and real-time data available and simulating and evaluating many possible scenarios (Wagner and Kontny, 2017). In this chapter, we review the various digital technologies and how they impact risk management in supply chains.

Supply Chain Mapping

While firms usually have relatively good information regarding their first-tier suppliers, they typically have limited visibility into the lower tiers in their supply chains (Basole and Bellamy, 2014). In fact, 65% of chief procurement officers have little to no visibility beyond their first-tier suppliers (Umbenhauer *et al.*, 2018). While a relatively smaller number of parts that go into its products allow Apple to have almost full visibility of its extended supply chain (Apple Inc., 2012), this is a lot harder for an automotive manufacturer like Honda (Giannoccaro *et al.*, 2018) due to the sheer amount of parts that go into a car. Toyota has reported that it did not know many of its second, third, or fourth tier suppliers before the devastating tsunami hit Japan in 2011 (Novotny, 2012) and disrupted Toyota's many suppliers in different tiers of the supply chain. Not surprisingly, Toyota was not alone. Many global firms had a similarly limited visibility into lower tiers of their supply chains, which resulted in similar disruptions both in the aftermath of the 2011 Japan tsunami and the flooding that happened later that year in Thailand (Vakil, 2021). After more than a decade of these incidents, many firms experienced similar disruptions during COVID-19 since many of them knew very little about their lower-tier suppliers (Lund *et al.*, 2020) and most of them tried to manually identify suppliers located in regions that were under lockdown in China (Choi *et al.*, 2020). More than 40% of COVID-related supply chain disruptions occurred in tier-2 suppliers and below (Elliott, 2021). As of 2019, less than a quarter of the firms surveyed by Elliott (2021) reported that they were using technology to help with supply chain mapping. This figure has increased significantly to 40% in 2020 when COVID-19 forced firms to make such investments. The growing demand for sustainable business practices also driving the need for firms to have visibility into their extended supply chains (Choi *et al.*, 2021).

Having a digital map of the entire supply chain can provide solid information that can help in identifying and foreseeing supply chain weaknesses.

Basole and Bellamy (2014) illustrate that an electronics hardware manufacturer's supply network includes well-connected tier-2 and tier-3 suppliers that are either at moderate risk or high risk. More formally, Wang *et al.* (2021) show that the sub-tier supply network structure and the degree of commonality of tier-2 suppliers among tier-1 suppliers are important risk sources for a firm. Thus it is imperative to map the supply chain beyond tier-1 to identify high-risk parts of the supply chain. The mapping can also enable a firm to take proactive actions and react to disruptions more quickly. GM, Cisco, IBM, and Amgen are some firms that benefited from supply chain mapping during COVID-19 as they had a clear picture of their supply base in multiple tiers (Vakil, 2021), and what locations, parts, and products are at risk (Choi *et al.*, 2020).

Mapping the entire supply chain is not an easy task. It requires a significant amount of resources in the form of time and money (Choi *et al.*, 2020). Xia and Lu (2014) and Braud and Gong (2016) illustrate the necessary steps for data collection in their work to map the supply chain of a large multinational chemical company and a garment manufacturer, respectively. They collected geographical location information for where supplies are manufactured and stored; used bill of materials to create the material flow from suppliers to manufacturing and customers; obtained specific inventory, demand, and revenue data at each location for each supply and finished goods. Xia and Lu's (2014) work only considers the first-tier suppliers, whereas Braud and Gong (2016)'s work includes only a few second-tier suppliers as well.

The data collection effort becomes much more difficult when mapping is expanded toward lower tiers. For example, the mapping of the extended supply chain of a firm took a year for a team of more than 100 people (Choi *et al.*, 2020). Mapping also requires the willingness of suppliers to share information regarding their suppliers. The challenging nature of this undertaking is illustrated by Toyota, which reported that half of its first-tier suppliers were not willing to disclose information about their suppliers (Masui and Nishi, 2012). Furthermore, as more firms start mapping their supply chains, a supplier may face repetitive requests for information from many of its customers. While major consulting firms provide some mapping services, recently, such specialized services are being offered by a new breed of firms such as Elementum, Llamasoft, Resilinc (Choi *et al.*, 2020), Elm Analytics and Sourcemap. These firms can reduce the overall effort and cost for all stakeholders. Since their primary method of information gathering is through questionnaires sent to suppliers, after a supplier responds to a questionnaire, the anonymized data can be used for other customers of that same supplier, reducing repetition (Sheffi, 2015).

Visualization for Supply Chain Risk Management

Visualization, as a scientific approach, uses graphical representations of data to identify trends, patterns, and outliers in data sets (Basole *et al.*, 2021). Risk assessment can benefit greatly from visualization since visual information is easier for people to process than textual information (Gardner & Cooper, 2003). Supply chain managers can quickly comprehend the supply chain network when a map is superimposed on it (Tripathi, 2021) and make better decisions in a more effective way (Lou *et al.*, 2020). With the help of a visualization tool, supply chain operations can be viewed clearly, and trends and bottlenecks can be identified (Goh *et al.*, 2013). Such tools can also allow for a better understanding of supply chain network structures (Singh *et al.*, 2019) and process flows (Sackett & Williams, 2003). While the ever-growing amount of available data and its speed of arrival makes it difficult to effectively use such data, visualization can help present such large and fast data for decision-makers.

Xia and Lu (2014) and Braud and Gong (2016) both illustrate how such visualization can be done using a visualization software for the data they gathered from a large multinational chemical company and a garment manufacturer, respectively. They both overlay risk exposure data of geographic locations using geographical disaster data they obtained from third-party sources. Moreover, they illustrate several relevant data such as revenue, inventory, disruption probability, and value at risk on the same geographically mapped supply chain, allowing supply chain managers to see data in meaningful ways.

Basole *et al.* (2017) illustrate a case where the visualization of the geographic footprint of a firm's supply chain, the interconnectedness between the entities in the supply chain, and firm innovativeness allowed the identification of knowledge risk since the knowledge capital (innovativeness) resides with the highest concentration outside of the home country of this firm.

Blackhurst *et al.* (2018) present a network clustering-based methodology to not only visualize a supply chain but also the path of disruption propagation from upstream to downstream in a supply chain when a disruptive event occurs. Moreover, they show how potential weaknesses in the supply chain network can be identified considering the topological properties of the network.

Interactive visualization can also be appealing as it presents different views of the same supply chain (Singh *et al.*, 2019). Similarly, manufacturing processes can be visualized for risk management purposes (Sackett & Williams 2003). The benefit of interactive visualization on supply network risk assessment is illustrated by Basole and Bellamy (2014) using data from the electronics industry. They illustrate how a hardware manufacturer's three-tier supply base and the connections among them can be visualized based on topological importance (connectedness of suppliers) and risk level using size and color coding. Their visualizations clearly show many of the well-connected tier-2 suppliers are either at moderate risk or high risk. Furthermore, some tier-3 suppliers are categorized as very risky and well-connected. Such visualization allows supply chain managers to easily identify and recognize the distribution of risk levels across the tiers of the firm's extended supply base.

Interactive visualization tools can also allow for "what if?" scenario analysis using simulation methods. As a manager creates different scenarios, such as by changing the supply chain structure, the simulation tool can translate these changes into business relationships (Patten *et al.*, 2001).

Internet of Things, Big Data Analytics, and Artificial Intelligence

More data has been generated in the last few years than ever before in human history and yet firms can use a very small amount of the data they have (Calvo, 2019). IoT devices, which are interconnecting devices embedded in physical objects, are responsible for a significant portion of this large amount of data. Access to real-time data from a growing number of sources is made possible by IoT, which can be very helpful in various risk management processes such as risk identification, assessment, and monitoring (Birkel & Hartmann, 2020). IoT makes it possible for disruptive technologies like AI and big data analytics as these technologies require comprehensive data collection (Whitmore *et al.*, 2015).

The use of big data analytics has the potential to help businesses mitigate supply chain disruptions better (Akter *et al.*, 2016; Papadopoulos *et al.*, 2017). Big data analytics and predictive analytics can increase the visibility, performance, and resilience of supply chains (Gunasekaran *et al.*, 2017). One area where big data analytics is used effectively by some firms is reducing demand risks. One of the most popular Chinese e-commerce firms, JD.com, uses big data analytics to forecast demand four weeks in advance by using ad click data (Fan *et al.*, 2015). Another firm that uses cutting-edge big data analytics to forecast demand is Amazon, which can predict demand based on the pattern of product searches (Sanders, 2014). DM, a very large drugstore chain in Germany, also uses big data analytics very successfully to forecast demand for its thousands of locations at the SKU level (BlueYonder, 2020). A closely related application domain is pricing, for which Li and Wang (2017) show how big data analytics can dynamically estimate the time–temperature profile of perishable products and modify prices using big data gathered by sensors in a food supply chain.

Big data analytics is also used in many other supply chain problems. For example, UPS uses big data analytics for preventative maintenance of its vehicle fleet, where sensor-generated data is monitored for deviations from the norm (van Rijmenam, 2014). Similarly, Unilever uses IoT sensor data to identify maintenance needs as well as quality problems (Smith, 2019). Supply chains with AI support were shown to be 45% more effective at making deliveries on time and with fewer mistakes (Bonner, 2020). Big data analytics can also be used to predict other types of potential disruptions. For example, for a food company sourcing agricultural goods as raw material, big data analytics and AI can predict which farms could be impacted by climate change by analyzing weather patterns and can suggest new sourcing options (Dani, 2020). Similarly, when a supplier is impacted by a local disaster, big data analytics can be used to assess the severity of the disruption and suggest a supply chain redesign if necessary (*ibid.*). Royal Dutch Shell, the world's largest oil company, uses digital twin technology to test how its assets would react to accidents (Woodroof, 2019).

While the use of big data analytics is accelerating in general, there is still ample room to exploit big data analytics for supply chain risk management (Choi *et al.*, 2018). Given that disruptions to supply chains occur frequently, firms should work to increase their flexibility by developing and implementing AI solutions that are tailored to their particular operations (Scholten *et al.*, 2019). There is also a great need for research on the use of big data analytics and AI in predictive supply chain risk management (Baryannis *et al.*, 2018) and research that considers the interplay between big data analytics, IoT, and blockchain technologies and supply chain risk management (Ivanov *et al.*, 2018).

Blockchain for Traceability and Visibility

A blockchain is a distributed, tamperproof database and ledger containing a chronologically ordered chain of transactions among various parties. A blockchain can keep relevant information related to a product as it moves downstream from the raw material stage to the finished product stage.

Many firms have very limited visibility beyond their first-tier suppliers. This makes it difficult for firms to trace the source of a material and component when a problem occurs. While IT service providers came up with a variety of traceability technologies, blockchain technology has been the one that received the most attention. For example, IBM and Walmart are investigating using blockchain technology to improve food supply chain safety (Baryannis *et al.*, 2018). Similarly, pharmaceutical firms use blockchain against stolen, counterfeit, or dangerous drugs (Gaur & Gaiha, 2020).

Blockchain can also enable faster and more efficient logistics operations (Yoon *et al.*, 2020). Walmart Canada uses blockchain with the trucking firms it works with to synchronize data and track shipments (Gaur & Gaiha, 2020). Blockchain can also improve coordination within the supply chain, as firms like Emerson and Hayward see great potential (*ibid.*).

The increasing market interest attracted many startups as well as large tech firms, including Amazon, Microsoft, IBM, and Oracle, which resulted in many blockchain platforms. As firms continue to deal with global supply chain risks, traceability, visibility, and coordination benefits of blockchain make it an important digital technology for supply chain risk management.

Risk Monitoring in Supply Chains

Timely identification of risks impacting (or potentially impacting) your firm directly (or indirectly by impacting your supply chain partners) can be very useful in business continuity and recovery (Hoffmann *et al.*, 2013). Sheffi (2015) describes the case of BNSF Railroad Co., which anticipated a potential disruption ahead of time in 2008 after it was notified of a complex and hazardous operation over its tracks by a mining company and took proactive actions that allowed them to minimize the negative impact of the disruption when it happened. Similarly, in our interviews with many global companies regarding their experiences in COVID-19, we learned that those companies which have offices in China or have close communication with their suppliers in China were able to sense the potential threat of the early pandemic-related developments in Wuhan, China, at the beginning of COVID-19 and act quicker than those firms that did not have such information. The time between "knowing that a disruptive event will take place and the event's first impact on the company" is defined as the detection lead time by Sheffi (2015). Detection lead time can be an important dimension to categorize disruptions, during which a firm can prepare for the impending disruption and mitigate its impact. Given the wide variety of natural and human-made risks that threaten global supply chains, relying on *ad hoc* information sharing between various supply chain partners to detect risks is not a robust approach. This is where risk monitoring and early warning systems can come into play and provide firms with critical information early, thus enabling longer detection lead times.

Risk monitoring has not received enough academic interest (Hoffmann *et al.*, 2013; Fan & Stevenson, 2018) and Ho *et al.* (2015) called on scholars to "extend the literature by developing an early warning monitoring system with adaptive risk indicators." COVID-19 made the need for such tools clear as firms that have invested in such technologies and services had reaped the benefits by being able to react to disruptions much faster than those that did not invest. For example, by utilizing a risk notification and visualization service, AGCO, an American agricultural machinery manufacturer, was able to detect COVID-19-related country shutdowns early. This allowed AGCO to ensure the availability of critical supplies and position them at locations where they are needed (Banker, 2020). Similarly, a U.S.-based electronics manufacturer, which utilizes supply chain risk monitoring services, acted quickly when it received an alert from the service provider about the potential supply chain impacts of a "flu-like illness" in China (Resilinc, 2020). Such quick disruption detections can provide a firm advantage over its competitors in ensuring critical supplies or capacity, which can be scarce and/or too expensive during disruptive events. Even though news about certain disruptions may be accessible to all firms, the precise nature, location, likelihood, and impact of such disruptions particular to a firm's supply chain network requires a sophisticated undertaking of mapping out the firm's entire supply chain, as discussed earlier, and utilizing a variety of data sources to overlay risk data over the firm's supply chain network.

Monitoring risk in real time across a geographically dispersed supply chain comprising various independent firms is not an easy task. It requires the ability to use a combination of sophisticated methodologies and technologies such as tracking and tracing systems, sensors, RFID, IoT, cloud computing, AI, and big data analytics. While real-time data collection can be challenging, the widespread use of technologies such as Enterprise Resource Planning systems, Transportation Management Systems, and Warehouse Management Systems can allow accessing key performance indicators.

There exist a few academic studies focusing on this topic. Blackhurst *et al.* (2008) developed a tool that monitors supplier and part-specific risk indices that can identify trends that may present high-risk levels for an automotive manufacturer and provide early warning signals. To offer early warning signals of manufacturing quality in the food production supply chains, Zhang *et al.* (2011) developed an integrated abnormality detection model incorporating fuzzy set theory and the radial basis function neural network. Yildiz *et al.* (2022) presented a methodology jointly utilizing a nonparametric cumulative sum control chart (CUSUM) chart and data envelopment analysis (DEA) to monitor the performance of a distribution network and provide signals when the performance indicators deviate.

In this domain, firms that provide supply chain event management applications, such as Oracle and Manhattan Associates, can also be quite useful. Such software can provide timely visibility on product movement and if there is any deviation from the plan, an alert is issued, which would allow a firm to take quick recovery actions (Sheffi *et al.*, 2012b).

In addition to process-related internal data, several sources of external data also present themselves as important opportunities for risk monitoring. These may include weather, global news (e.g., disasters, civil unrest, political actions), supply base-related information (e.g., financial data, operational data), social media, and government policies. Academic studies in this domain are very scarce.

Firms can take two routes in monitoring all that external data. They can invest resources and do it internally or they can utilize the services of third-party risk monitoring service providers, which emerged as valuable supply chain risk management partners in recent years. Some of the well-known firms in this domain are Resilinc, Everstream Analytics, Interos, and RiskMethods. These firms use AI to monitor many data sources and provide alerts to a customer based on the overlap between the risk events and the supply chain map of that customer. These services can also allow firms to prioritize information and allow decision-makers to focus on issues that require urgent attention. For example, Flextronics received a week's worth of notice about the potential disruption risks posed by the rising waters during the 2011 Thailand floods from a risk monitoring service provider. This allowed the firm to narrow down the critical set of suppliers and parts that need attention immediately (Sheffi *et al.*, 2012a).

One important aspect of such monitoring and early warning systems is accuracy and sensitivity. If a firm acts early based on an inaccurate early warning signal, the performance could suffer significantly. Moreover, a detection system can also miss important disruptions if it is undersensitive. So, when a firm considers implementing such technology or receiving such a service, the stringency of the accuracy performance has to be vetted very well.

Conclusion

Many new digital technologies have been developed in the last few decades, opening up many possibilities in coping with ever-growing supply chain risks in a global economy. Most firms rely on extended supply chains consisting of many tiers of suppliers in meeting the demands of their customers. Gaining visibility deep into the supply networks, visualizing the vast amount of data generated both internally and externally, analyzing such data to make inferences using big data analytics and AI, sharing and storing information in a secure way using blockchains, and real-time monitoring of supply chain activities and processes to identify risks are all now possible with such new digital technologies. The extant supply chain risk management literature has evolved at a fast pace providing many important insights in recent years. Still, there are many research opportunities and open questions. Similarly, recent years have seen a surge of both startups and larger firms investing in supply chain risk management technologies providing many new tools and services for the marketplace. It is quite likely that these trends will continue as supply chains keep experiencing disruptions and firms look for solutions to cope with them.

References

Akter, S., Wamba, S. F., Gunasekaran, A., Dubey, R., & Childe, S. J. (2016). How to improve firm performance using big data analytics capability and business strategy alignment? *International Journal of Production Economics*, **182**, 113–131.

Apple Inc. (2012). *Apple Supplier Responsibility: 2012 Progress Report*. Apple Inc.

Baryannis, G., Validi, S., Dani, S., & Antoniou, G. (2019). Supply chain risk management and artificial intelligence: State of the art and future research directions. *International Journal of Production Research*, **57**(7), 2179–2202.

Banker, S. (2020). A Very Agile Supply Chain: The Inside Story of AGCO's Response To COVID-19. *Forbes*. https://www.forbes.com/sites/stevebanker/2020/04/15/a-very-agile-supply-chain-the-inside-story-of-agcos-response-to-covid-19/?sh=305a1a75574d.

Basole, R. C., & Bellamy, M. A. (2014). Visual analysis of supply network risks: Insights from the electronics industry. *Decision Support Systems*, **67**, 109–120.

Basole, R. C., Bellamy, M. A., & Park, H. (2017). Visualization of innovation in global supply chain networks. *Decision Sciences*, **48**(2), 288–306.

Basole, R., Bendoly, E., Chandrasekaran, A., & Linderman, K. (2021). Visualization in operations management research. *INFORMS Journal on Data Science*, **1**(2), 172–187.

Birkel, H. S., & Hartmann, E. (2020). Internet of Things — The future of managing supply chain risks. *Supply Chain Management: An International Journal*, **25**(5), 535–548.

Blackhurst, J., Rungtusanatham, M. J., Scheibe, K., & Ambulkar, S. (2018). Supply chain vulnerability assessment: A network based visualization and clustering analysis approach. *Journal of Purchasing and Supply Management*, **24**(1), 21–30.

Blackhurst, J., Scheibe, K. P., & Johnson, D. J. (2008). Supplier risk assessment and monitoring for the automotive industry. *International Journal of Physical Distribution & Logistics Management*, **38**(2), 143–165.

BlueYonder (2020). Successful Demand Forecasting at dm. https://blueyonder.com/knowledge-center/collateral/dm-drugstore-case-study.

Bonner, H. (2020). Artificial Intelligence in Supply Chain Management. https://riskpulse.com/blog/artificial-intelligence-in-supply-chain-management/.

Braud, J. A., & Gong, S. (2016). *Quantifying and Visualizing Risk in the Garment Manufacturing Supply Chain* (Doctoral Dissertation, Massachusetts Institute of Technology).

Calvo, J. (2019). Digital Transformation — Is Your Supply Chain Ready to Compete? https://www.thefuturefactory.com/blog/22.

Choi, T. Y., Narayanan, S., Novak, D., Olhager, J., Sheu, J. B., & Wiengarten, F. (2021). Managing extended supply chains. *Journal of Business Logistics*, **42**(2), 200–206.

Choi, T. Y., Rogers, D., & Vakil, B. (2020). Coronavirus is a wake-up call for supply chain management. *Harvard Business Review*, **27**(1), 364–398.

Choi, T. M., Wallace, S. W., & Wang, Y. (2018). Big data analytics in operations management. *Production and Operations Management*, **27**(10), 1868–1883.

Dani, S. (2020). Utilising AI in Supply Chain Risk Management. https://www.thefuturefactory.com/blog/54.

Elliott, R. (2021). Supply Chain Resilience Report 2021. BCI. https://www.thebci. org/static/e02a3e5f-82e5-4ff1-b8bc61de9657e9c8/BCI-0007h-Supply-Chain-Resilience-ReportLow-Singles.pdf.

Fan, Y., Heilig, L., & Voß, S. (2015). Supply chain risk management in the era of big data. In *Design, User Experience, and Usability: Design Discourse: 4th International Conference, DUXU 2015, Held as Part of HCI International 2015, Los Angeles, CA, USA, August 2–7, 2015, Proceedings, Part I* (pp. 283–294). Cham: Springer.

Fan, Y., & Stevenson, M. (2018). A review of supply chain risk management: Definition, theory, and research agenda. *International Journal of Physical Distribution & Logistics Management*, **48**(3), 205–230.

Gardner, J. T., & Cooper, M. C. (2003). Strategic supply chain mapping approaches. *Journal of Business Logistics*, **24**(2), 37–64.

Gaur, V., & Gaiha, A. (2020). Building a Transparent Supply Chain. *Harvard Business Review*, (May–June), 94–103.

Giannoccaro, I., Nair, A., & Choi, T. (2018). The impact of control and complexity on supply network performance: An empirically informed investigation using NK simulation analysis. *Decision Sciences*, **49**(4), 625–659.

Goh, R. S. M., Wang, Z., Yin, X., Fu, X., Ponnambalam, L., Lu, S., & Li, X. (2013, August). RiskVis: Supply chain visualization with risk management and real-time monitoring. In *2013 IEEE International Conference on Automation Science and Engineering (CASE)*, pp. 207–212. IEEE.

Gunasekaran, A., Papadopoulos, T., Dubey, R., Wamba, S. F., Childe, S. J., Hazen, B., & Akter, S. (2017). Big data and predictive analytics for supply chain and organizational performance. *Journal of Business Research*, **70**, 308–317.

Ho, W., Zheng, T., Yildiz, H., & Talluri, S. (2015). Supply chain risk management: A literature review. *International Journal of Production Research*, **53**(16), 5031–5069.

Hoffmann, P., Schiele, H., & Krabbendam, K. (2013). Uncertainty, supply risk management and their impact on performance. *Journal of Purchasing and Supply Management*, **19**(3), 199–211.

Ivanov, D., Dolgui, A., & Sokolov, B. (2019). The impact of digital technology and Industry 4.0 on the ripple effect and supply chain risk analytics. *International Journal of Production Research*, **57**(3), 829–846.

Li, D., & Wang, X. (2017). Dynamic supply chain decisions based on networked sensor data: An application in the chilled food retail chain. *International Journal of Production Research*, **55**(17), 5127–5141.

Liao, Y., Deschamps, F., Loures, E. D. F. R., & Ramos, L. F. P. (2017). Past, present and future of Industry 4.0 — A systematic literature review and research agenda proposal. *International Journal of Production Research*, **55**(12), 3609–3629.

Lou, C. X., Bonti, A., Prokofieva, M., Abdelrazek, M., & Kari, S. M. C. (2020). Literature Review on Visualization in Supply Chain & Decision Making. In *2020 24th International Conference Information Visualisation (IV), September*, pp. 746–750. IEEE.

Lund, S., Manyika, J., Woetzel, J., Barriball, E., & Krishnan, M. (2020). Risk, Resilience, and Rebalancing in Global Value Chains. https://www. mckinsey.com/business-functions/operations/our-insights/risk-resilience-and-rebalancing-in-global-value-chains.

Masui, Y., & Nishi, N. (2012). *Toyota's Supply Chain Disruption in the Great East Japan Earthquake.* Technical Report, Stanford University, Stanford, CA.

Minner, S., Battini, D., & Çelebi, D. (2017). Innovations in production economics. *International Journal of Production Economics*, **194**, 1–2.

Monostori, L., Csáji, B. C., Kádár, B., Pfeiffer, A., Ilie-Zudor, E., Kemény, Z., & Szathmári, M. (2010). Towards adaptive and digital manufacturing. *Annual Reviews in Control*, **34**(1), 118–128.

Novotny, P. (2012). Japan Manufacturers in Post-Tsunami Rethink. *IndustryWeek*, March 5. http://www.industryweek.com/planning-amp-forecasting/japan-manufacturers-post-tsunami-rethink.

Papadopoulos, T., Gunasekaran, A., Dubey, R., Altay, N., Childe, S. J., & Fosso-Wamba, S. (2017). The role of Big Data in explaining disaster resilience in supply chains for sustainability. *Journal of Cleaner Production*, **142**, 1108–1118.

Patten, J., Ishii, H., Malone, T., Hines, J., Murphy-Hoye, M., Koo, B., Quimby, J., Herman, G., Strong, C., & Goncalves, P. Supply Chain Visualization. https:// tangible.media.mit.edu/project/supply-chain-visualization/.

Resilinc (2020). Annual Report 2019 with 2020 MidYear Review. https://resource. resilinc.com/rs/863-OTG-034/images/Resilinc%20Annual%20Report%20 2019-Q2%202020.pdf.

Sanders, N. R. (2014). *Big Data Driven Supply Chain Management: A Framework for Implementing Analytics and Turning Information into Intelligence.* Upper Saddle River, NJ: Pearson Education.

Sackett, P. J., & Williams, D. K. (2003). Data visualization in manufacturing decision making. *Journal of Advanced Manufacturing Systems*, **2**(2), 163–185.

Scholten, K., Scott, P. S., & Fynes, B. (2019). Building routines for non-routine events: Supply chain resilience learning mechanisms and their antecedents. *Supply Chain Management: An International Journal*, **24**(3), 430–442.

Schlüter, F., Diedrich, K., & Güller, M. (2017). Analyzing the Impact of Digitalization on Supply Chain Risk Management. In *IPSERA Conference: International Purchasing and Supply Education and Research Association*, Budapest/Balatonfüred, Hungary.

Sheffi, Y. (2015). Preparing for disruptions through early detection. *MIT Sloan Management Review*, **57**(1), 31.

Sheffi, Y., Vakil, B., & Griffin, T. (2012a). Risk and Disruptions: New Software Tools. Unpublished MS. https://web.mit.edu/sheffi/www/documents/Risk_and_Disruptions_V9.pdf.

Sheffi, Y., Vakil, B., & Griffin, T. (2012b). New Software Tools to Manage Risk and Disruptions: Part II. https://www.logisticsmgmt.com/article/new_software_tools_to_manage_risk_and_disruptions1.

Singh, S. K., Jenamani, M., Garg, C., & Alirajpurwala, H. (2019). Multi-echelon supply network analysis with interactive visualization. In *2019 International Conference on Machine Learning, Big Data, Cloud and Parallel Computing (COMITCon), February*, pp. 481–484. IEEE.

Smith, J. (2019). Unilever Uses Virtual Factories to Tune Up Its Supply Chain. *The Wall Street Journal*. https://www.wsj.com/articles/unilever-uses-virtual-factories-to-tune-up-its-supply-chain-11563206402.

Tripathi, P. (2021). *Building Resilient Supply Chain using Interactive Visualization*. Doctoral Dissertation, Massachusetts Institute of Technology.

Umbenhauer, B., & Younger, L. (2018). Leadership: Driving innovation and delivering impact. The Deloitte Global Chief Procurement Officer Survey 2018. https://www2.deloitte.com/content/dam/Deloitte/at/Documents/strategy-operations/deloitte-global-cpo-survey-2018.pdf.

Vakil, B. (2021). Resiliency Starts with Supplier Mapping. *CSCMP's Supply Chain Quarterly*. https://www.supplychainquarterly.com/articles/4298-supply-chain-resiliency-starts-with-supplier-mapping.

van Rijmenam, M. (2014). Why UPS Spends Over $1 Billion on Big Data Annually. https://datafloq.com/read/ups-spends-1-billion-big-data-annually/.

Wagner, J., & Kontny, H. (2017). Use case of self-organizing adaptive supply chain. In *Digitalization in Supply Chain Management and Logistics: Smart and Digital Solutions for an Industry 4.0 Environment. Proceedings of the Hamburg International Conference of Logistics (HICL)* (Vol. 23, pp. 255–273). Berlin: epubli GmbH.

Wang, Y., Li, J., Wu, D., & Anupindi, R. (2021). When ignorance is not bliss: An empirical analysis of subtier supply network structure on firm risk. *Management Science*, **67**(4), 2029–2048.

Whitmore, A., Agarwal, A., & Da Xu, L. (2015). The Internet of Things — A survey of topics and trends. *Information Systems Frontiers*, **17**(2), 261–274.

Woodroof, N. (2019). Extending Simulation Technology from the Design World into the Operational World. *OilField Technology*. https://www.oilfieldtechnology.com/special-reports/17062019/extending-simulation-technology-from-the-design-world-into-the-operational-world/.

Xia, D., & Lu, K. (2014). *Application of Supply Chain Risk Management through Visualization and Value-At-Risk Quantification.* Doctoral Dissertation, Massachusetts Institute of Technology.

Yildiz, H., Talluri, S., Xie, X., Yoon, J., Qiu, P., & Wassick, J. M. (2022). Evaluating and monitoring distribution network efficiency with multivariate process control methods. *International Journal of Production Research*, **60**(2), 517–533.

Yoon, J., Talluri, S., Yildiz, H., & Sheu, C. (2020). The value of blockchain technology implementation in international trades under demand volatility risk. *International Journal of Production Research*, **58**(7), 2163–2183.

Zhang, K., Chai, Y., Yang, S. X., & Weng, D. (2011). Pre-warning analysis and application in traceability systems for food production supply chains. *Expert Systems with Applications*, **38**(3), 2500–2507.

https://doi.org/10.1142/9789811286636_0004

CHAPTER 4

Blockchain for the Supply Chain: What Is It? Where Is It Being Used?

Ronald Lembke

University of Nevada, Reno, Nevada, USA

ronlembke@unr.edu

Abstract

We describe many leading blockchain supply chain projects in shipping, trucking, grocery, pharmaceuticals, retail, mining and information technology. After an explanation of blockchain technology and terms, we explain how hashing algorithms provide security to blockchains. Blockchains allow individual items or lots of items to be tracked for traceability and provenance. This also helps protect against counterfeits and deters theft. Non-Fungible Tokens can be used to track individual products, and ISO is developing such a standard. Universal Serial Numbers are necessary to ensure all parties are referring to the same individual item.

Keywords: Blockchain; Hashing; Non-fungible tokens; Provenance; Retail; Universal Serial Numbers.

Introduction

Blockchain is one of the most widely covered technologies in the business press. Many articles have suggested that it offers tremendous potential benefits for the supply chain. A recent database search for articles with both supply chain and blockchain in their abstracts yielded more than one thousand articles in the popular press, and 288 articles in peer-reviewed journals (EBSCOhost, 2022).

From the stream of headlines and newsletters talking about blockchain supply chain projects, a person could be given the impression that blockchain is already widely utilized throughout the supply chain. As we will see, although there are important successes, blockchain is not yet widely used in the supply chain.

In this chapter, we will provide a detailed introduction to blockchain technology and an overview of many supply chain blockchain projects that have been announced or implemented.

For a number of industries, we will describe many blockchain efforts, but for a growing technology like blockchain, the list cannot be comprehensive. Hopefully, it will provide the reader an overview of the types of efforts in each sector, and a useful introduction to the efforts.

Overview of Blockchain Technology

First and foremost, a blockchain is a database. Unlike traditional databases, which are controlled by a single entity (like a bank's list of account balances and transactions), a blockchain is a *distributed ledger*, because identical copies are held by all of the participants in the system. This is why blockchain is also referred to as "distributed ledger technology" (DLT).

Readers interested in a highly detailed understanding of blockchain systems may want to consider Voshmgir (2020).

What is a "Blockchain?"

All of the members participating in the blockchain have a computer, known as a "node," storing copies of the blockchain.

Nodes forward transactions from their customers to all of the other nodes in the network. Every so often, recent transactions are grouped into a "block," and run through a "hashing" algorithm, which creates a "hash" of the block. Also included in the block, before the hashing, is the hash of the previous block. We will explain more about the hash below, but in this way, every new block is "chained" to the block before it by containing the hash of the previous block. Once a block is created, it cannot be changed.

The hash has two important properties: firstly, it is small, always the same size (64 hexadecimal characters), and secondly, if any change is made to the inputs, the resulting hash would be totally different. If someone tried to change a transaction to say that instead of X giving Y $10,000, the amount was $100,000, the fraud would be discovered immediately, because the hash of the block with that transaction would have changed.

To summarize, a blockchain is an immutable record of transactions, grouped into blocks, and they are chained together, because each block contains the hash of the previous block, so any attempted change to any of the data would immediately be discovered, because any future hash of the block would no longer match the previously announced hash of the block.

Security of distributed ledger technology

Blockchains are either public or private, also known as "permissioned." In a public blockchain, like Bitcoin, anyone can look at any transaction. However, the accounts are all anonymous, so there is no way to know whose transactions they are. In a private, or permissioned blockchain, participation in the blockchain is limited to authorized parties, and access to information about each transaction can be controlled.

The distributed nature of the system plays an important security role. If someone tried to change a transaction in the copy of the database on one computer (and they couldn't, as previously explained, because the hash wouldn't match anymore), that computer would ask all of the other copies of the database if they had the same information. Because the others would all have the correct information, not the attempted fraudulent one, the fraud would be replaced with the correct information.

In this way, blockchain provides multiple sources of security. To try to falsify a transaction, thieves would have to make a change and insert a new hash into their copy of the database (which they can't do) and then sneak the same change into the databases held on over 51% of the computers in the network, which they definitely also can't do.

Because the blocks are chained together, it is not possible to go back and even make corrections to transactions in the case of an error. Instead, a second transaction needs to be made, correcting the inaccurate initial transaction.

Proof of work and mining

When transactions are recorded onto the blockchain, the process of creating blocks is known as "mining." To record a new block, a new block is "mined" by one of the "miners" on the network, and that miner receives a financial reward. In the case of Bitcoin, the reward is 6.25 Bitcoins in 2023, but the reward is halved roughly every four years.

If a miner knew that they were going to be given the opportunity to record the new block, there could be a temptation to attempt to engage in fraud. To prevent this, the miner is selected randomly. In Bitcoin, the process used is "proof of work" (PoW), but "proof of stake" (PoS) is another process gaining popularity.

When Bitcoin miners are generating the hash of the transactions, in addition to the data to be hashed (including the previous hash), one more term is added to the string of information being hashed, and this is called a "nonce" (which stands for "number used once"). Each miner chooses whatever random nonce they want and creates the hash. Although the hash can be represented as a 64 hexadecimal character string, it is also a number, composed of 256 binary digits, ones and zeroes. The miners are told a target value, and the first miner to generate a hash smaller than the target gets to mint the transaction and receives the reward.

Because the outputs from the hashing algorithm are (apparently) random, many nonces must be tried to find a value smaller than a certain number. For example, if the hash is thought of as a number between 0 and 1, and the target were one one-millionth (0.000001), then one million different nonces would have to be tried, on average, to get a hash smaller than that amount.

Once a nonce has been found, it is extremely easy for anyone to verify that using this nonce creates a hash output that satisfies the target value. The method is called proof of work because it is easy to very that someone has really done the work necessary to identify a suitable nonce.

In PoW, a miner would need processing power equal to more than 50% of the processing power on the network to control the network and generate fraudulent transactions.

A blockchain must decide how often it will ideally record a block of transactions. In the case of Bitcoin, the target is that every ten minutes, a new block should be recorded. As the speed of computers increases, and as the number of computers being used for mining increases, more and more nonces can be tried per second. The Bitcoin network therefore adjusts the difficulty of the target periodically, to balance the difficulty with the amount of computing power currently deployed on the network.

Proof of stake

We will discuss the environmental costs of proof of work below, which are enormous, but they have led to a quest for a more environmental-friendly approach. The leading contender to replace proof of work is proof of stake.

Proof of stake systems do not choose the miner based on being the first to find a hash small enough. Rather, the miner is chosen directly through a random process, a lottery. The number of tokens (described next), or "stake" that the miner has in the system, represents their odds of being chosen.

The lack of complex mathematical problems does not incentivize the utilization of ever more and more computational power and avoids the worst of PoW's environmental costs.

With PoS, to engage in fraud, a miner would have to amass a stake equal to 51% of the coins staked in the network.

Paying for network transactions: Tokens, coins, and gas

Regardless the blockchain, a cost is incurred to run the network. The people running the network expect to receive benefits from their work at least as great as the costs. For a private network, the parties involved may be running the DLT because it reduces costs or improves service so much that they believe the cost is worth it.

For a public network, however, the parties running nodes expect to be paid for their services. For most networks, *reading* information *from* the ledger is free. This seems reasonable, as there is very little cost involved in reading information off of the blockchain: information is simply being looked up in an existing database.

However, *writing* information *to* the ledger generally incurs a cost. For new transactions to be recorded, new blocks must be created. Regardless of whether proof of work, proof of stake, or some other method is used, computing cycles are being used to record the transaction.

The cost to have a transaction written is generally referred to as a "gas fee." Gas fees are not paid in "fiat currency" of dollars, pounds, euros, or yuan, etc. Every blockchain has a native token, or coin, that must be used for paying gas fees on the network. In the Bitcoin network, Bitcoins are used. In the Ethereum network, the tokens are ETH (pronounced "eeth"). In the Cosmos network, the coins are Atom.[1]

---

[1]In the interest of full disclosure, the author purchased $100 worth of Atom tokens in October, 2021, his only cryptocurrency holding. As of November, 2023, it was worth $27, having lost 73% of its value.

In the Ethereum network, a sender creating a transaction specifies how much they are willing to pay in gas fees for the transaction. The more someone is willing to pay, the more quickly their transaction will be executed.

The study of the economics of the tokens (how many to have, what they should be worth, etc.) is called token economics, or "tokenomics."

Customers pay the node holders for their services in tokens, so they have to buy them from a pool, likely trading fiat currency for tokens. The node holders later sell their tokens via the pool, converting them to fiat. As usage of the network increases, demand for the token increases, and the price of the token may go up. Speculators can also buy tokens, if they believe that this particular blockchain is going to be important and buy tokens as a speculative investment.

SHA-256 hashing algorithms

Because hashing is such an important part of the system, it is worth describing in some detail. The hash is kind of like an X-ray of the input, because it is a summary or distillation. An X-ray loses a lot of information (compared to reality), but it can show what is inside an object. Another analogy is a microfiche (the obsolete library technology). The microfiche loses many details but still presents the most important information. However, both X-rays and microfiche provide representations of the original, while the hash is a meaningless string of 64 letters and numbers.

Unlike an X-ray, a hashing algorithm provides information about the data, without revealing any of the data. For example, two very bad hashing methods would be counting the number of letters in the input, or a list of how many times each letter appeared. A clever fraudster could easily change the contents in such a way that it would not be detectable under either of these methods. But the hash itself does not reveal any the input directly.

The most widely used hash algorithm is SHA-256, which was published by the US National Institute of Standards and Technology in 2004 and patented by the US National Security Agency. It is considered extremely secure.

No matter how long the input, the resulting hash is always 64 hexadecimal characters. If you input "Hello, world," or the complete works of William Shakespeare, the hash is the same length. This is important because this makes it impossible to reverse-engineer the input string that was entered into the algorithm.

For example, here is the hash of "Hello, world":

4ae7c3b6ac0beff671efa8cf57386151c06e58ca53a78d83f36107316cec125f

Here is the hash of "Hello, world!":

315f5bdb76d078c43b8ac0064e4a0164612b1fce77c869345bfc94c75894edd3

Adding one character completely changed the resulting hash and demonstrates the most powerful property of the algorithm, namely, that any change to the inputs results in a completely different output. If you remove one comma from the works of Shakespeare, the resulting hash is totally different.

The output appears to be random. But in fact, it is not. It follows an extremely complicated algorithm. Any two people who put the same input into the algorithm will always get the same hash.

A hash is 256 binary numbers (represented as 64 hexadecimal characters), which means there are only 2^{256} possible output hashes. This is $1.157 * 10^{77}$, or 1 followed by 77 zeroes. The number of possible hashes is not infinite, but it is so large that it is very difficult to conceive of. For comparison, the number of grains of sand on Earth is 7.5×10^{18}, or only 18 zeroes (Krulwich, 2012).

Environmental Considerations of Blockchains

Carbon emissions from proof of work

Unfortunately for Bitcoin enthusiasts, the proof of work method requires massive amounts of computing power, which requires massive amounts of electricity. As of May 2022, Bitcoin mining consumed 150 terawatt-hours of electricity annually, equal to the annual consumption of Argentina, a country of 45 million people (Hinsdale, 2022).

Companies have realized that the way to make money by mining Bitcoin is to put as much computing power on the problem as they possibly can. The more computing power a firm uses, the more likely it is to find a winning nonce.

A single Bitcoin transaction uses as much electricity as a typical US household uses in 50 days (Hern, 2022). In July 2022, Digiconomist estimated the carbon footprint of a single Bitcoin transaction at 808.36 kg of CO_2, which it says is equivalent to watching 134,727 hours of YouTube, or to 1,791,606 Visa transactions (Digiconomist, 2022b).

In July 2017, Bitcoin was estimated to be using 13.67 tera-watt hours (TWh) of electricity per year. By May 2022, the estimate was 204.50 TWh (Digiconomist, 2022a). The higher the price of Bitcoin rose, the more profitable mining became. However, as the price began to fall in 2022, miners using more expensive electricity sources were no longer profitable, and many closed down their operations.

E-Waste from proof of work

Another large environmental effect from Bitcoin mining is the generation of e-waste. In the beginning, hobbyists could mine Bitcoin on their desktop computers. But as miners sought to become more efficient, PCs were replaced by graphics processing units (GPUs), and then by Application-Specific Integrated Circuits (ASIC). ASICs are so specialized that they can only be used to mine Bitcoin. They cannot be used even to mine any other cryptocurrencies (de Vries & Stoll, 2021).

As Bitcoin became increasingly valuable, corporate mining efforts grew. The result was that in May 2021, the annual amount of e-waste from Bitcoin mining was estimated at 30.7 metric kilotons, which is the same as the amount of e-waste produced by the Netherlands each year (de Vries & Stoll, 2021).

Need for Unique Serialization

Serialization and non-fungibility

In order an item to be trackable in a blockchain (or database of any kind), the item must be unique and have some type of serial number (SN).

If items are interchangeable, they are "fungible." If items can readily be differentiated, they are "non-fungible." Fungible items cannot be stored on a blockchain, because there is no way to know which particular item is being sold, transported, inspected, or modified, etc.

To be trackable, an item must be made non-fungible, through some type of serialization process, in which a SN is added directly onto the item, ideally in a permanent way.

Computers and electronic devices already have SNs applied by the manufacturer. For some products there is no SN, but one could theoretically be applied. For example, for apples, a serial number could be applied to each item, however, it seems unlikely to be economically warranted. However, a license plate or temporary serial number could also be assigned to a larger quantity, such as a box or pallet.

For even smaller discrete items, like coffee beans or corn kernels, serializing individual items is impractical, and larger quantities would need to be used. Finally, for products like powders and liquids, individual serialization is impossible and can only be done for larger quantities, such as sacks, drums, or tanks.

It seems likely that the number of products being given SNs will continue to increase. In the past, no one would have considered giving SNs to cell phone headphones. Now, left and right Apple AirPods have different SNs.

Universal Serial Numbers

A manufacturer's SN, unfortunately, may not be enough to guarantee that the item in someone's possession is exactly the item being looked for. Manufacturers create SNs using whatever combination of letters, numbers, and symbols they prefer. This leaves open the possibility that two products from different manufacturers (or even different products from the same manufacturer) could have the same SN.

To track individual products using blockchain, (or any other database technology), the products must be *uniquely* identified. In some industries, such as cell phones and automobiles, industry-wide SN systems such as IMEI and VIN have been developed. However, the likelihood of developing similar systems across all other product types seems unlikely.

One proposal for meeting this need is a Universal Serial Number (USN) (Lembke & Sukhia, 2023). The authors propose first combining together the manufacturer's name, the product name, and the item's SN. This avoids the problem of two products from different manufacturers, or different products from the same manufacturer, having the same SNs.

However, the resulting USN could easily be 30 or more characters long. To avoid this, once the three data elements are combined, the resulting string is run through the SHA-256 hashing algorithm, resulting in an apparently random string of 64 characters. Under the proposal, characters 1–12 are used as the USN. If that matches one previously used, characters 2–13 would be used, etc. This proposal is currently under consideration for inclusion in a new ISO standard by ISO Technical Committee 307 Working Group 8.

Blockchain History

Bitcoin

Because Bitcoin was the first use of blockchain, it remains the only use many people have heard of. Bitcoin was proposed in 2008 by the pseudonymous author, Satoshi Nakamoto (2008), but the tools necessary to build blockchains had been developed over time. Permanently chaining blocks together with hash functions was proposed by Merkle (1979). The concept of blockchains was presented by Haber and Stornetta (1991). They suggested time stamping documents by including bits from the previously time-stamped document. Nakamoto (2008) cites their work in his initial presentation of Bitcoin. The Bitcoin network was launched, and mining began in January 2009.

There were other previous efforts to create digital cash. Chaum (1979) described a system for maintaining a distributed computer system, between parties who do not trust each other (Sherman *et al.*, 2019). In 1990, Chaum founded DigiCash to implement a secure, private digital cash solution (Pitta, 1997).

Ethereum

Bitcoin was created as a digital currency, but in 2013, a young programmer and Bitcoin enthusiast, Vitalik Buterin, thought of the idea of a blockchain with a built-in programming language to be used as a platform for many more applications (Finley, 2014; Frank & Silverstein, 2021).

The network went live in 2015. Ethereum is the second-best known blockchain platform, after Bitcoin, and the Ethereum token, Ether, is second only to Bitcoin, in terms of market capitalization.

Ethereum has been very successful and its use of non-fungible tokens (NFTs, described below), has allowed for the creation of some very popular speculative assets. However, NFTs do also offer possibilities for other types of supply chain coordination, described below. Lastly, Ethereum also created the very important concept of "smart contracts."

Like Bitcoin, Ethereum was created using proof of work, but in September 2022, Ethereum switched to Proof of stake, in a process known as "the Merge" (Kessler, 2022). The switch is expected to reduce Ethereum's energy consumption by 99.95% (Ethereum, 2022b).

Smart contracts and decentralized apps, dapps

One of the key advances that Ethereum pioneered was the idea of "smart contacts." The concept was created in 1994 (Szabo, 1994). For security purposes, Bitcoin has limited programming capabilities. But Ethereum was designed to allow transactions to be automatically executed if certain conditions are met. Smart contracts can be thought of as computer programs that live on a blockchain and execute automatically when the proper conditions are met (Ethereum, 2022a), and generally written in the Solidity programming language. Smart contracts have allowed the creation of decentralized applications, known as dApps.

Non-fungible tokens: Digital art

Ethereum standard ERC-20 allows individual tokens to be created and tracked on the blockchain. But each of these tokens refers to a particular specific item, so these tokens are non-fungible.

In 2021, the use of these NFTs exploded into the public's attention. The most visible use of them is the buying and selling of digital art, generally simple, cartoonish drawings. The CryptoPunks and Bored Ape Yacht Club being two of the most well-known examples, but their values have fallen far from the peak (Hetzner, 2022).

Also, NFT transactions are not as private as people believe. TV host Jimmy Fallon showed off his Bored Ape NFT on TV, which told the world that he owned that individual NFT. Because the Ethereum blockchain is public, it was simple for anyone to find the address of the wallet that owned this NFT. In a public blockchain, anyone can send tokens to anyone they want to. In late 2021, someone sent 1,776 politically themed NFTs to his account, regardless of whether he wanted them or not (Ravenscraft, 2022).

Non-fungible tokens: Physical assets (pNFTs)

Beyond managing digital art, NFTs can potentially be a useful and powerful way to track physical assets. The term pNFT is being introduced, which is shorthand for "representing physical assets using NFTs." Working Group 8 of ISO Technical Committee 307 is proposing development of a global standard to use pNFTs to track physical devices (ISO.org).

The proposal would standardize methods for: (1) identifying physical items and creating digital identifiers for them, (2) verifying the identity of people and software performing transactions, and (3) storing and sharing transactions.

Hyperledger

In 2015, the Linux Foundation announced a project to produce an open-source, "enterprise grade" distributed ledger, listing more than twenty major multi-national corporations who committed to work with the project (Hyperledger, 2015). There were initially two main products, Hyperledger Fabric, and Hyperledger Sawtooth, but Hyperledger Cactus has been added, which facilitates the integration of multiple blockchains (Kerner, 2022).

Hyperledger allows companies to build permissioned, or private, blockchains. As we will see below, many supply chain industry solutions have been built using Hyperledger. Many of these solutions were created for an industry consortium, or small number of companies, to facilitate the widespread sharing, within their group, of a limited scope of information, but keeping other details private. As private, permissioned blockchains, a gas fee is not charged.

Blockchain interoperability

As will be seen below, numerous blockchains have been created for particular industries or sectors. A blockchain allows trading partners to easily share the desired information with their partners who are in the blockchain.

However, companies may need to transact with companies who are part of another blockchain and not theirs. Maybe they are in their same industry but joined different blockchains or are in different industries and joined the blockchains for those industries.

The process of transferring information between two different blockchains is called cross-chain communication, or a bridge. Bridges have been targeted by hackers, causing enormous losses. In three different attacks in early 2022, more than $1 billion worth of cryptocurrencies was stolen (Page, 2022b). The largest, in which $625 million in mostly Ethereum was stolen, was linked by US officials to a North-Korean-backed hacking group (Page, 2022a). In August 2022, $200 million was stolen from a bridge when a software update created a vulnerability, and after an initial theft, copycat hackers deployed armies of bots to replicate the attack (Browne, 2022).

Because interoperability is so important, and bridges are so attractive for attackers, newer blockchains have been designed for interoperability from the beginning. The Cosmos blockchain platform is designed to allow different blockchains built on the Cosmos platform to easily communicate and move assets back and forth (Kessler & Young, 2022). Polkadot has a more hub-and-spoke approach for securely sharing data between chains (*ibid.*).

The Cosmos whitepaper was published in 2016 (Kim, 2019), and Cosmos introduced the Inter Blockchain Communication Protocol (IBC) in 2021 (Radmilac, 2022). In June 2022, the Hyperledger Foundation announced YUI, their project to achieve interoperability between different blockchains and it uses the IBC developed by Cosmos (Kimura, 2021).

Permissioned blockchains versus distributed ledger technology (DLT)

Many permissioned blockchain applications have been built for commercial enterprises using blockchain technology. These applications store transactions in blocks and hash the contents, including the hash of the previous block, so they would seem to meet the definition of a blockchain.

However, many of these private ledgers are not highly distributed. They are controlled by a central entity and therefore lack the distributed, communal nature that is central to something like Bitcoin. This led some to claim these are not "real" blockchains (e.g., Konashevych, 2021).

When a company sets up an internal blockchain, the ledger is not decentralized in the same way, even if multiple copies exist on different servers. When a consortium of organizations works together to build a blockchain, it is also not highly decentralized.

Blockchains are designed to be usable by parties who do not necessarily trust each other, so it is not surprising they work equally well with trusting ones. Given the amount of corporate interest in DLTs, it seems likely that these centralized blockchains will find many valuable and useful applications in the future.

Permissioned blockchains are also less likely to need a token system for payments. If the whole system is underneath one entity, and all of the costs are incurred by that same entity, transfer payments for the services may not be necessary (Furlonger & Uzureau, 2019).

Supply Chain Opportunities for Blockchain

Blockchains are designed to track all of the transactions involving a particular asset or item. This means that blockchains are potentially well suited to tackling a number of supply chain challenges:

- provenance: authenticity and embargoes,
- recalls,
- counterfeit prevention, and
- theft deterrence and recovery.

Provenance

Blockchain makes it possible for a retailer to be able to easily prove to a customer exactly where an item has come from. The customer could know the exact geographic origin of the item, where it was sent for processing and guarantees that no child labor or forced labor was involved. This is the primary focus of many current blockchain projects.

Recalls

Every year, millions of pounds of food are recalled. Because retailers and producers lack detailed visibility of where every item was produced, and where it ended up, much food is thrown away unnecessarily. A blockchain solution could allow a retailer to know exactly where every unit from a given lot from a supplier ended up and minimize wastage. By tracking the provenance of food products, where they come from and where they go, blockchain systems for tracking food are also well equipped to facilitate improved recalls (Sajja, 2022).

Counterfeit prevention

One of the areas where producers of consumer goods are particularly interested in blockchain is in the area of counterfeit prevention. Traditional anti-counterfeiting programs have generally applied some type of mark to the product, which should be as difficult as possible for counterfeiters to replicate. The problem for producers is that the counterfeiters have always quickly gained the ability to replicate the marking.

Many anti-counterfeiting efforts also include the use of a SN, but counterfeiters can simply find a SN from a legitimate product and put it on every single counterfeit unit they produce. Or perhaps cycle through multiple SNs to reduce the odds of a customer noticing that they are reusing SNs, or generate fake SNs, using the structure of the legitimate SNs.

However, in order for SNs to be truly effective in preventing fraud, customers need to register that they have purchased a given unit. If a counterfeiter has used a SN from a legitimate product on multiple copies, and none of the units are ever registered, no one will ever know about the counterfeiting. But if every customer were to attempt to register their units, all of the counterfeit units would immediately be identified.

This is where blockchain may be particularly helpful in the fight against counterfeits. Blockchain systems can streamline and simplify the process of SN registration and tracking.

It is worth mentioning that even without a blockchain, one of the most effective ways firms could battle counterfeits (and also fraudulent warranty claims) would be to capture the SN of every device as it is sold. Unfortunately, most point-of-sale systems require a second barcode to be scanned to do this today. As Lembke (2020, 2022) outlined, a new ANSI standard known as MH10.8.2.12N allows a single QR code on the packaging to contain both the UPC and the SN. With a single scan, the point-of-sale terminal can retrieve the sales price, using the UPC, and register the SN.

It is worth stressing that a blockchain is not necessary to provide this history; a traditional database could easily be used. However, using a blockchain is more likely to make it easier and faster to access this information.

Theft deterrence and recovery

If the SN of a product is captured at the point of sale (PoS), this could reduce the desirability of shoplifting. This would not make it harder to steal an item, but it could make it much harder to profit from the stolen item. Currently, once items are stolen, some are returned to the store for full refunds or store credit. But if the retailer tracks the SN of every item that was sold, and someone attempts to return an item that has not been sold by that retailer, the return will be denied.

Currently, when police recover stolen goods, retailers have difficulty in proving that they were the source of the items. If the SN of each item has been tracked through a blockchain, a retailer could prove to law enforcement that the item was previously in one of their stores and recover the item.

Transportation and Logistics Industry

Transportation would seem like a discipline ready to benefit from the incorporation of blockchain and much has been written about the possibilities (Patel, 2017).

Trucking

The Blockchain in Transport Alliance (BiTA) was founded in 2017 to develop blockchain standards to be used across the transportation and logistics industry (Baker, 2018). FedEx, DHL Express and UPS are all members, working together to develop common standards (Merian, 2019). By 2019, the organization grew to over 500 member companies (*ibid.*).

Unfortunately, despite its promise, blockchain adoption in the transportation industry has been slower than many might have expected. As of 2022, no significant benefits have yet been seen in the industry (Fisher, 2022). In 2019, Gartner predicted that by 2023, 90% of blockchain initiatives would suffer "blockchain fatigue" due to lack of strong use cases (Gartner, 2019).

In 2019, BiTA commissioned Arthur D. Little to study perceptions and adoptions of blockchain (Kilefors *et al.*, 2020). Executives from more than 100 companies were surveyed. Over 70% believed it could increase efficiencies and nearly 60% said it could disrupt business models. Respondents believed blockchain allows traceability and security from a single source of trust. They also believed smart contracts should speed processing and settlement of transactions. Sixty-seven percent of respondents either had no plans to implement blockchain or had not moved beyond the planning stage.

The biggest factors that executives felt were holding back blockchain adoption were lack of proven benefits and lack of technical expertise. The study authors also felt that many organizations also lack the technical foundation necessary to begin a blockchain project (*ibid.*).

One well-publicized success for blockchain in transportation has been Walmart Canada (Vitasek *et al.*, 2022). It was experiencing difficulties and delays with the invoices from its carriers. Information systems that did not talk to each other led to manual processing. They partnered with DLT Labs, and after a 2019 a pilot version, it was rolled out to all of the other 69 carriers in March 2021.

Before the system, over 70% of freight invoices were disputed. After, less than 1% were, and those that are, are resolved quickly (*ibid.*). Building the system as a permissioned blockchain, using Hyperledger, allowed them to control information visibility to only the parties involved. Another suggestion, based on their experience, was to not replace existing information systems as part of a blockchain implementation. This prevents any loss of existing data and companies continue to benefit from the strengths of their existing systems.

Shipping

The global shipping industry is more actively pursuing blockchain solutions. In 2018, Maersk partnered with IBM to design a Hyperledger blockchain to streamline the paperwork associated with international shipments (Moise, 2018), subsequently named TradeLens. Hapag-Lloyd of Germany and Japan's ONE joined in 2019 (Paris, 2019). MSC subsequently joined, and Hapag-Lloyd left, meaning three of the five largest container shipping lines were participating (Ledger Insights, 2021c).

In 2022, IBM claimed that TradeLens had handled over 150 million "shipping events" and saved users 20% on documentation costs (Pessaraly, 2022). However, in November 2022, IBM and Maersk announced TradeLens would shut down in the first quarter of 2023, saying the platform had not reached the level of commercial viability needed (Wragg, 2022).

The Global Shipping Business Network (GSBN) was started by CMA CGM and Cosco Shipping (*ibid.*). As of 2022, other members include OOCL, Hapag-Lloyd, Qindao Port, PSA International, and Shanghai International Port Group (GSBN, 2022). With COSCO and Hapag-Lloyd, they have two of the world's largest ocean carriers (Ledger Insights, 2021c). They claim that one out of three containers are handled by their members. GSBN runs on Hyperledger Fabric, with hosting by Oracle, but nodes in China are provided by AntChain (Ledger Insights, 2021d).

In March 2018, APL announced it had partnered with AB InBev, Accenture, and Kuehne + Nagel and successfully tested an Etherereum blockchain solution (Knowler, 2018; Ledger Insights, 2018).

In July 2018, APL announced a plan to introduce a blockchain platform, hoping other carriers, forwarders and shippers would join them

(Johnson, 2018). In August 2018, APL announced it would be joining the BiTA (Sok, 2018).

Parcel shipping

In 2017, UPS announced its participation in BiTA, looking for increased efficiencies and transparency (Patel, 2017). In 2018, it filed for a patent for using blockchain to track packages (Hamilton, 2018). In 2019, UPS announced a partnership to use blockchain to track beef from the United States to Japan (Cosgrove, 2019), apparently built on Hyperledger (Bandoim, 2019).

FedEx also joined BiTA (Merian, 2019), and in 2018, CEO Fred Smith said that blockchain has *big, big implications in supply chain, transportation, and logistics* (Norton, 2018). FedEx also said they had some projects built on Ethereum and Hyperledger (*ibid.*). In April 2019, CIO Rob Carter said collaboration across the industry is necessary for the technology to take off (Castellanos, 2019).

DHL Express USA agrees. *Blockchain won't work in a perfect environment unless everyone is cooperating*, said CIO Eugene Laney (*ibid.*).

Food Products

Many blockchain projects have been initiated to bring transparency and visibility to food supply chains. Walmart, as the world's largest brick and mortar retailer, has been very interested in blockchain. In 2017, it announced it was teaming up with Unilever, Nestle, Dole, and Kroger to develop a blockchain system for traceability of foodstuffs (Peterson, 2017). A primary goal was improving traceability for food safety, to reduce the time to identify unsafe food, and minimize the amount of food wasted unnecessarily. IBM built the system using Hyperledger.

In 2017, a supply chain manager asked Walmart staff to trace back a package of mangoes that were purchased in a store. It took six days and 18 hours. With their blockchain implementation, the time was reduced to 2.2 seconds (Charlebois, 2017).

This system is now known as the Food Trust (Nash, 2018). After 18 months of testing, in September 2018, Walmart notified direct suppliers of lettuce, spinach, and other greens that they had to join the blockchain by September 2019. Millions of bags and heads of lettuce had been thrown away the year before because of an *E.coli* outbreak.

Since 2019, green bell peppers and other categories have been added and the expanded list of suppliers has grown from 12 to around 100. Frank Yiannas was the vice president of food safety at Walmart who helped lead the effort. In 2022, while serving as the deputy commissioner for food policy and response at the US FDA, he said he thought lessons learned from the pandemic, as well as proposed food traceability rules, would help increase adoption of blockchain in the food industry (Bhattacharyya, 2022).

In 2018, Coca-Cola announced that it was partnering with the US State Department to fight the use of forced labor worldwide (Chavez-Dreyfuss, 2018). Subsequent searches have failed to yield any further announcements about the project unfortunately. Not all blockchain projects move forward smoothly. In 2022, Coca-Cola announced it was partnering with Diginex to build a new ESG blockchain tool (Ledger Insights, 2022a). Coke One North America announced it is using an SAP Hyperledger solution to coordinate production among 70 suppliers (Wood, 2019). In 2020, Coke One North America announced it was developing an Ethereum solution that allows participants to synchronize inventories (Ledger Insights, 2020b).

PepsiCo is partnering with Security Matters, to use an invisible chemical marker system that will allow them to track plastic packaging waste via blockchain (George, 2022).

Raw Seafoods, in Massachusetts, worked with IBM and their fishing fleet to develop a system that puts a two-dimensional QR barcode on each bag of scallops as it is filled, on the boat. The identifying number in the QR code allows consumers to track where and when they were harvested, and downstream partners add in where and when the seafood was processed and packaged (Holmyard, 2019).

IBM has introduced a FoodTrust solution for tracking wine through the distribution chain, including monitoring for proper temperatures (Ledger Insights, 2020d). Everledger announced a Hyperledger solution for tracking fine wines, in which consumers can scan an near-field communication (NFC) tag contained in the label to discover the full provenance of the bottle (Ledger Insights, 2020a). In 2019, EY announced it had developed an Ethereum solution for tracking bottles of wine (Makrygiannis, 2019). In 2020, a dozen Australian wine companies started tracking their wines, using a solution called Hedera, which is a DLT, but not a blockchain, rather a hashgraph (Ledger Insights, 2020c).

Starbucks has partnered with Microsoft's Azure platform to allow customers to see where their beans have come from, and farmers to see where their beans have gone (Almeida, 2020).

Pharmaceuticals

The World Health Organization estimates that one in ten medical products in the developing world is substandard or falsified (WHO, 2017). According to BSI, the British standards agency, over $1 billion worth of pharmaceuticals are stolen every year (BSI, 2020). Every year, 2–3% of pharmaceuticals are returned, which could represent as much as $21 billion worth of returns per year (Morris, 2018b).

To fight fraud, and ensure that medications are legitimate, the EU created the Falsified Medicine Directive (FMD), which requires drugs to be serialized or barcoded. A centralized database was required. The US enacted the Drug Supply Chain Security Act (DSCSA), which requires serialization or barcoding at the package level (Morris, 2018a). The US system did not require a centralized database.

The Mediledger Network tracks the sale and movement of individual packages. Using the SNs, if drugs are returned to a manufacturer, the manufacturer can verify that they did, in fact, come from them. The network includes manufacturers such as Pfizer and Amgen, and distributors like Genentech and McKesson and is built on Ethereum (Morris, 2018a). Walmart and Walgreens participated in a 2020 pilot of the system's track and trace capabilities (McCauley, 2020).

SAP created a blockchain that generates unique identifiers and stores the GS1 item number, the batch number, and expiration date. SAP said the solution is built using the MultiChain protocol (Morris, 2018a). The blockchain went live in January 2019, including partners of GlaxoSmithKline, Merk, and AmerisourceBergen (Ledger Insights, 2019a). Verification requests about the legitimacy of a given package can be satisfied by the blockchain, rather than the original manufacturer.

Retail Consumer Goods

As described above, Walmart has made many efforts related to food traceability using the IBM FoodTrust platform.

In 2018, Target began working on an open-source supply chain block-chain called ConsenSource, focused on certification of paper suppliers. In 2019, Target announced it was supporting the Hyperledger Grid project (Baydakova, 2019). In 2020, Target announced it was working with The Coupon Bureau using Hedera's Hashgraph DLT to minimize fraud in the use of customer coupons (Pollock, 2020).

Home Depot has worked with IBM to build a blockchain solution to minimize disputes with vendors. The system provides vendors visibility into their receiving process, letting the vendors see exactly how much Home Depot has received (King, 2021).

In December 2022, Lowe's announced a plan to use RFID chips to activate power tools at the PoS and then track their provenance using a block-chain built in Ethereum. Stolen tools will be inoperable. However, subsequent buyers of legitimately purchased tools will be able to verify their authenticity (Tobin, 2023; Wolfson, 2023).

Amazon Web Services announced Ethereum and Hyperledger templates in 2018, designed to help companies build their own blockchains more easily (Town, 2018). To date, Amazon has not made any public statements about using blockchain in its own distribution operations.

French retailer Carrefour began offering customers the ability to track mashed potatoes using the IBM Food Trust platform in 2019 (Khatri, 2019). Information available to consumers includes the production date and the farmers who grew the potatoes. Previously, Carrefour worked on its own blockchain in Ethereum (Morris, 2018c). In 2021, Carrefour announced it was using the Food Trust to track 450 organic cotton bed linen and baby products in France and Spain, and to track citrus fruits in Brazil (Ledger Insights, 2021a).

The United Nations Economic Commission for Europe (UNECE) has a goal of increasing traceability and sustainability in the footwear and garment industries. UNECE has launched an Ethereum blockchain for tracking cotton production and a pilot project for tracking leather (UNECE, 2021).

The Organic Traceability Project is sponsored by the C&A Foundation, the Organic Cotton Accelerator, and Fashion for Good, along with C&A, Zalando, PVH Corp, and the Kering Group. A quantity of cotton is tracked as a token on the Bext360 blockchain, which uses the Stellar blockchain network (Knapp, 2019).

Computers and Consumer Electronics

Dell is working with its subsidiary, VMware, to track the provenance of plastic that has been recovered from e-waste recyclers and then used in its computers using VMware's blockchain solution (Ledger Insights, 2019c). VMware's blockchain solution is central to the Australian stock market's efforts to replace its core trading systems. Unfortunately, this project has been delayed due to difficulties with scalability and resilience (Sharwood, 2022).

Intel was a major contributor to the development of Hyperledger Sawtooth but has not announced any blockchain usage within its own supply chain (Baydakova & Allison, 2019).

Hewlett Packard has released an Ethereum-based swarm learning blockchain for AI (Ledger Insights, 2022c) but has not announced any supply chain related efforts.

There has been media coverage when it considered accepting cryptocurrencies for payment, but no supply chain blockchain projects have been announced.

Lifecycle tracking of electronics

In 2017, the Open Blockchain for Asset Disposition Architecture (OBADA) Foundation was created. Its goal is to build a blockchain for tracking IT assets throughout their lifetimes. When a device is sold, resold, and refurbished, its hard drive is wiped, or it is properly disassembled and/or recycled, these actions will be stored to the blockchain. All histories are stored securely in the blockchain built on the Cosmos platform (OBADA.io, 2022). The blockchain creates NFTs for each physical item, pNFTs, as discussed above.

High-Tech Supply Chain: Fungible Raw Materials

Once they are assembled, technology devices are serialized, as are many of their components. But before the semiconductors, batteries, screens, and other components can be combined to make a device, they all begin as fungible raw materials.

Batteries: Cobalt

Batteries use different materials to produce three primary components: the anode, cathode, and electrolyte. All of these materials begin as ore, which is naturally fungible.

One of the most important minerals for batteries today is cobalt, used in the cathode. Cobalt extends the battery's life and ensures that the batteries will not catch fire. It is also very expensive.

Unfortunately, there are ethical concerns related to sourcing cobalt. The Democratic Republic of Congo holds the largest economically accessible cobalt deposits in the world, but in 2016 was accused by Amnesty International of child labor and other human rights abuses in its cobalt mining. More than 20% of Congo's production comes from artisanal miners using hand tools and often using child labor (Amnesty International, 2016). Because the artisanal mining industry is so decentralized, progress on safety and child labor has been difficult despite significant efforts (Barich, 2022).

Companies are therefore trying hard to improve their tracking and tracing abilities. London-based Circulor is providing tracing and carbon emissions tracking for nickel and cobalt, which involves auditors on site at the artisanal sites, ensuring standards are being met (Barich, 2022). In 2019, Volvo began working with Circulor to use blockchain to trace cobalt (Hampel, 2020), built on Hyperledger (Sloane, 2020).

Tesla is working with the ReSource consortium to track its cobalt sourcing (Crider, 2021). The solution is being developed by Kryha, which is *leveraging a private blockchain with a public mindset* (Ledger Insights, 2021b), although their LinkedIn page does list *blockchain, Ethereum* as the first two of eighteen specialties (LinkedIn, 2022).

Another consortium using blockchain to track the sourcing of cobalt is the Responsible Sourcing Blockchain Network (RSBN), built by IBM on Hyperledger. Fiat, Ford, Volkswagen, Volvo, and LG are all working together on a project aimed at tracking cobalt production (Ledger Insights, 2019d).

Going one step further, Volvo is using its blockchain built by Circulor using Hyperledger and Oracle to track recycled cobalt that is sourced from older lithium-ion batteries (Banks-Louie, 2020).

Because of the cost and the ethical sourcing concerns, some companies are using lithium phosphate (LFP) batteries that do not use cobalt. LFP batteries are cheaper to make but result in lower driving range, which still allows them to be popular for urban driving in China (Desai, 2021). However, LFP technology improved so much that it makes economic sense in more vehicles. In 2022, Tesla announced that nearly half of the vehicles it produced in the previous quarter were LFP (Lambert, 2022).

Nickel, tantalum, and lithium

Another key metal for battery production is nickel, and Tesla has announced plans to build a blockchain solution with BHP for tracing its nickel supplies (BHP, 2021). Volvo plans to use the RSBN Hyperledger platform to track nickel and lithium (Ledger Insights, 2019b).

The RSBN group also plans to use Hyperledger to track mica, tungsten, tantalum, tin, and gold (Ledger Insights, 2019d).

Tantalum, also known as coltan, was another metal whose mining was causing ethical sourcing dilemmas. Miners running illegal mining operations in the DRC were killing endangered gorillas (Temperton, 2016). Circulor has also begun a Hyperledger-based solution to track tantalum production in Rwanda (Khatri, 2018).

High-End Retail: Diamonds, Jewelry, and Luxury Goods

As a new technology, it is perhaps not surprising that some of the first industries using blockchain solutions have been producers of expensive, high-end products because they can afford the expenses required to work with a new technology. Their products are expensive and highly desirable, so consumers have greater concerns about counterfeiting, provenance, and ethical sourcing.

Diamonds

Consumer concerns about ethical sourcing and avoiding so-called "blood diamonds" have led retailers and suppliers to believe customers value access to provenance information about diamonds. Secondly, because diamonds are so small and clear, applying any type of registration or SN was impractical, which made it very difficult to track stolen or unethically sourced stones.

The Gemological Institute of America (GIA) certification process for gems creates a unique identification number for each stone and evaluates the weight, color, cut, and clarity (including drawings showing the size and location of inclusions), dimensions, fluorescence, and geographical origin. Technology now allows the identification number to be inscribed on the girdle of the diamond (Palmer, 2022).

Working with the GIA, starting in 2018, Everledger has built a Hyperledger-based solution for diamonds. The SN and 40 measurements about the diamond are stored in the blockchain (Escobar, 2022; Everledger, 2021).

In 2018, diamond producer DeBeers announced its own blockchain solution, called Tracr, to track diamonds from the point of mining through polishing and sales (Shapshak, 2018) and built using Ethereum (del Castillo & Schifrin, 2020). The process includes a scan of the rough diamond, then of the cut stone, and documenting it at each step of the process (Becker, 2021).

In 2018, Russian-based Alrosa, the world's largest producer of rough diamonds, also joined the Tracr pilot program but eventually opted to work instead with Everledger (Ledger Insights, 2022d).

Russia accounts for 28% of global rough diamonds, and Alrosa mines at least 90% of Russia's diamonds and is partly owned by the Kremlin. Because of Russia's invasion of Ukraine, in February 2022, many American firms wanted guarantees that the diamonds they were selling were not Russian. Because of Tracr, DeBeers was able to prove the provenance of their diamonds and provide non-Russian diamonds to US retailers (Godsen, 2022).

Gemstones

Everledger has also built a Hyperledger-based solution for other gemstones (Palmer, 2022) in which microscopic artificial DNA particles are allowed to seep into the microscopic cracks in the gemstones and remain intact throughout the shaping process, making it possible to prove the origin of the stones throughout the supply chain and usage (Becker, 2021).

Jewelry

Technology has been developed to put an RFID chip inside of a nucleus of a cultured pearl, which allows an individual pearl to be tracked via blockchain (Swedberg, 2013). For natural pearls, no identification number can be inscribed on the pearl, but Everledger has created a Hyperledger solution to track individual pearls. The pearls are digitally scanned and precision measurements are stored in the database (Chiu, 2021).

In 2021, the Aura Blockchain Consortium for luxury goods was announced, created by Consensys and Microsoft, built on Ethereum, and started with LVMH, including Cartier, Bulgari, and Christian Dior

(Thompson, 2019). Bulgari has begun some limited use of the Aura blockchain (Ledger Insights, 2022b).

In Hong Kong, jewelry retailer Chow Tai Fook partnered with GIA and Everledger to share grading information about the stones used in their jewelry (GIA, 2018).

Chinese e-tailer JD.com has partnered with Everledger to allow shoppers to access GIA data about diamonds, prior to purchase, to prove legitimacy, including previous owners (Wright, 2020).

In 2018, IBM announced TrustChain, built on Hyperledger, to track engagement rings. The intent was that by 2019, a jewelry shopper could scan a QR code to see the ring's complete history (Miller, 2018). However, as of July 2022, the website still says that the project is in the *trial and development phase* (Trustchainjewelry.com, 2018).

Luxury goods

Using the Aura Hyperledger blockchain, Louis Vuitton places NFC sensor chips inside their bags, which allow sales associates with the proper app to read the bag's identification number and look it up on the blockchain. Counterfeiters have, of course, begun to make counterfeit bags also with NFC chips that direct the person reading the NFC tag to go to the Louis Vuitton website (Zhang, 2020).

Summary and Conclusions

We have presented a detailed introduction to blockchains, providing details and a historical overview of blockchain development.

We have also provided the reader with an understanding of the places where supply chain blockchain solutions have, and have not, been pursued. Many benefits have been expected from blockchain for the supply chain. From reading the business press, an impression might be created that blockchain implementations are succeeding everywhere. As we have seen, this is not the case.

In the ocean shipping sector, two major blockchain alliances were created, both built on Hyperledger. In the trucking sector, despite the efforts of the BiTA, very little common ground has been found and companies are waiting for more consensus before proceeding. In parcel shipping, the same holds true.

In the food supply chain, the Food Trust, based on Hyperledger, seems to have delivered satisfactory results for its members, but further application is dependent on either more industry consensus or legislative mandates.

In the supply chain for raw materials for technology products, leading industry players are engaged in solutions, mainly built on Hyperledger, but also Ethereum.

Perhaps surprisingly, the supply chain for diamonds, gemstones, jewelry, and luxury goods has a great deal of activity from leading players, built mainly on Hyperledger, but also Ethereum.

What we can conclude from this detailed look across industries is that although blockchain has been expected to provide many benefits to supply chains, blockchain efforts have not yet made significant inroads into the domestic delivery phase of most supply chains.

The food supply chain seems to have demonstrated the ability to accurately track and trace goods, but there is not enough demand for those solutions yet for wider implementation.

Motivated by consumer concerns, the supply chains for high-tech raw materials, jewelry, and luxury goods have made significant progress. Motivated by theft concerns, a major home improvement retailer has begun tracking power tool provenance using blockchain.

The creation, through ISO and OBADA, of an international standard for tracking physical assets on blockchains should simplify all of these efforts.

Going forward, as software and consulting firms gain more experience with the technology, if benefits are realized from existing projects, blockchain may become more widely adopted. Within industries, consensus may be reached about which platforms to use, further aiding development.

Consumers also may increasingly demand traceability and provenance features that are best served by blockchain. Additionally, regulation regarding traceability may also increase adoption.

Time will tell whether sufficient benefits will be generated to propel blockchain solutions forward throughout global supply chains.

References

Almeida, I. (2020). Starbucks clients can now trace their coffee, and so can farmers. *Bloomberg.com*, August 25.

Amnesty International (2016). 'This is what we die for:' Human Rights Abuses in the Democratic Republic of the Congo Power the Global Trade in Cobalt. London.

Baker, M. (2018). The business of blockchain with BiTA. *Freightwaves*, August 30, https://www.freightwaves.com/news/the-business-of-blockchain-with-bita (accessed July 21, 2022).

Bandoim, L. (2019). Can blockchain and chip technology improve beef sourcing transparency? *Forbes*, April 30, https://www.forbes.com/sites/lanabandoim/2019/04/30/can-blockchain-and-chip-technology-improve-beef-sourcing-transparency/ (accessed July 21, 2022).

Banks-Louie, S. (2021). Volvo mines blockchain to keep ethical sourcing promise. *Forbes*, January 27, https://www.forbes.com/sites/oracle/2020/01/27/volvo-mines-blockchain-to-keep-ethical-sourcing-promise/ (accessed July 20, 2022).

Barich, A. (2022). Responsible cobalt from Congo artisanal mining proving a challenge for industry. *S&P Global Market Intelligence*, March 25, https://www.spglobal.com/marketintelligence/en/news-insights/latest-news-headlines/responsible-cobalt-from-congo-artisanal-mining-proving-a-challenge-for-industry-69137290 (accessed July 20, 2022).

Baydakova, A., & Allison, I. (2019). Retail giant Target is quietly working on a blockchain for supply chains. *CoinDesk*, June 10, https://www.coindesk.com/markets/2019/06/10/retail-giant-target-is-quietly-working-on-a-blockchain-for-supply-chains/ (accessed August 9, 2022).

Becker, V. (2021). The good gem guide. *Financial Times*, October 18, https://www.ft.com/content/9ec1b86d-b9b8-46c6-9e1b-57b13b0aef93 (accessed July 19, 2022).

Bhattacharyya, S. (2022). FDA official says new rule could boost blockchain-based food tracking. *Wall Street Journal*, February 1, https://www.wsj.com/articles/fda-official-says-new-rule-could-boost-blockchain-based-food-tracking-116437 11402 (accessed July 21, 2022).

BHP (2021). BHP enters into nickel supply agreement with Tesla Inc. *BHP Press Release*, https://www.bhp.com/news/media-centre/releases/2021/07/bhp-enters-into-nickel-supply-agreement-with-tesla-inc (accessed July 20, 2022).

Browne, R. (2022). Hackers drain nearly $200 million from crypto startup in 'free-for-all' attack. *CNBC*, August 2, https://www.cnbc.com/2022/08/02/hackers-drain-nearly-200-million-from-crypto-startup-nomad.html (accessed August 6, 2022).

BSI (2020). Theft and counterfeiting: Global threats to pharmaceutical supply chains. https://www.bsigroup.com/en-US/blog/supply-chain-blog/risk-management/theft-and-counterfeiting-global-threats-to-pharmaceutical-supply-chains/ (accessed August 7, 2022).

Castellanos, S. (2019). FedEx CIO looks to industry collaboration to scale blockchain. *Wall Street Journal*, April 29, https://www.wsj.com/articles/fedex-cio-looks-to-industry-collaboration-to-scale-blockchain-11556572820 (accessed July 21, 2022).

Charlebois, S. (2017). How blockchain could revolutionize the food industry. *The Globe and Mail*, December 12, https://www.theglobeandmail.com/

report-on-business/rob-commentary/how-blockchain-could-revolutionize-the-food-industry/article37305425/ (accessed July 21, 2022).

Chaum, D. L. (1979). *Computer Systems Established, Maintained, and Trusted by Mutually Suspicious Groups.* Memorandum No. UCB/ERL M79/10, College of Engineering, University of California, Berkeley.

Chavez-Dreyfuss, G. (2018). Coca-Cola, U.S. State Dept to use blockchain to combat forced labor. *Reuters*, March 16, https://www.reuters.com/article/us-blockchain-coca-cola-labor-idUSKCN1GS2PY (accessed July 21, 2022).

Chiu, R. (2021). New blockchain platform can track pearl provenance and ownership. *Jeweller Magazine*, December 6, https://www.jewellermagazine.com/Article/10263/New-blockchain-platform-can-track-pearl-provenance-and-ownership (accessed July 19, 2022).

Cosgrove, E. (2019). UPS creates digital tools to deliver blockchain-verified beef. *Supply Chain Dive*, November 11, https://www.supplychaindive.com/news/ups-herdx-blockchain-verified-beef/567038/ (accessed July 21, 2022).

Crider, J. (2021). Tesla's resource blockchain collaboration for cobalt aims to prove that Tesla ethically sources its cobalt. *CleanTechnica*, August 27, https://cleantechnica.com/2021/08/27/teslas-resource-blockchain-collaboration-for-cobalt-aims-to-prove-that-tesla-ethically-sources-its-cobalt/ (accessed July 20, 2022).

del Castillo, M., & Schifrin, M. (2020). Forbes blockchain 50: De Beers. *Forbes*, https://www.forbes.com/sites/michaeldelcastillo/2020/02/19/blockchain-50/#1b2f5bdc7553 (accessed July 18, 2022).

Desai, P. (2021). Explainer: Costs of nickel and cobalt used in electric vehicle batteries. *Reuters*, February 3, https://www.reuters.com/business/autos-transportation/costs-nickel-cobalt-used-electric-vehicle-batteries-2022-02-03 (accessed July 20, 2022).

deVries, A., & Stoll, C. (2021). Bitcoin's growing e-waste problem. *Resources, Conservation, and Recycling*, **175**(December), 1–11.

Digiconomist (2022a). Bitcoin energy consumption. https://digiconomist.net/bitcoin-energy-consumption/ (accessed July 13, 2022).

Digiconomist (2022b). Single bitcoin transaction footprints. https://digiconomist.net/bitcoin-energy-consumption/ (accessed July 13, 2022).

EBSCO*host* (2022). Search for peer reviewed articles with "supply chain" and "blockchain" in the Abstract. Online Database, https://web-s-ebscohost-com.unr.idm.oclc.org/ehost/resultsadvanced?vid=6&sid=8fdff57b-6000-4a6e-b8a7-71236c5ee3b0%40redis&bquery=AB+supply+chain+AND+AB+blockchain&bdata=JmRiPWFwaCZjbGkwPVJWJmNsdjA9WSZ0eXBlPTEmc2VhcmNoTW9kZT1TdGFuZGFyZCZzaXRlPWVob3N0LWxpdmUmc2NvcGU9c2l0ZQ%3d%3d (accessed July 8, 2022).

Escobar, S. (2022). How this company is using blockchain to buff up the image of diamonds. *Barrons*, March 15, https://www.barrons.com/articles/brilliant-earth-blockchain-diamonds-51647294829 (accessed July 18, 2022).

Ethereum (2022a). Smart contracts. https://ethereum.org/en/smart-contracts/ (accessed July 16, 2022).

Ethereum (2022b). The merge. https://ethereum.org/en/upgrades/merge/ (accessed July 14, 2022).

Everledger (2021). What is the Everledger blockchain network? https://hs.everledger.io/knowledge/what-is-the-everledger-blockchain-network (accessed July 17, 2022).

Finley, K. (2014). Out in the open: Teenage hacker transforms web into one giant bitcoin network. *Wired*, January 27.

Fisher, J. (2022). Still waiting on blockchain to catch up with the hype. *FleetOwner*, July 28, https://www.fleetowner.com/technology/article/21247568/still-waiting-on-blockchain-to-catch-up-hype-trucks (accessed August 6, 2022).

Frank, J., & Silverstein, S. (2021). Ethereum co-founder Vitalik Buterin on how he created one of the world's largest cryptocurrencies in his early twenties. *Insider*, May 14, https://www.businessinsider.com/vitalik-buterin-created-ethereum-one-of-the-worlds-three-largest-cryptocurrencies-2019-1?r=US&IR=T (accessed July 14, 2022).

Furlonger, D., & Uzureau, C. (2019). The 5 kinds of blockchain projects (and which to watch out for). *Harvard Business Review*, October, updated December 2019. https://hbr.org/2019/10/the-5-kinds-of-blockchain-projects-and-which-to-watch-out-for (accessed July 14, 2022).

Gartner (2019). Gartner predicts 90% of blockchain-based supply chain initiatives will suffer 'blockchain fatigue' by 2023. Press Release, May 7, https://www.gartner.com/en/newsroom/press-releases/2019-05-07-gartner-predicts-90--of-blockchain-based-supply-chain (accessed July 21, 2022).

George, S. (2022). PepsiCo funnels funding into plastic recycling innovation projects. *edie.net*, July 26, https://www.edie.net/pepsico-funnels-funding-into-plastic-recycling-innovation-projects/ (accessed August 12, 2022).

GIA (2018). Chow Tai Fook and GIA bring diamond grading reports to consumers via blockchain. Press release, May 23, https://www.gia.edu/gia-news-press/chow-tai-fook-gia-blockchain (accessed July 19, 2022).

Godsen, E. (2022). DeBeers has new spotlight on diamonds. *The Times* (London), May 16.

GSBN (2022). GSBN: Our ecosystem. https://www.gsbn.trade/our-ecosystem (accessed July 21, 2022).

Haber, S., & Stornetta, W. S. (1991) How to time-stamp a digital document. *Journal of Cryptography*, 3, 99–111.

Hamilton, D. (2018). A look into the UPS blockchain. December 23, https://coincentral.com/ups-blockchain/ (accessed July 21, 2022).

Hampel, C. (2020). Volvo invests in Circulor for blockchain technology. *electrive. com*, July 9, https://www.electrive.com/2020/07/09/volvo-invests-in-circulor-for-blockchain-technology/ (accessed July 20, 2022).

Hern, A. (2022). Electricity used to mine bitcoin plummets as crypto crisis widens. *The Guardian*, June 24, https://www.theguardian.com/technology/2022/jun/24/electricity-consumption-mine-bitcoin-plummets-crypto-crisis-widens-cryptocurrency (accessed July 13, 2022).

Hertzner, C. (2022). Death of the NFT? CryptoPunk bought for $1 million sells for just $139,000 just 6 months later. *Fortune*, May 9, https://fortune.com/2022/05/09/death-of-cryptopunk-nft-bayc-bored-apes-yuga-larva/ (accessed July 20, 2022).

Hinsdale, J. (2022). Cryptocurrency's dirty secret: Energy consumption. *State of the Planet, Columbia Climate School*, https://news.climate.columbia.edu/2022/05/04/cryptocurrency-energy/ (accessed July 10, 2022).

Holmyard, N. (2019). Raw seafoods wants Americans to regain trust in their seafood. *SeafoodSource*, October 24, https://www.seafoodsource.com/news/supply-trade/raw-seafoods-wants-americans-to-regain-trust-in-their-seafood (accessed July 17, 2022).

Hyperledger (2015). Linux foundation unites industry leaders to advance blockchain technology. https://www.hyperledger.org/announcements/2015/12/17/linux-foundation-unites-industry-leaders-to-advance-blockchain-technology (accessed July 11, 2022).

ISO.org (2016). ISO/TC 307: Blockchain and distributed ledger technologies. https://www.iso.org/committee/6266604.html (accessed August 12, 2022).

Johnson, E. (2018). APL adds to carrier jostle for industry blockchain platform. July 26, https://www.joc.com/technology/apl-adds-carrier-jostle-industry-blockchain-platform_20180726.html (accessed July 21, 2022).

Kerner, S. M. (2022). Hyperledger expands open source blockchain efforts. *TechTarget*, February 17, https://www.techtarget.com/searchdatamanagement/news/252513560/Hyperledger-expands-open-source-blockchain-efforts (accessed July 20, 2022).

Kessler, S. (2022). "Ethereum merge explained: What investors should know about the shift to proof-of-stake. *CoinDesk*, September 19, 2022, https://www.coindesk.com/learn/ethereum-merge-explained-what-investors-should-know-about-the-shift-to-proof-of-stake/ (accessed January 11, 2023).

Kessler, S., & Young, S. D. (2022). A major crypto exchange abandons ethereum: Is the world's computer falling behind? *CoinDesk*, June 29, https://www.coindesk.com/layer2/2022/06/29/a-major-crypto-exchange-abandons-ethereum-is-the-worlds-computer-falling-behind/ (accessed July 21, 2022).

Khatri, Y. (2018). Rwanda starts tracking conflict metal tantalum with blockchain. *Coindesk*, October 17, https://www.coindesk.com/markets/2018/10/17/

rwanda-starts-tracking-conflict-metal-tantalum-with-blockchain/ (accessed July 20, 2022).

Khatri, Y. (2019). Nestle, Carrefour team up to feed consumers data with IBM blockchain. *CoinDesk*, April 16, https://www.coindesk.com/markets/2019/04/16/nestle-carrefour-team-up-to-feed-consumers-data-with-ibm-blockchain/ (accessed August 12, 2022).

Kilefors, P., Döemer, F., af Sandeberg, I., Andric, T., Mudersbach, P., Samuelsson, G., & Schmidtke, S. (2020). Blockchain in transport — Awaiting the breakthrough. *Arthur D. Little*, https://www.adlittle.com/en/insights/prism/blockchain-transport-%E2%80%93-awaiting-breakthrough (accessed July 21, 2022).

Kim, C. (2019). A blockchain to connect all blockchains, Cosmos is officially live. *CoinDesk*, March 14, https://www.coindesk.com/markets/2019/03/13/a-blockchain-to-connect-all-blockchains-cosmos-is-officially-live/ (accessed July 21, 2022).

Kimura, J. (2021). Meet YUI. June 9, https://www.hyperledger.org/blog/2021/06/09/meet-yui-one-the-new-hyperledger-labs-projects-taking-on-cross-chain-and-off-chain-operations (accessed July 21, 2022).

King, B. (2021). Faster invoicing solutions build stronger relationships. https://www.ibm.com/case-studies/the-home-depot/ (accessed August 9, 2022).

Knapp, A. (2019). This blockchain startup is partnering with fashion giants to make organic cotton traceable. *Forbes*, March 4, https://www.forbes.com/sites/alexknapp/2019/03/04/this-blockchain-startup-is-partnering-with-fashion-giants-to-make-organic-cotton-traceable.

Knowler, G. (2018). Consortium puts new blockchain solution to the test. *Journal of Commerce*, March 15, https://www.joc.com/technology/consortium-puts-new-blockchain-solution-test_20180315.html (accessed July 21, 2022).

Konashevych, O. (2021). Private distributed ledger technology or public blockchain? *CoinTelegraph*, October 2, https://cointelegraph.com/news/private-distributed-ledger-technology-or-public-blockchain (accessed July 14, 2022).

Krulwich, R. (2012). Which is greater, the number of sand grains on earth or stars in the sky? *NPR.org*, September 17, https://www.npr.org/sections/krulwich/2012/09/17/161096233/which-is-greater-the-number-of-sand-grains-on-earth-or-stars-in-the-sky (accessed January 12, 2023).

Lambert, F. (2022). Tesla is already using cobalt-free LFP batteries in half of its new cars produced. *electrek*, April 22, https://electrek.co/2022/04/22/tesla-using-cobalt-free-lfp-batteries-in-half-new-cars-produced (accessed July 20, 2022).

Ledger Insights (2018). Accenture completes blockchain test for beer logistics. March 15, https://www.ledgerinsights.com/accenture-completes-beer-supply-chain-blockchain-test/ (accessed July 21, 2022).

Ledger Insights (2019a). SAP's pharmaceutical blockchain goes live. January 16, https://www.ledgerinsights.com/saps-pharmaceutical-blockchain-goes-live/ (accessed August 7, 2022).

Ledger Insights (2019b). Volvo joins VW, Ford, IBM for blockchain cobalt traceability. November 6, https://www.ledgerinsights.com/volvo-vw-ford-ibm-blockchain-cobalt-traceability-responsible-minerals-rsbn/ (accessed July 20, 2022).

Ledger Insights (2019c). Dell using VMware's blockchain to track recycled packaging. November 15, https://www.ledgerinsights.com/dell-vmware-blockchain-recycled-plastic/ (accessed August 12, 2022).

Ledger Insights (2019d). Fiat Chrysler joins Ford, VW blockchain consortium for ethically sourced minerals. December 11, https://www.ledgerinsights.com/fiat-chrysler-blockchain-ford-vw-consortium-minerals/ (accessed July 20, 2022).

Ledger Insights (2020a). Tencent, Fidelity backed Everledger launches blockchain bottle closures for wine industry. April 20, https://www.ledgerinsights.com/everledger-blockchain-bottle-closures-wine-anti-counterfeit/ (accessed August 7, 2022).

Ledger Insights (2020b). Coca-Cola bottles to trial public Ethereum for supply chain transparency. August 5, https://www.ledgerinsights.com/coca-cola-bottlers-coke-blockchain-ethereum-baseline/ (accessed August 7, 2022).

Ledger Insights (2020c). Australian fine wines tracked by Entrust on Hedera's Hashgraph DLT. September 21, https://www.ledgerinsights.com/australia-fine-wine-traceability-entrust-hedera-hashgraphs-dlt/ (accessed August 7, 2022).

Ledger Insights (2020d). eProvenance, IBM launch blockchain wine quality solution. December 10, https://www.ledgerinsights.com/eprovenance-ibm-blockchain-wine-solution/ (accessed August 7, 2022).

Ledger Insights (2021a). Carrefour expands blockchain traceability to textile products. March 16, https://www.ledgerinsights.com/carrefour-expands-blockchain-traceability-to-textile-products/ (accessed August 12, 2022).

Ledger Insights (2021b). World's largest mining firm Glencore pilots blockchain cobalt traceability. May 20, https://www.ledgerinsights.com/mining-glencore-pilots-blockchain-cobalt-traceability-resource-cmoc-erg/ (accessed July 20, 2022).

Ledger Insights (2021c). IBM, Maersk's TradeLens blockchain signs 10 Chinese partners. June 17, https://www.ledgerinsights.com/ibm-maersk-tradelens-blockchain-signs-10-chinese-partners/ (accessed July 21, 2022).

Ledger Insights (2021d). Blockchain shipping network GSBN using Oracle, AntChain for hosting. September 10, https://www.ledgerinsights.com/blockchain-shipping-network-gsbn-using-oracle-antchain-for-hosting/ (accessed July 21, 2022).

Ledger Insights (2022a). Coca-Cola partners Diginex for ESG supply chain traceability using blockchain. March 17, https://www.ledgerinsights.com/coca-cola-partners-diginex-for-esg-supply-chain-traceability-using-blockchain/ (accessed July 21, 2022).

Ledger Insights (2022b). Bulgari's exclusive watch to include NFTs. March 28, https://www.ledgerinsights.com/bulgaris-exclusive-watch-to-include-nfts/ (accessed July 19, 2022).

Ledger Insights (2022c). HPE launches Swarm Learning using blockchain for AI, machine learning. April 29, https://www.ledgerinsights.com/hpe-launches-swarm-learning-using-blockchain-for-ai-machine-learning/ (accessed August 12, 2022).

Ledger Insights (2022d). De Beers' diamond provenance blockchain Tracr launched at scale. May 6, https://www.ledgerinsights.com/de-beers-diamond-provenance-blockchain-tracr-launched-at-scale/ (accessed July 18, 2022).

Lembke, R. (2020). Reducing cybersecurity vulnerabilities through the use of 12N QR codes. In Carnovale, S. & Yeniyurt, S. (Eds.), *Cyber Security and Supply Chain Management: Risks, Challenges, and Solutions*. World Scientific Publishing Co., Singapore.

Lembke, R. (2022). Serial number capture with a single scan: Increasing satisfaction and reducing fraud. *Reverse Logistics Magazine*, 118th edition (pp. 8–12).

Lembke, R., & Sukhia, R. (2023). Universal Serial Numbers, in preparation for submission.

LinkedIn (2022). Kryha. https://www.linkedin.com/company/kryha/about/ (accessed July 20, 2022).

Makrygiannis, K. (2019). EY blockchain platform Blockchain Wine Pte. Ltd. to launch TATTOO Wine marketplace across Asia Pacific. November 13, https://www.ey.com/en_gl/news/2019/11/ey-blockchain-platform-supports-blockchain-wine-pte-ltd-to-launch-tattoo-wine-marketplace-across-asia-pacific (accessed August 7, 2022).

McCauley, A. (2020). Why big pharma is betting on blockchain. *Harvard Business Review*, May 29, https://hbr.org/2020/05/why-big-pharma-is-betting-on-blockchain (accessed August 7, 2022).

Merian, L. (2019). FedEx CIO: It's time to mandate blockchain for international shipping. *Computerworld*, April 25, https://www.computerworld.com/article/3391070/fedex-cio-its-time-to-mandate-blockchain-for-international-shipping.html (accessed July 21, 2022).

Merkle, R. (1979). Secure communications over insecure channels. *Communications of the ACM*, **21**(4), 294–299.

Miller, R. (2018). IBM introduces a blockchain to verify the jewelry supply chain. *TechCrunch*, April 26, https://techcrunch.com/2018/04/26/ibm-introduces-trustchain-a-blockchain-to-verify-the-jewelry-supply-chain (accessed July 18, 2022).

Moise, I. (2018). Maersk and IBM partner on blockchain for global trade. *Wall Street Journal*, January 16, https://www.wsj.com/articles/maersk-and-ibm-partner-on-blockchain-for-global-trade-1516111543 (accessed July 21, 2022).

Morris, N. (2018a). SAP leads pharma supply chain blockchain. *Ledger Insights*, July 7, https://www.ledgerinsights.com/sap-pharma-supply-chain/ (accessed August 7, 2022).

Morris, N. (2018b). MediLedger: Pharmaceutical industry's blockchain network. *Ledger Insights*, July 27, https://www.ledgerinsights.com/mediledger-pharmaceutical-blockchain/ (accessed August 7, 2022).

Morris, N. (2018c). Carrefour extends food traceability blockchain. *Ledger Insights*, August 6, https://www.ledgerinsights.com/carrefour-food-traceability-blockchain/ (accessed August 12, 2022).

Nakamoto, S. (2008). Bitcoin: A peer-to-peer electronic cash system. http://bitcoin.org/bitcoin.pdf.

Nash, J. S. (2018). Walmart requires lettuce, spinach suppliers to join blockchain. *Wall Street Journal*, September 24, 2018. https://www.wsj.com/articles/walmart-requires-lettuce-spinach-suppliers-to-join-blockchain-1537815869 (accessed July 21, 2022).

Norton, S. (2018). FedEx CIO says blockchain a 'Game Changer' for supply chain visibility. *Wall Street Journal*, May 14, https://www.wsj.com/articles/fedex-cio-says-blockchain-a-game-changer-for-supply-chain-visibility-1526328067 (accessed July 21, 2022).

OBADA.io (2022). Introducing the pNFT standard. https://www.obada.io/ (accessed August 12, 2022).

Page, C. (2022a). US officials link North Korean Lazarus hackers to $625M Axie Infinity crypto theft. *TechCrunch*, April 15, https://techcrunch.com/2022/04/15/us-officials-link-north-korean-lazarus-hackers-to-625m-axie-infinity-crypto-theft/ (accessed July 21, 2022).

Page, C. (2022b). Hacker exploits Harmony blockchain bridge, loots $100M in crypto. *TechCrunch*, June 24, https://techcrunch.com/2022/06/24/harmony-blockchain-crypto-hack/ (accessed July 21, 2022).

Palmer, A. (2022). For the Gem industry, the trusted expert is not obsolete yet. *Forbes*, March 22, https://www.forbes.com/sites/columbiabusinessschool/2022/03/22/for-the-gem-industry-the-trusted-expert-is-not-obsolete-yet/ (accessed July 18, 2022).

Paris, C. (2019). Shipping blockchain initiative gathers steam. *Wall Street Journal*, July 2, https://www.wsj.com/articles/shipping-blockchain-initiative-gathers-steam-11562061601 (accessed July 21, 2022).

Patel, D. (2017). UPS bets on blockchain as the future of the trillion-dollar shipping industry. *Tech Crunch*, December 15, https://techcrunch.com/2017/12/15/ups-bets-on-blockchain-as-the-future-of-the-trillion-dollar-shipping-industry/ (accessed July 21, 2022).

Pessaraly, W. (2022). How blockchain technology can revolutionize international trade. *Coin Telegraph*, August 1, https://cointelegraph.com/news/how-blockchain-technology-can-revolutionize-international-trade (accessed August 7, 2022).

Peterson, B. (2017). IBM wants to use the technology that underlies bitcoin to help prevent major foodborne outbreaks like salmonella. *Business Insider*, August 22, https://www.businessinsider.com/ibm-and-walmart-are-using-blockchain-in-the-food-supply-chain-2017-8 (accessed July 21, 2022).

Pitta, J. (1997). David Chaum: The cybermint. *Forbes*, July 7, 320–321.

Pollock, D. (2020). Target, General Mills getting look in at Hedera blockchain technology through couponing. *Forbes*, April 27, https://www.forbes.com/sites/darrynpollock/2020/04/27/target-general-mills-getting-look-in-at-hedera-blockchain-technology-through-couponing/?sh=69324ee14023 (accessed August 9, 2022).

Radmilac, A. (2022). Cosmos' Inter-Blockchain Communication Protocol (IBC) surpassed 11 million transfers in February. *Cryptoslate*, March 9, https://cryptoslate.com/cosmos-inter-blockchain-communication-protocol-ibc-surpassed-11-million-transfers-in-february (accessed July 21, 2022).

Ravenscraft, E. (2022). NFTs are a privacy and security nightmare. *Wired*, April 5, https://www.wired.com/story/nfts-privacy-security-nightmare/ (accessed July 20, 2022).

Sajja, P. (2022). Can blockchain solve the problem of food recalls? *SupplyChainBrain*, February 18, https://www.supplychainbrain.com/blogs/1-think-tank/post/34470-can-blockchain-solve-the-problem-of-food-recalls (accessed August 5, 2022).

Shapshak, T. (2018). Blockchain used to track gems to counter blood diamonds and fakes. *Forbes*, May 10, https://www.forbes.com/sites/tobyshapshak/2018/05/10/blockchain-used-to-track-gems-to-counter-blood-diamonds-and-fakes/ (accessed July 18, 2022).

Sharwood, S. (2022). Financial exchange's efforts to replace core systems with blockchain founder — Again. *The Register*, August 4, https://www.theregister.com/2022/08/04/asx_blockchain_delayed_again/ (accessed August 12, 2022).

Sherman, A. T. Javani, F., Zhang, H., & Golaszewski, E. (2019). On the origins and variations of blockchain technologies. *IEEE Security & Privacy*, **17**(1), 72–77.

Sloane, R. (2020). Conflict minerals and child labour: Enabling better business with blockchain traceability. *Hyper Ledger Foundation*, https://www.hyperledger.org/blog/2020/01/17/conflict-minerals-and-child-labour-enabling-better-business-with-blockchain-traceability (accessed July 20, 2022).

Sok, H. (2018). APL logistics joins blockchain in transport alliance. *Global Trade Magazine*, August 8, https://www.globaltrademag.com/apl-logistics-joins-blockchain-in-transport-alliance/ (accessed July 21, 2022).

Swedberg, C. (2013). Pearl company creates authentication solution. *RFID Journal*, October 2, https://www.rfidjournal.com/pearl-company-creates-authentication-solution (accessed July 19, 2022).

Szabo, N. (1994). Smart contracts. https://www.fon.hum.uva.nl/rob/Courses/InformationInSpeech/CDROM/Literature/LOTwinterschool2006/szabo.best.vwh.net/smart.contracts.html (accessed July 14, 2022).

Temperton, J. (2016). Gorillas are being killed and eaten by miners in the Congo. *Wired*, December 7, https://www.wired.co.uk/article/grauers-gorillas-bush-meat-conflict-minerals-technology (accessed July 20, 2022).

Thompson, S. (2019). LVMH, ConsenSys, Microsoft announce AURA, to power luxury industry with blockchain tech. May 18, https://finance.yahoo.com/news/lvmh-consensys-microsoft-announce-aura-100008984.html (accessed July 18, 2022).

Tobin, B. (2023). Lowe's to sell power tools that won't work if they're stolen, as retailers take increasingly desperate measures to prevent theft. *Insider*, January 10, https://www.businessinsider.com/lowes-plans-stop-theft-power-tools-organized-crime-with-blockchain-system-2023 (accessed January 12, 2023).

Town, S. (2018). Amazon web services launches instant blockchain templates for Ethereum and Hyperledger. *Crypto Slate*, April 20, https://cryptoslate.com/amazon-web-services-launches-instant-blockchain-templates-for-ethereum-and-hyperledger/ (accessed August 9, 2022).

Trustchainjewelry.com (2018). The TrustChain initiative. https://www.trustchain-jewelry.com/ (accessed July 18, 2022).

UNECE (2021). UNECE and FAO join forces on cotton traceability to connect sustainable rural producers in Latin America to global value chains. United Nations Economic Commission for Europe, December 17, https://unece.org/media/press/363667 (accessed August 12, 2022).

Vitasek, K., Bayliss, J., Owen, L., & Srivastava, N. (2022). How Walmart Canada uses blockchain to solve supply-chain challenges. *Harvard Business Review*, January 5, https://hbr.org/2022/01/how-walmart-canada-uses-blockchain-to-solve-supply-chain-challenges (accessed July 21, 2022).

Voshmgir, S. (2020). *Token Economy: How the Web3 Reinvents the Internet*. Token Kitchen, Berlin.

Wolfson, R. (2023). Using blockchain technology to combat retail theft. *Coin Telegraph*, January 7, https://cointelegraph.com/news/using-blockchain-technology-to-combat-retail-theft (accessed January 12, 2023).

Wood, M. (2019). Coca-Cola bottlers adopt SAP blockchain for supply chain. *Ledger Insights*, November 5, https://www.ledgerinsights.com/coca-cola-sap-blockchain-bottling-supply-chain/ (accessed August 7, 2022).

World Health Organization (WHO) (2017). 1 in 10 medical products in developing countries is substandard or falsified. November 28, https://www.who.int/news-room/detail/28-11-2017-1-in-10-medical-products-in-developing-countries-is-substandard-or-falsified (accessed August 7, 2022).

Wragg, E. (2022). Maersk and IBM pull the plug on TradeLens. *Global Trade Review*, November 11, https://www.gtreview.com/news/fintech/maersk-and-ibm-pull-the-plug-on-tradelens/ (accessed January 12, 2023).

Wright, T. (2020). DLT tracking partnership to fight fake diamonds in China. *Coin Telegraph*, August 26, https://cointelegraph.com/news/dlt-tracking-partnership-to-fight-fake-diamonds-in-china (accessed July 19, 2022).

Zhang, T. (2020). Louis Vuitton uncovers a mole and 'High-tech' counterfeits in China. *Yahoo! Finance*, https://finance.yahoo.com/news/louis-vuitton-uncovers-mole-high-135732806.html (accessed July 18, 2022).

https://doi.org/10.1142/9789811286636_0005

CHAPTER 5

Improving Supply Chain Resilience Through a Blockchain-Based System Architecture

Yu Cui[*,‡], Prakash J. Singh[†,§], and Huashan Li[†,¶]

*Graduate School of Business Administration and Economics,
Otemon Gakuin University, Osaka, Japan
†Department of Management and Marketing,
University of Melbourne, Melbourne, Australia
‡yucui@otemon.ac.jp
§pjsingh@unimelb.edu.au
¶huashan.li@unimelb.edu.au

Abstract

Many companies and their associated supply chains are now operating in an increasingly digitalized way. On the other hand, with increasing levels of disruptive events taking place around the world, global supply chains are exposed to more complex risks that threaten their short- or long-term viability. Compared to ordinary conditions, supply chains affected by emergency events are more prone to significant delays of supply or even breakage due to the suddenness, complexity, and destructiveness of these events. To overcome the disruptions caused by emergency events, many companies have been building supply chain resilience (SCR) to quickly restore ordinary operations. Consistent with this trend, this chapter analyzes the architecture of traditional supply chain systems and proposes a new system architecture based on blockchain technology. Examples from Japan are used to demonstrate that blockchain technology can minimize the losses caused by the disruption of the supply chain system when emergency events occur, and fundamentally improve and strengthen SCR.

Keywords: SCR; Blockchain; System architecture.

Introduction

Based on the widespread usage of internet in industries around the world and the rapid development of digitalization, digital transformation in the field of supply chain management is considered an effective and necessary path (Tavana *et al.*, 2022). Over recent years, with the support of digital technologies such as big data, cloud computing, artificial intelligence, Internet of Things (IoT), digital twins, and blockchain, the perception of the supply chain system has changed from the traditional passive and independent mode to the active, fusion mode (Al-Qudah, 2021). These changes enable the Internet of everything, ecosystem networking, intelligent manufacturing in the supply chain, and the traversing and integration between virtual and reality in the Web3.0[1] environment.

The digital machine-to-machine interconnection required in the digital supply chain has been gradually completed, such as the cyber physical system (CPS) described in Industry 4.0. A digital supply chain could be described as an intelligently optimized system that performs functions such as massive data processing and excellent collaboration and communication with the usage of digital hardware and software that synchronize and support the interactions between organizations (Büyüközkan & Göçer, 2020). The digital supply chain mediates the activities of the partners in the supply chain through hardware, software, and communication networks to support the interaction in the process of procurement, manufacturing, inventory, transportation, and sales among organizations around the world (Bhargava *et al.*,

---

[1]"Web3.0 is an era of computing where the critical computing of applications is verifiable. And there are three key categories of infrastructural enablers for Web3.0: individual smart-contract capable blockchains, federated or centralized platforms capable of publishing verifiable states, and an interoperability platform to hyperconnect those state publishers to provide a unified and connected computing platform for Web3.0 applications" (Liu *et al.*, 2022).

2013). All stages of the digital supply chain are interconnected, which enables robust data collection and intelligent decision-making based on real-time communication (Wu *et al.*, 2016). Ivanov *et al.* (2019) combined the digital supply chain with the SCOR model, defined it as a system based on emerging digital technologies such as big data analysis, CPS network and additive manufacturing, including planning execution, traceability, and manufacturing and delivery functions.

Kinnett (2020) defines a digital supply chain as an intelligent, value-driven network that leverages new technologies and approaches to create new forms of revenue and business value through an ecosystem platform that captures and maximizes the use of real-time data from a variety of sources. To build an ecosystem network of a digital supply chain, it is necessary to start from the components of cloud, network, platform, and terminal, and adjust measures according to their own conditions. Cloud refers to the infrastructure based on cloud computing and big data technology; Network refers to the Internet and IoTs; Platform refers to the business systems established by the Internet and IoTs; Terminal refers to computers, mobile and wearable devices, sensors, and various application functions in the form of embedded software used by enterprises. Pricewaterhouse Coopers (PwC) defines a digital supply chain as a system that focuses on the digital connection of all physical assets beyond the automation of each machine and process, as well as the integration of supply chain partners into a digital ecosystem (Pyun & Rha, 2021). Various resources of the supply chain are gathered in the ecosystem network, which not only forms the relationship between the upstream and downstream enterprises but also promotes the linkage between the producer and the consumer, forming a low-cost and high-efficiency peer-to-peer (P2P) connection.

In terms of intelligent manufacturing, the IoT-based management is incorporated into network management, so that human beings, machines, and objects are integrated in the virtual space (Shi *et al.*, 2020). Calatayud *et al.* (2019) defined a digital supply chain as a self-thinking supply chain that predicts and detects risks by analyzing big data collected from various sources and proactively takes preventive measures before risks occur, thereby enabling continuous monitoring of performance. The development of cloud computing further enables the storage, business processing, and integrated management of massive data generated by the IoT. Big data technologies provide a reliable technical guarantee for analyzing these massive data, exploring its potential value and making decisions. The development of artificial intelligence technologies has significantly improved the ability to analyze big data independently. By reading video and audio, it can analyze a large amount of trivial unstructured data in the IoT context so as to support intelligent decision-making and solve the compatibility of various communication protocols between IoT devices.

With the continuous breakthroughs in new-generation digital technologies such as acquisition, mass storage, data mining, quantum information transmission, and blockchain trust mechanism, the multilevel integration of business processes, supply chains, and digital business ecosystems has been promoted (Cacciapuoti *et al.*, 2020). Moreover, it promotes the interactive development of networks, services, and terminals and opens up new paths for technology diffusion, knowledge sharing, and knowledge acquisition (Ranganathan *et al.*, 2014). In addition, a new model of enterprise cooperation, upstream and downstream associations, and industrial alliances has been created in the digital supply chain so as to maximize the value of cyberspace, which also provides sufficient conditions for the creation and development of virtual space.

Different from the previous innovations based on information technologies, the particularity of the new generation of digital technologies focused on the fact that they form a coherent and coordinated digital supply chain around the generation, transmission, processing, and decision-making of massive amounts of information (Abdelshafy & Walther, 2022). Therefore, a new ecosystem that integrates cyberspace and physical space is established, while the transition and transformation of enterprises and supply chains in this direction are promoted, which might called as the Web3.0 infrastructure (Park *et al.*, 2022). The Web3.0-based digital supply chain has gradually formed brand-new digital-driven innovations and management processes through the alternation and evolution in the virtual and physical space (Li & Chen, 2022).

However, in the digitalization process, supply chains have been exposed to greater risks. Supply chain disruptions have become a prominent risk among organizations whatever their digitization levels are (Azad *et al.*, 2013; Hu *et al.*, 2017; Cui & Singh, 2022). For example, natural and human-made events, such as natural disasters, terrorist activities, political turmoil, economic crisis, and operational accidents cause significant supply chain disruptions, leading to the interruption of the normal flow of goods and materials in the supply chain, delay the production or logistics processes, and deviate from the expected management goals, thereby affecting the operation of the entire supply chain (Hendricks *et al.*, 2003; Chopra *et al.*, 2004; Kleindorfer *et al.*, 2005; Tang, 2007).

In view of the negative consequences caused by disruptive events, dealing with supply chain disruptions has become a major challenge in the field of supply chain security operations. Building resilience is a way to overcome the fragility of the supply chain (Peck, 2005). The resilience of the supply chain enables companies to respond quickly and proactively to shocks (Sheffi & Rice, 2005). Christopher and Peck (2004) defined SCR as the ability to restore the supply chain system to its original state or a new and more ideal state after being disrupted. Due to the increased vulnerability to supply chain risks, supply chain resilience has become a core issue in supply chain management research. For example, Lam *et al.* (2016) used the offshore supply chain as an example to illustrate the applicability of the quality function deployment method to the elastic construction of the supply chain. Ji *et al.* (2012) discussed the characteristics of emergency logistics and the elasticity of emergency logistics network from the flexibility and reliability perspective. Tang (2007) used a complex network method to identify and evaluate the invulnerability of the emergency logistics network. In general, according to the different response times of supply chain interruption, the supply chain interruption response can be divided into three situations: before, during, and after a major disruption. Compared with the early warning and formulating a thorough plan that is valued by risk management, in terms of before a major disruption, the focus of SCR is on how to quickly respond to various emergency conditions while minimizing losses, and how to quickly restore the entire supply chain system to a normal state after the incident.

The traditional supply chain has a focus on people and efficiency, with a centralized structure. In such a framework, both the plan formulation and the emergency response during an incident are centralized. The maintenance of this framework has restricted the improvement of the flexibility of the supply chain, and the supply chain as a whole can be negatively affected by sudden risks. The introduction of decentralized network structure and blockchain technology with smart contracts and consensus mechanisms as the core function can be the best solution and choice for dealing with sudden risks. In a traditional centralized network, if one of the central nodes is damaged, it is likely to disrupt the entire system. The decentralized network uses distributed recording, distributed storage, and P2P communication. The rights and obligations of any node are equal, and all the data is jointly maintained by all nodes. In this way, when any node is attacked or stops working, the entire system will not be affected (Li *et al.*, 2018).

Since the operation of the entire system is open and transparent, the data is also open and transparent. Once the data is written into the block, it cannot be revised. Therefore, within the scope of the rules and time specified by the system, nodes cannot deceive each other. This reduces the reliance on third-party intervention (Kang *et al.*, 2018). In the blockchain, data can be modified when half or more than half of the nodes agree on the revision. However, in the blockchain system, there are a large number of participants, which makes it difficult to obtain half of the nodes of the blockchain. Therefore, the supply chain system is more robust (Aoki *et al.*, 2019).

This chapter is organized as follows. In the following section, we review research on SCR. We then discuss the issues for traditional supply chains in dealing with disruptions. In the fourth section, we discuss the characteristics of blockchain technology and how it can be applied to supply chain management. In the fifth section, we present the new architecture of the supply chain system. In the sixth section, we discuss how the new architecture of the supply chain system can be applied to a couple of examples from the food supply chains in Japan.

Literature Review

SCR

The first study of SCR was carried out in the United Kingdom following transportation disruptions resulting from fuel protests in 2000 and the outbreak of the foot-and-mouth disease in early 2001 (Pettit *et al.*, 2010). Based on the complex system theory, Holling (1973) proposed that systems have two distinct properties: resilience and stability. Resilience determines the ability of systems to absorb changes. The concept of resilience has been investigated in multiple disciplines and has congruence around specific characteristics. In material sciences, resilience characterizes the ability of a material to return to its original state after an alteration or deformation. According to Sapountzaki (2007), resilience has an adaptive characteristic and was described as a *dynamic process indicating the adaptive functioning of individuals at risk*. Resilience is widely regarded as involving the ability to adapt to adversity (Stewart, 2009; Sapountzaki, 2007; Schoon, 2006). According to

Pettit *et al.* (2010), firms should achieve a balance between vulnerability and capability as firms will be most profitable over the long term.

Emerging from the fields of material and behavioral science, business research has described resilience as the ability of companies to return to pre-disaster levels of performance (Sheffi, 2009). According to Christopher and Peck (2004), SCR addresses a supply chain's capability to deal with the consequences of unavoidable risk events. It captures the ability to return to original operations or move to a new, more desirable state after being disturbed. Christopher and Peck (2004) developed an initial framework for a resilient supply chain and asserted that SCR can be established through four key principles: (1) building resilience into a system before the occurrence of a disruption (i.e., re-engineering), (2) establishing a high level of collaboration and cooperation to identify and manage risks, (3) maintaining agility as an essential means to react quickly to unforeseen events, and (4) focusing on the culture of risk management. They also proposed secondary factors in this framework, including availability, efficiency, flexibility, redundancy, velocity, and visibility. Ponomarov *et al.* (2009) suggested that the concept of resilience is multidimensional. They define SCR as *the adaptive capability of the supply chain to prepare for unexpected events, respond to disruptions, and recover from them by maintaining continuity of operations at the desired level of connectedness and control over structure and function* (Ponomarov *et al.*, 2009). All of these definitions share the view that SCR assists an organization in responding and recovering at a similar or better state of operations and thus comprises system renewal. There is no conceptual difference among the definitions of a supply chain's adaptive resilience ability at the system level.

Research on SCR takes a broad perspective to capture the dynamics of turbulence and complexity. Gunderson and Holling (2000) define resilience as the capacity of a system to go through disturbances while maintaining its functions and controls. The United Nations International Strategy for Disaster Reduction defines resilience as the capability of a system, community, or society potentially exposed to hazards to adapt, by resisting or changing to reach and maintain an acceptable level of functioning and structure. Stewart *et al.* (2009) define resilience as a process linking a set of adaptive capabilities to a positive trajectory of functioning and adaptation after a disturbance. Given the destructive nature of certain hazards, this definition provides an extensive scope of recovery and does not incorporate a return to pre-hazard performance. This extensive contextual domain for resilience is important because there are times when returning to pre-hazard levels of performance is not in the best interests of stakeholders (Stewart *et al.*, 2009).

The Centralized Supply Chain System Architecture

The supply chain has become an important part of competitive strategies since the 1980s. The competition among firms has gradually shifted from the corporate level to the supply chain level. However, due to the dynamics and asymmetry of information among the participants in the supply chain, traditional internal management methods cannot be used to coordinate the complex situation in emergence conditions. The coordination between the participants has also become the core issue in the theoretical research and practice of the supply chain. The major deterrents to the collaboration between supply chain partners can be listed as follows:

1. The existing supply chain ecosystem is mostly dominated by the leading companies in the industry. The self-interested leaders take away most of the cooperation premium, making the cooperation to deviate from the optimal win–win Nash equilibrium (Chern *et al.*, 2014).
2. Supply chain participants are dynamic. Other than a small number of long-term strategic partnerships, members of the supply chain are always in dynamic changes. This makes members ignore long-term benefits and act opportunistically to pursue short-term goals (Cheng *et al.*, 2012).
3. Small and medium-sized suppliers are unable to certify their credits. This leads to adverse selection problems. This also induces the failure of the entire market mechanism (Fabbri *et al.*, 2016).
4. Supply chain members adopt different management information systems. The interfaces between different information systems are not compatible with each other; this adds difficulties to the information exchange between different supply chain members. Furthermore, information is disconnected from business processes and applications, leading to the formation of "information islands" among participants (Li, 2011).

The key to these problems is to solve the information barriers and ensure the authenticity of information between all participants in the supply chain. As a result, a human-centered centralized network structure and third-party intermediaries are required to strengthen regulation and to ensure the normal operation of the trust mechanism (see Figure 1).

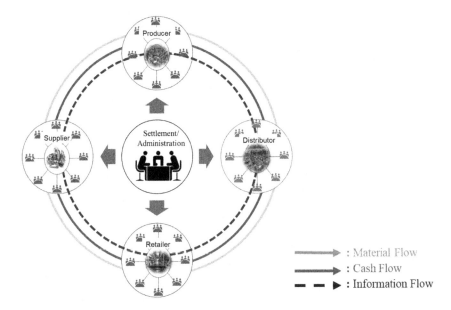

Figure 1. A Simplified Transaction Structure in the Traditional Supply Chain System

In a centralized supply chain system, it is difficult to avoid temporary supply chain disruption when emergencies occur. Especially in cases such as coronavirus outbreak when people and the major enterprises and government cannot work and function normally. In such a situation, the traditional supply chain system becomes quite vulnerable. Therefore, to solve this problem fundamentally, a new system framework needs to be developed.

Features and Advantages of Blockchain Technology

Blockchain is a decentralized and highly intelligent framework model. Specifically, blockchain is a distributed ledger in which any node participating in the system is packed into associated blocks and connected through the digital fingerprint generated by the encrypted hash algorithm. Each block contains all the transaction data of the system within a certain period and then combined into a chained data structure. Moreover, cryptography is used to ensure data transmission and access security. This ensures that each ledger cannot be tampered (Wang *et al.*, 2020).

The technical structure of blockchain determines that it has three functional characteristics. First, it is multicentered, which means that there are multiple institutions in the blockchain network to simultaneously complete computing, authentication, and storage tasks. Since access to data should be verified through consensus algorithms, data tampering becomes unachievable. This ensures the security of the data (Maesa *et al.*, 2019). Second, the blockchain is highly intelligent. In the blockchain, the "smart contract" can be repeatedly executed (Huang *et al.*, 2019). This type of contract does not rely on manpower and is actively and dynamically executed by the machine; this saves a lot of transaction costs and greatly reduces the hidden dangers caused by human intervention (Muzammal *et al.*, 2019). The third characteristic is trustworthiness. The data stored in the blockchain is immutable and traceable. Credit can be established in no time, ensuring value exchange and the uniqueness of circulation (Lyu *et al.*, 2019).

The blockchain includes six core technologies, including consensus mechanism, storage data, encryption algorithms, P2P network protocols, side chain technology, and smart contracts. The decentralized consensus mechanism is the key of blockchain technology.

I. *Consensus Mechanism*: The consensus mechanism is the key to blockchain technology. This mechanism makes it possible for the blockchain to be decentralized. In a distributed network, special nodes carry out voting and generate new blocks for storing data. By reaching a consensus on the selection of new blocks, decentralization can be achieved. In the meantime, the data will not be tampered with. The proof of work consensus mechanism is currently the most widely used, followed by the proof of stake consensus mechanism and the delegated proof of stake consensus mechanism (Dorri *et al.*, 2019; Liu *et al.*, 2019).

II. *Data Storage*: As a distributed ledger database, blockchain can store detailed information of all the data. Its information is carried by the blocks. Each block contains the information of the prepositioned block and the information of the current block. Moreover, the information can only be added but cannot be deleted. As a result, the data information in the block will be tamper-resistant and continue an increasing trend. As long as the information is stored, the data will be irreversible and cannot be modified unless the usurper uses considerable cost and resources which are more than the benefit to attack more than 51% of the blockchain nodes (Cheng *et al.*, 2019; Wang *et al.*, 2019).

III. *Encryption Algorithm*: Blockchain technology uses asymmetric encryption algorithms that require both the encryption key (namely the public key) and the decryption key (namely the private key). The public key contains information that can be encrypted to the receiver. In contrast, the private key belongs to the individual and can decrypt the encrypted information of the sender. If the recipient does not have the private key, the information encrypted by the public key cannot be decrypted (Fan *et al.*, 2019; Chen *et al.*, 2019). This ensures the safety of the information.

IV. *P2P Network Protocol*: The P2P network is network topology and is a P2P network. Each peer site can transmit and receive information and data from each other. Due to the existence of the P2P network protocols, blockchain technology can revolutionize the value transmission between peers. Therefore, all the blockchain nodes can protect the information and data on the blockchain without relying on the central agency. This avoids the data being attacked or tampered (Chen *et al.*, 2019; Tang *et al.*, 2019).

V. *Side Chain Technology*: A side chain is another blockchain that is parallel to the main chain, but there is a certain distance between them. The side chain technology mainly includes two types: two-way and joint wedging. They help to realize the two-way communication and value transmission between the side chain and the main chain. Meanwhile, it protects the main chain to a great extent so that the main chain will not be damaged. The deficiencies of the main chain are made up of sideward; this extends the application range of the blockchain technology (Xu *et al.*, 2019).

VI. *Smart Contract*: The smart contract is a new way to reach consensus among different nodes. In essence, it is a non-dangerous and usable computer program. In a decentralized system when the set initial conditions are met, the blockchain technology that can store intelligent programming and run the code will forcibly execute the contract content automatically (Meeuw *et al.*, 2019; Jamison *et al.*, 2018; Shala *et al.*, 2019; Biswas *et al.*, 2019).

This chapter proposes a new architecture of the blockchain-based supply chain system by referring to the characteristics and advantages of the above-mentioned blockchain technology and catering to the functional operation mode of the existing supply chain system.

Proposed Architecture of the Supply Chain System

The distributed subject occupies an important position in the blockchain database. The updates and maintenance of the database require the function of all subjects and are not performed by a core institution in the traditional database. This exactly manifests the typical characteristics of the decentralization of blockchain (Helo *et al.*, 2019). The supply chain includes different types of firms, such as material suppliers, production plants, sales intermediaries, and final customers. The main body of the supply chain is very diverse, and information and resources are exchanged and shared based on the supply chain (Schmidt *et al.*, 2019). The supply chain has a multiagent, multifunction, and multilevel chain organization. The application of blockchain technology in the supply chain system should be aligned with the characteristics of blockchain technology and should avoid the absolute central position of a certain subject (Choi *et al.*, 2019). In the supply chain, different subjects are equal. As a result, from the perspective of the subject, there is a relatively large coupling between the blockchain and the supply chain system, as indicated in Figure 2.

The chain structure in the blockchain is the basis for different nodes to form a consensus mechanism with each other. Different blocks will form a continuous chain structure, which is safe, transparent, traceable, and tamperproof. However, in the supply chain system, the transaction relationships between different entities are complicated. The relevant contents of decentralization in the blockchain can be introduced into the supply chain system to reduce the opportunity cost caused by the lack of trust between different entities in the supply chain.

In the actual operation process, each supply chain member will set up a corresponding information file when registering for the supply chain. The file contains information regarding the company, employer, and qualification. After successful registration, the participant will receive a public key and a private key. The public key is disclosed to all members of the blockchain, and

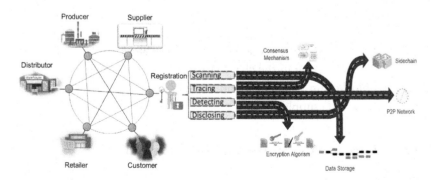

Figure 2.   A New Framework of Supply Chains with Blockchain Mechanisms

the private key is the individual key to verify identity and information during the transaction. All the participants can use the registered ID to log into the user interface and access the specified blockchain network. In terms of information flow, all information is stored in the blockchain and is supported by authorized nodes. The right to access information depends on the participants' roles and positions in the supply chain. The operation rules of blockchain are defined by the codes, which cannot be modified by a certain participant in the blockchain. As a result, the authenticity and validity of data can be ensured. If operation rules of the blockchain need to be changed, broadcast needs to be made to all the nodes and verification needs to be performed by the key departments, like the way data is stored.

Furthermore, blockchain is a relatively complete mechanism, including processing transactions, data storage, acceptance of smart contracts, and related processing. After the confirmation of the information on the event has been transferred to the smart contract, it is necessary to update the status of the contract information and resources in time. The status of the contract is then verified. Meanwhile, the supply chain will automatically execute a series of contracts to ensure the completion of transactions. Blockchain-based smart contracts can avoid malicious interference of related factors and affect the ordinary execution of the contract. Both of them have obvious advantages in terms of cost, so it is apparent that they also have a relatively large coupling in terms of smart contracts.

Case Studies

The supply chain system based on blockchain as discussed above is described and analyzed.

From 2018, we conducted surveys that focused on firms that were applying blockchain technologies to develop their food supply chain systems. Through interviews with relevant managers and archival data, we analyzed and clarified their efforts and characteristics of supply chain systems. We focused on key factors that were important in rebuilding their supply chains by introducing the blockchain architecture; results they achieved through utilizing blockchain mechanisms; and how they could improve their SCR after they transitioned to the new architecture. In this section, the key elements of the resilient supply chain system are described with the aid of two Japanese case studies.

Case Study 1: A Fishery Blockchain-Based Supply Chain System

In recent years, many Japanese fisheries companies have become active in acquiring Chain of Custody (CoC) certificate from the Marine Stewardship Council (MSC), and the entire supply chain from fishing to production, distribution, and final product manufacturing has an established system for producing MSC-certified marine products.

At the same time, there is a growing need for greater transparency in the supply chain from retailers, food-service companies, and consumers who want to know whether even food that has not been certified was produced with consideration for the environment and human rights, and whether it was delivered with controlled freshness. A growing trend in the food industry to meet demand is the use of blockchain technology. To prove its provenance, it takes advantage of its characteristics that make it difficult to falsify information from production to distribution and processing.

Company K, a sea bass aquafarmer in Tokyo, was one of the first companies to adopt blockchain technology and launched the "Ocean to Table" project to prove the provenance of seafood. A QR code attached to the fish is used to track information from fishing to processing and shipping. For example, if a customer scans a QR code on a menu for a sea bass dish served at a restaurant, they will get information on who took the fish, when and where, as well as processing and certification information. The company also plans to add restaurant recipes and recipe information (Fujita, 2020).

In order to preserve the freshness of the sea bass, it is killed immediately after being caught and the nerves are removed, before being shipped as "instant sea bass killing." The sea bass fishery is also engaged in the Fishery Improvement Project (FIP) to obtain MSC certification. There are many participating members of this project, such as aquafarmers, processing and production companies, central wholesale market, MSC, logistics and/or distributor, retailer and restaurants, and the entire supply chain is working together (see Figure 3).

In Japan, the Fisheries Act was amended in 2018, and the government is considering introducing a Catch Documentation Scheme (CDS) to certify that fish are caught legally and properly by fishery operators. Blockchain tracking information could also be used to certify catches. Even in export, if you can prove that the fish is sustainably taken, it will be a differentiator.

It will add value if they can tell the story of the producers about the hardships involved in obtaining certification and removing nerves to preserving

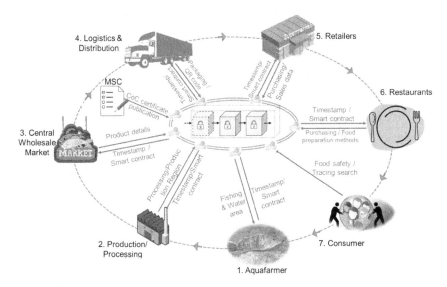

Figure 3. The Fishery Supply Chain System Based on Blockchain Technology

freshness. The use of blockchain technology is expected to bring about an era in which transparency in supply chain traceability will prove sustainable eating and create new added value.

Case Study 2: A Blockchain-Based Cloud Business Platform

Company A, one of Japan's leading chemical manufacturers, is engaged in the development and promotion of utilization of technologies such as hydrogen extraction by electrolysis of alkaline water using renewable energy and the production of electrolyte materials for high-performance plastics and lithium-ion batteries using carbon dioxide (CO_2) as a raw material (Koyama, 2022). Recycling of used plastics and the use of recycled plastics have become major social issues for the formation of a resource-recycling society. The Japanese government has set a policy of using 60% recycled plastic by 2030 and 100% by 2035. In the near future, the realization of a resource-recycling society will naturally increase the value of recycled products. However, it is difficult to prove the recycling chain of products made from recycled plastic or the recycling ratio of raw materials.

To solve this problem, Company A launched the green plastics initiative, which aims to recycle plastic resources. The green plastics is defined as a project to develop a digital platform to visualize the resource circulation of recycled plastics, and it is expected that companies and consumers involved in the supply chain will realize the recycling certification and the creation of recycling culture by building an open platform with all participants.

Recycling certification is issued when consumers choose recycled plastic, and they will be correctly told that it comes from recycled materials. This will encourage consumers to buy recycled products with peace of mind and help promote recycling by making their environmental contributions visible. In this way, Company A aims to create a new recycling culture by turning the plastic resource cycle around.

When consumers pick up a plastic item, it is hard to prove scientifically if it comes from recycling. Therefore, the green plastics project administers the information with a blockchain technology that is nearly impossible to tamper with. Users joining the network keep data on each other to prove they are recycled plastic. The team then built an app that was meant to be used by consumers on a platform in the cloud and completed a prototype (see Figure 4).

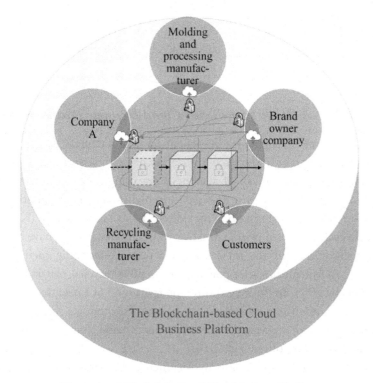

Figure 4.   A Blockchain-Based Cloud Business Platform

The development of the platform is marked by a concerted effort by members of the supply chain. The first feature of the platform is all supply chain members, including recycling manufacturers, resin manufacturers, molding and processing manufacturers, and brand owner companies, participated in the development, which was supported by IBM Japan that has a rich track record in blockchain business.

The second is proof of recycling. Consumers can scan QR codes on recycled plastic products with their smartphone cameras to see the percentage of recycled plastic used. The recycling rate is managed by blockchain, which acts as a certification.

The third is the visualization of companies involved in recycling. By scanning a QR code on a smartphone, a consumer can trace back through the recycling chain to see the player's history. In other words, the consumer can see what the plastic has been through. They call it the traveling plastic. The effect is that transparency of provenance allows consumers to use products with confidence.

The fourth is the introduction of a system to record consumers' environmental contributions. They hypothesized that consumers value experiences, not just money exchanges, because plastic bottles and other items are properly sorted and put into the collection boxes at supermarkets and other stores.

Under the platform, when recycled plastic products are placed in a collection box, an environmental contribution index named the green leaf is accumulated to record environmental contribution experiences. By visualizing the national ranking of accumulated leaves and the amount of carbon dioxide reduction, the supply chain partners aim to raise consumer awareness and foster a culture of recycling.

The green plastics initiative is not just a contribution to promote a resource-recycling society, but also the strategy of creating a new economic system using digital platforms. Company A will continue to invite other companies that resonate and sympathize with it from across the field and expand the types and applications of resins.

Discussion

Blockchain is a typical collaboration tool. The blockchain-based supply chain system architecture can be analyzed from three different aspects. Figure 5, adapted from Cui and Singh (2022), is a schematic diagram of the content and relationships contained in different dimensions. The most fundamental purpose of developing a supply chain system is to provide the best service while minimizing costs under certain conditions. The traditional supply chain system simply connects different subjects on the chain. Since the way of connecting is relatively simple, it will inevitably lead to some of the problems that are difficult to solve. The blockchain can provide comprehensive technical support from one point to the whole chain, and then, to the network. The blockchain technology is directly embedded in the internal IoT of a company. Through the application of more advanced sensor technology and identification technology in the IoT, information exchange and transmission can be achieved. Internet technology is used as the basis for the effective application of blockchain technology (Pereira *et al.*, 2019).

As a traceable, immutable, secure and verifiable distributed database, the blockchain has changed the rigid model of the traditional bureaucratic organization and replaced it with a decentralized autonomous organization (DAO) structure, and through a unique incentive mechanism, given full play to the network effect and better adapt to the requirements of the organizational model in the digital age (Lumineau *et al.*, 2021). The DAO structure of blockchain provides a new method to ensure the ownership and origin of data and intellectual property rights (see Figure 5). The security and accuracy of the assets stored in the ledger are guaranteed through a consensus mechanism and asymmetric encryption mechanism.

In the new architecture, every member of the supply chain system will design their operational procedures based on blockchain mechanisms, such as smart contracts, rather than conduct transactions with each other based on a system based on labor. Since transactions that are executed through blockchain mechanisms are accurate and creditable, many troubles and negotiations derived from a traditional supply chain model can be avoided. On the other hand, when unexpected events happen, for example, a human-made disaster or natural catastrophe like the COVID-19 pandemic, the supply chain system can quickly coordinate and recover itself with the aid of the blockchain network. The architecture of the blockchain-based supply chain system is resilient and robust due to its decentralized pattern originally and can self-organize after receiving damages.

Moreover, joining the blockchain network with the supply chain system can expand global relationships. This resolves the problem of the increase of opportunity cost caused by the fragile trust relationship and significantly

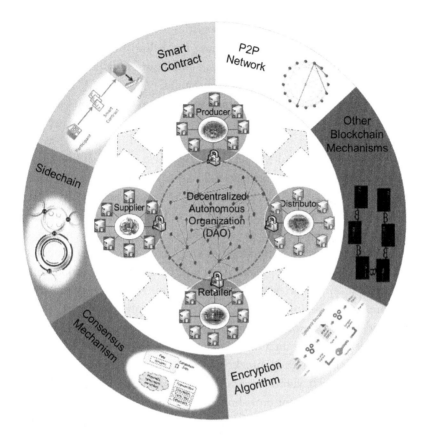

Figure 5. An Architecture of Blockchain-Based Supply Chain System (Adapted from Cui & Singh, 2022)

improves the transaction efficiency between different entities (Yang, 2019). Due to the existence of distributed coexistence technology and decentralized technology, every transaction of the firm on each node in the system can be effectively verified. A unique chain that will not be broken can be constructed, which improves the management of supply chain efficiency and ensures that each transaction is unique. Figure 5 shows the content of the object dimension.

Due to the existence of core technologies in the blockchain, such as the application of distributed databases, smart contracts, etc., data will not be forged and tampered in actual operations. Furthermore, due to the application of advanced technologies, its application scope has been extended to the relevant supply chain enterprises as a whole (Zhang *et al.*, 2019). In the digital era, capital, information, and logistics between supply chain companies use information networks to achieve rapid flow. Although the foundation of the supply chain structure is cash and logistics, the information flow is an important link connecting different nodes.

In terms of logistics, the combination of related technologies in logistics information and blockchain technology can help to improve the security of network systems (Azzi *et al.*, 2019). With the help of operations, any information can form a special Merkle tree. After packaging, it will be stored in the blockchain without any artificial behaviors. With encryption technology, security and logistics efficiency are improved automatically. In terms of information flow, the information of different links will be stored in the system of each link, resulting in the situation that numerous information cannot be effectively traced back and therefore lack transparency (Longo *et al.*, 2019). The introduction of blockchain technology can help various entities to effectively capture relevant data information. Moreover, enhancing the transparency of the information flow in the supply chain will assist the prompt identification of problems. As a result, appropriate measures can be taken to deal with them in a timely manner. In terms of capital flow, adopting related technologies in blockchain can reduce financial disputes and improve the efficiency and processing speed of the payment. The effect is particularly significant for cross-border payments (Wang *et al.*, 2019). The secure database technology applied in blockchain can ensure that the transaction data in each node is authentic and reliable and cannot be tampered at a later stage.

The blockchain system can exchange data anonymously without mutual trust and can effectively avoid relevant violations of the subject during data processing. Besides, there will not be a special central agency in the blockchain for supervision and management. The subjects are in an equal relationship and can exchange data freely. Since blockchain is a decentralized and intelligent system architecture, when an emergency happens, the supply chain system can reorganize and figure it out immediately and automatically by utilizing blockchain technology.

The blockchain-based supply chain system includes the function of intelligent logistics. The implementation of intelligent logistics includes applying video technology, voice technology, RFID technology, and logistics services such as identification, positioning, sorting, and measurement (Yi *et al.*, 2019). Meanwhile, it can also accurately locate raw materials, parts, and navigation systems through adopting navigation systems such as Global Positioning System. With the technical support provided by storage technologies, such as Storage Area Network technology and Network Attached Storage technology, the logistics central information system can focus on warehouse management (Pustišek *et al.*, 2018; Alharby *et al.*, 2018).

Taking the "accounting principle" as the basis can ensure the data in the intelligent warehouse not be tampered with. The lockers are effectively connected by a distributed ledger platform, which can help customers to track the real-time dynamic situation of the packages. In short, the application of blockchain technology not only increases the transparency of the entire supply chain but also ensures the company to conduct related transaction activities in a secure environment with the adoption of smart terminals to track parcels. Most of transactions and operations can be conducted by machines rather than human beings in the blockchain-based supply chain system. Therefore, the risks caused by human beings will be minimized and new trust mechanisms will be ensured. The issues such as "information asymmetry" and power asymmetry will be solved as a whole.

Conclusion

Since blockchain is a decentralized and intelligent system architecture, when emergency events happen, the supply chain system can reorganize and detect and react immediately and automatically by utilizing blockchain technology. Most transactions and operations can be conducted by machines rather than people in the blockchain-based supply chain system; therefore, the risks caused by human behaviors will be minimized and new trust mechanisms will be ensured. In this chapter, we used case studies of two Japanese food supply chains to illustrate how the new supply chain system architecture model and blockchain technology can minimize the losses caused by the stagnation of the supply chain system when an emergency occurs. The new supply chain system architecture model can also improve and strengthen supply chain resilience. This demonstrates the application of the new architecture of a resilient supply chain system based on blockchain technology. The blockchain technologies are still at an early stage. As a result, the efficiency and costs are higher than the current supply chain system under a normal state. However, these problems will be resolved in the near future with new solutions developed and the advancement of blockchain technologies.

References

Abdelshafy, A., & Walther, G. (2022). Exploring the effects of energy transition on the industrial value chains and alternative resources: A case study from the German federal state of North Rhine-Westphalia (NRW) resources. *Conservation and Recycling*, **177**, 1–10.

Alharby, M., & Moorsel, A. (2018). The impact of profit uncertainty on miner decisions in blockchain systems. *Electronic Notes in Theoretical Computer Science*, **340**, 151–167.

Al-Qudah, L. (2021). The perception of implementing Industry 4.0 on supply chain: A review on sustainability pillars. *Cross Cultural Management Journal, Fundaţia Română pentru Inteligenţa Afacerii*, **1**, 57–69.

Aoki, Y., Otsuki, K., Kaneko, T., Banno, R., & Shudo, K. (2019). SimBlock: A blockchain network simulator. *IEEE INFOCOM 2019 — IEEE Conference on Computer Communications Workshops (INFOCOM WKSHPS)*, Paris, France, pp. 325–329.

Arend, R (2006). SME–supplier alliance activity in manufacturing: Contingent benefits and perceptions. *Strategic Management Journal*, **27**(8), 741–763.

Azad, N., Saharidis, G. K. D., Davoudpour, H., Malekly, H., & Yektamaram, S. A. (2013). Strategies for protecting supply chain networks against facility and transportation disruptions: An improved Benders decomposition approach. *Annals of Operations Research*, **146**, 125–163.

Azzi, R., Chamoun, R. K., & Sokhn, M. (2019). The power of a blockchain-based supply chain. *Computers & Industrial Engineering*, **135**, 582–592.

Bhargava, B., Ranchal,R., & Othmane, L. B. (2013). Secure information sharing in digital supply chains. *3rd IEEE International Advance Computing Conference (IACC 2013)*, pp. 1636–1640. https://doi: 10.1109/IAdCC.2013.6514473.

Biswas, B., & Gupta, R. (2019). Analysis of barriers to implement blockchain in industry and service sectors. *Computers & Industrial Engineering*, **136**, 225–241.

Büyüközkan, G., & Göçer, F. (2018). Digital supply chain: Literature review and a proposed framework for future research. *Computers in Industry*, **97**, 157–177. https://doi.org/10.1016/j.compind.2018.02.010.

Cacciapuoti, A. S., Caleffi, M., Tafuri, F., Cataliotti, F. S., Gherardini, S., & Bianchi, G. (2020). Quantum internet: Networking challenges in distributed quantum computing. *IEEE Network*, **34**(1), 137–143. https://doi: 10.1109/MNET.001.1900092.

Calatayud, A., Mangan, J., & Christopher, M. (2019). The self-thinking supply chain. *Supply Chain Management*, **24**(1), 22–38. https://doi.org/10.1108/SCM-03-2018-0136.

Chen, Y., Xie, H., Lv, K., Wei, S., & Hu, C. (2019). DEPLEST: A blockchain-based privacy-preserving distributed database toward user behaviors in social networks. *Information Sciences*, **501**, 100–117.

Chen, J., Lv, Z., & Song, H. (2019). Design of personnel big data management system based on blockchain. *Future Generation Computer Systems*, **101**, 1122–1129.

Cheng, J. H., & Sheu, J. B. (2012). Inter-organizational relationships and strategy quality in green supply chains — Moderated by opportunistic behavior and dysfunctional conflict. *Industrial Marketing Management*, **41**(4), 563–572.

Cheng, L., Liu, J., Su, C., Liang, K., Xu, G., & Wang, W. (2019). Polynomial-based modifiable blockchain structure for removing fraud transactions. *Future Generation Computer Systems*, **99**, 154–163.

Chern, M. S., Chan, Y. C., Teng, J. T., & Goyal, S. K. (2014). Nash equilibrium solution in a vendor–buyer supply chain model with permissible delay in payments. *Computers & Industrial Engineering*, **70**, 116–123.

Choi, T., Wen, X., Sun, X., & Chung, S. H. (2019). The mean-variance approach for global supply chain risk analysis with air logistics in the blockchain technology era. *Transportation Research Part E: Logistics and Transportation Review*, **127**, 178–191.

Chopra, S., & Sodhi, M. S. (2004). Managing risk to avoid supply-chain breakdown: by understanding the variety and interconnectedness of supply-chain risks, managers can tailor balanced, effective risk-reduction strategies for their companies. *MIT Sloan Management Review*, **46**(1), 53–62.

Christopher, M., & Peck, H. (2004). Building the resilient supply chain. *The International Journal of Logistics Management*, **15**(2), 1–13.

Craighead, C. W., Blackhurst, J., Rungtusanatham, M. J., & Handfield, R. B. (2007). The severity of supply chain disruptions: Design characteristics and mitigation capabilities. *Decision Sciences*, **38**(1), 131–156.

Cui, Y., & Singh, P. J. (2022). Blockchain-based supply chain architecture adapted to digital business ecosystems. In Baumann, S. (Ed.), *Handbook on Digital Business Ecosystems: Strategies, Platforms, Technologies, Governance and Societal Challenges* (Chapter 24, pp. 387–404). Edward Elgar Publishing, Cheltenham, UK. DOI: https://doi.org/10.4337/9781839107191.00033.

Davis, Z., Zobel, C.W., Khansa, L., & Glick, R. E. (2019). Emergency department resilience to disaster–level overcrowding: A component resilience framework for analysis and predictive modeling. *Journal of Operations Management*, **66**(1–2), 54–66.

Dorri, A., Kanhere, S. S., Jurdak, R., & Gauravaram, P. (2019). LSB: A lightweight scalable blockchain for IoT security and anonymity. *Journal of Parallel and Distributed Computing*, **134**, 180–197.

Fabbri, D., & Klapper, L. F. (2016). Bargaining power and trade credit. *Journal of Corporate Finance*, **41**, 66–80.

Fan, K., Sun, S., Yan, Z., Pan, Q., Li, H., & Yang, Y. (2019). A blockchain-based clock synchronization scheme in IoT. *Future Generation Computer Systems*, **101**, 524–533.

Fujita, K. (2020). Food tray reclamation, blockchain explicit, consumer tracking experiment on plastic containers. *Nikkei Business Daily*, September 11, p. 2.

Gaonkar, R., & Viswanadham, N. (2004). A conceptual and analytical framework for the management of risk in supply chains. *Proceedings of IEEE International Conference on Robotics and Automation*, pp. 2699–2704.

Helo, P., & Hao, Y. (2019). Blockchains in operations and supply chains: A model and reference implementation. *Computers & Industrial Engineering*, **136**, 242–251.

Hendricks, K. B., & Singhal, V. R. (2003). The effect of supply chain glitches on shareholder wealth. *Journal of Operations Management*, **21**(5), 501–522.

Holling, C. S. (1973). Resilience and stability of ecological systems. *Annual Review of Ecology and Systematics*, **4**, 1–23.

Hu, H., Shi, L., & Ran, H. M. B. (2017). Stability of the supply chain based on disruption classification. *Engineering — Technical Gazette*, **24**(4), 1187–1195.

Huang, J., Li, S., & Thürera, M. (2019). On the use of blockchain in industrial product service systems: A critical review and analysis. *Procedia CIRP*, **83**, 552–556.

Ivanov, D., Dolgui, A., & Sokolov, B. (2019). The impact of digital technology and Industry 4.0 on the ripple effect and supply chain risk analytics. *International Journal of Production Research*, **57**(3), 829–846. https://doi.org/10.1080/00207543.2018.1488086.

Ji, G., & Zhu, C. (2012). A study on emergency supply chain and risk based on urgent relief service in disasters. *Systems Engineering Procedia*, **5**, 313–325.

Johnson, N., Elliott, D., & Drake, P. (2013). Exploring the role of social capital in facilitating supply chain resilience. *Supply Chain Management*, **18**(3), 324–336.

Kang, E. S., Pee, S. J., Song, J. G., & Jang, J. W. (2018). A blockchain-based energy trading platform for smart homes in a microgrid. *3rd International Conference on Computer and Communication Systems (ICCCS 2018)*, Nagoya, pp. 472–476. https://doi.org/10.1109/CCOMS.2018.8463317.

Kleindorfer, P. R., & Saad, G. H. (2005). Managing disruption risks in supply chains. *Journal of Production and Operations Management*, **14**(1), 53–68.

Korpela, K., Hallikas, J., & Dahlberg, T. (2017). Digital supply chain transformation toward blockchain integration. *Proceedings of the 50th Hawaii International Conference on System Sciences*, pp. 4182–4101.

Koyama, M. (2022). Visualizing the regeneration process of industrial waste plastics such as Asahi Kasei. *Nikkei Business Daily*, October 5, p. 5.

Lam, J. S., & Bai, X. (2016). A quality function deployment approach to improve maritime supply chain resilience. *Transportation Research Part E: Logistics and Transportation Review*, **92**(August), 16–27.

Li, D. (2011). Information architecture for supply chain quality management. *International Journal of Production Research*, **49**, 183–198.

Li, J., & Wang, X. (2018). Research on the application of blockchain in the traceability system of agricultural products. *2nd IEEE Advanced Information Management, Communicates, Electronic and Automation Control Conference (IMCEC 2018)*, Xi'an, pp. 2637–2640. https://doi.org/10.1109/IMCEC.2018.8469456.

Li, S., & Chen, Y. (2022). How non-fungible tokens empower business model innovation. *Business Horizons*, **S0007-6813(22)00132-X**, 1–20. https://doi.org/10.1016/j.bushor.2022.10.006.

Liu, X., Muhammad, K., Lloret, J., Chen, Y. W., & Yuan, S. W. (2019). Elastic and cost-effective data carrier architecture for smart contract in blockchain. *Future Generation Computer Systems*, **100**, 590–599.

Liu, Z., Xiang, Y., Shi, J., Gao, P., Wang, H., Xiao, X., Wen, B., Li, Q., & Hu, Y. C. (2022). Make Web3.0 connected. *IEEE Transactions on Dependable and Secure Computing*, **19**(5), 2965–2981. https://doi.org/10.1109/TDSC.2021.3079315.

Longo, F., Nicoletti, L., Padovano, A., Atri, G., & Forte, M. (2019). Blockchain-enabled supply chain: An experimental study. *Computers & Industrial Engineering*, **136**, 57–69.

Lu, Q., Xu, X., Liu, Y., Weber, I., Zhu, L., & Zhang, W. (2019). uBaaS: A unified blockchain as a service platform. *Future Generation Computer Systems*, **101**, 564–575.

Lumineau, F., Wang, W., & Schilke, O. (2021). Blockchain governance — A new way of organizing collaborations? *Organization Science*, 32(2), 500–521.

Lyu, Q., Qi, Y., Zhang, X., Liu, H., Wang, Q., & Zheng, N. (2019). SBAC: A secure blockchain-based access control framework for information-centric networking. *Journal of Network and Computer Applications*, **49**, 1–17.

Maesa, D. F., Mori, P., & Ricci, L. (2019). A blockchain based approach for the definition of auditable access control systems. *Computers & Security*, **84**, 93–119.

Meeuw, A., Schopfer, S., & Wortmann, F. (2019). Experimental bandwidth benchmarking for P2P markets in blockchain managed microgrids. *Energy Procedia*, **159**, 370–375.

Muzammal, M., Qu, Q., & Nasrulin, B. (2019). Renovating blockchain with distributed databases: An open source system. *Future Generation Computer Systems*, **90**, 105–117.

Park, A., Wilson, M., Robson, K., Demetis, D., & Kietzmann, J. (2022). Interoperability: Our exciting and terrifying Web3 future. *Business Horizons*, **S0007-6813(22)00131-8**, 1–22. https://doi.org/10.1016/j.bushor.2022.10.005.

Peck, H. (2005). Drivers of supply chain vulnerability: An integrated framework. *International Journal of Physical Distribution & Logistics Management*, **35**(4), 210–232.

Pereira, J., Tavalaei, M. M., & Ozalp, H. (2019). Blockchain-based platforms: Decentralized infrastructures and its boundary conditions. *Technological Forecasting and Social Change*, **146**, 94–102.

Pettit, T. J., Fiksel, J., & Croxton, K. L. (2010). Ensuring supply chain resilience: Development of a conceptual framework. *Journal of Business Logistics*, **31**(1), 1–21.

Ponomarov, S. Y., & Holcomb, M. C. (2009). Understanding the concept of supply chain resilience. *International Journal of Logistics Management*, **20**(1), 124–143.

Pustišek, M., & Kos, A. (2018). Approaches to front-end IoT application development for the ethereum blockchain. *Procedia Computer Science*, **129**, 410–419.

Pyun, J., & Rha, J. S. (2021). Review of research on digital supply chain management using network text analysis. *Sustainability*, **13**(17), 9929. https://doi.org/10.3390/su13179929.

Ranganathan, C., Dhaliwal, J. S., & Teo, T. S. H. (2014). Assimilation and diffusion of web technologies in supply-chain management: An examination of key drivers and performance impacts. *International Journal of Electronic Commerce*, **9**(1), 127–161. https://doi.org/10.1080/10864415.2004.11044319.

Sapountzaki, K. (2007). Social resilience to environmental risks. *Management of Environmental Quality*, **18**(3), 274–297.

Schmidt, C. G., & Wagner, S. M. (2019). Blockchain and supply chain relations: A transaction cost theory perspective. *Journal of Purchasing and Supply Management*, **25**(4), 1–13.

Schoon, I. (2006). *Risk and Resilience — Adaptations in Changing Times*. Cambridge University Press, New York.

Shala, B., Trick, U., Lehmann, A., Ghita, B., & Shiaeles, S. (2019). Novel trust consensus protocol and blockchain-based trust evaluation system for M2M application services. *Internet of Things*, **7**, 1–25.

Sheffi, Y. (2009). MIT center for transportation and logistics. *Journal of Commerce*, (January), 147–148.

Sheffi, Y., & Rice Jr., B. J. (2005). A supply chain view of the resilient enterprise. *MIT Sloan Management Review*, **47**(1), 41–48.

Sherman, E. (2020). 94% of the Fortune 1000 are seeing coronavirus supply chain disruptions: Report. *Fortune*, February 22, 2020. https://fortune.com/2020/02/21/fortune-1000-coronavirus-china-supply-chain-impact/.

Shi, Z., Xie, Y., Xue, W., Chen, Y., Fu, L., & Xu, X. (2020). Smart factory in Industry 4.0. *Systems Research and Behavioral Science*, **37**, 607–617. https://doi.org/10.1002/sres.2704.

Stewart, G. T., Kolluru, R., & Smith, M. (2009). Leveraging public-private partnerships to improve community resilience in times of disaster. *International Journal of Physical Distribution & Logistics Management*, **39**(5), 343–364.

Tang, C. S. (2007). Robust strategies for mitigating supply chain disruptions. *International Journal of Logistics Research and Applications*, **9**(1), 33–45.

Tang, H., Shi, Y., & Dong, P. (2019). Public blockchain evaluation using entropy and TOPSIS. *Expert Systems with Applications*, **117**, 204–210.

Tavana, M., Shaabani, A., Raeesi Vanani, I., & Kumar Gangadhari, R. (2022). A review of digital transformation on supply chain process management using text mining. *Processes*, **10**, 842. https://doi.org/10.3390/pr10050842.

Wang, E. K., Liang, Z., Chen, C. M., Kumari, S., & Khan, M. K. (2020). PoRX: A reputation incentive scheme for blockchain consensus of IIoT. *Future Generation Computer Systems*, **102**, 140–151.

Wang, L., Shen, X., Li, J., Shao, J., & Yang, Y. (2019). Cryptographic primitives in blockchains. *Journal of Network and Computer Applications*, **127**, 43–58.

Wang, Y., Singgih, M., Wang, J., & Rit, M. (2019). Making sense of blockchain technology: How will it transform supply chains. *International Journal of Production Economics*, **211**, 221–236.

Wu, L., Yue, X., Jin, A., & Yen, D. C. (2016). Smart supply chain management: A review and implications for future research. *The International Journal of Logistics Management*, **27**(2), 395–417. https://doi.org/10.1108/IJLM-02-2014-0035.

Xu, X., Lu, Q., Liu, Y., Zhu, L., Yao, H., & Vasilakos, A. V. (2019). Designing blockchain-based applications a case study for imported product traceability. *Future Generation Computer Systems*, **92**, 399–406.

Yang, C.-S. (2019). Maritime shipping digitalization: Blockchain-based technology applications, future improvements, and intention to use. *Transportation Research Part E: Logistics and Transportation Review*, **131**, 108–117.

Yi, H. (2019). Securing instant messaging based on blockchain with machine learning. *Safety Science*, **120**, 6–13.

Zhang, A., Zhong, R. Y., Farooque, M., Kang, K., & Venkatesh, V. G. (2020). Blockchain-based life cycle assessment: An implementation framework and system architecture. *Resources, Conservation and Recycling*, **152**, 1–11.

https://doi.org/10.1142/9789811286636_0006

CHAPTER 6

Blockchain Adoption in Maritime Supply Chain: Another Catch-Up Game for African Maritime Industry?

Olugbenga Ayo Ojubanire[*,§], Hicham Sebti[†,¶], and Sabrina Berbain[‡,||]

*Euromed Business School, Euromed University of Fes, Morocco

†ESSEC Business School Africa, Campus Rabat, Morocco

‡ISG International Business School, Paris, France

§o.ojubanire@ueuromed.org

¶sebti@essec.edu

||sabrina.berbain@isg.fr

Abstract

With over 90% of the world's goods relying on the maritime industry for transport, the digitalization of the maritime supply chain and logistics is greatly due. The real-world utility of blockchain technologies is hardly a subject of concern today, even in Africa. The application and success stories are evident in key economic sectors with the digitalization of payments as a predominant example. Although classical maritime logistics has a poor end-to-end supply chain integration, digitalization of shipping operations leads to the creation of new and innovative business models capable of generating real values across the global value chain. While several studies have been done on digitalization with a focus on technologies of digitalization and the manufacturing industry, maritime supply chain issues in emerging economies such as Africa are yet to get much attention. This study, therefore, expounds on the challenges and opportunities of blockchain adoption in the African maritime industry.

Keywords: Blockchain; Digitalization; Digital Transformation; Logistics; Maritime; Supply chain.

Introduction

The transition to the digital economy is changing the face of everything, from the production system to logistics and supply chain across all industries and sectors (Kohler & Weisz, 2018). The strategic and operational importance of digitalization cannot be denied, as early adopters report that they can work more efficiently and make a significant contribution to the business bottom line (Wellener *et al.*, 2020). The digitalization of all parts of the industrial production system, with interoperability, integration, real-time control and monitoring, easy production, rapid response to changes in market forces, state-of-the-art sensors, and extensive analysis of big data, can increase productivity (Lu *et al.*, 2016). The processes, technologies, and modes of organization associated with digitalization are gradually maturing and their scope is expanding to cover more industrial sectors (Arromba *et al.*, 2020). These applications now go beyond the pioneering industries of digital transformation such as aeronautics, automotive or defense, and the maritime industry. Nevertheless, transitioning into a fully digitalized industry may be a slow process and may also take some time to upgrade the components from the existing intra-organizational business system and inter-organizational ecosystem.

Although classical maritime logistics has a poor end-to-end supply chain integration (Voorspuij & Becha, 2020), digitalization of shipping operations leads to the creation of new and innovative business models capable of generating real values across the global value chain (Colbert, 2016). To put digitalization in the maritime context, Lambrou *et al.* (2019) describe *digitalization as an innovative process that entails the continuous scanning of the shipping markets and competitors, but foremost industry-spanning search for relevant business models and practices to adopt (e.g., autonomous vehicles).* With over 90% of the world's goods relying on the maritime industry for transport, the digitalization of maritime logistics is greatly due (Kapidani *et al.*, 2021) and the integration of customers into this development is fundamental for both industry and global value chain.

The currency for digitalization is data. Data is nothing new to the maritime sector as maritime informatics focuses on the collection, recording, processing, and use of necessary maritime data to support trade and operations in the industry (Ward & Bjørn-Andersen, 2021). Addressing digitalization from a technology point of view is not enough. Taken in isolation, digitalization of shipping operations through technology adoption and implementation does not solve critical business issues on shipping digitalization without due credence to total vertical and horizontal integration, which includes the customer segment. There has been a growing number of highly innovative technologies in recent years, and blockchain is one of the foremost of these technologies (Boison & Antwi-Boampong, 2020; Pilkington, 2016). Blockchain technology offers an innovative platform for transparent and decentralized business transactions (Boison & Antwi-Boampong, 2020), and it is the heart of modern-day distributed ledger.

Providing custody of vital documents requires trust. Conventional record keeping uses a centralized system where designated government agencies and private entities such as banks are entrusted with this responsibility (Casey & Vigna, 2018; Bohemen, 2020). *Blockchains can replace these intermediaries with a technology which verifies transactions through algorithms instead of trust* (Bohemen, 2020). The first and prominent application of blockchain technology today is found in the finance industry, which is a very sensitive economic factor. The next major sector where blockchain has a high disruptive potential is supply chain and logistics, an industry that has evaded digital overhaul for many years (Tapscott & Tapscott, 2018), especially in developing economies. This chapter, therefore, expounds on the potential of blockchain adoption in the African maritime sector, the issues and challenges, opportunities, and the possible way forward.

Digital Transformation of Supply Chain: An Evolution to "Supplychain4.0"

The fourth industrial revolution is rapidly transitioning the world and altering business models in its wake (Schrauf & Berttram, 2016). This transition extends to supply chain management (SCM) — the management of the entire flow of goods and services from the point of origin to the point of consumption — which cuts across different industries, businesses, and locations (Pflaum, 2017).

The supply chain is the lifeline of any business. It affects every aspect of business such as quality, production, delivery, and customer satisfaction (GSCI, 2018). According to Lee and Billington (1992), *The supply chain is a network of producers and distributors that supply raw materials, convert them into intermediate goods and final products, and distribute final products to customers* (Lee & Billington, 1992). It encompasses transportation and storage of raw materials, record/catalog of ongoing production, and catalog of final products. This string of processes demands interdisciplinary, interrelated, and interconnected effort across channels of production and delivery. The supply chain is crucial to the operations of companies that manufacture and distribute products and is in itself a business (Schrauf & Berttram, 2016).

A review of the pitfalls of supply chain inventory in 1992 identified a range of issues such as lack of supply chain metrics, lack of delivery status data, the inadequate definition of customer service, inefficient information systems, simplistic inventory stocking policies, poor coordination, incomplete inventory shipment coordination, and incorrect assessment of inventory costs (Lee & Billington, 1992). Digitalization of the supply chain solves this string of challenges by providing easier, faster, more effective, and more flexible ways to manage long and complex supply operations (Pflaum, 2017).

A digital supply chain is customer-centric. The goal of the technological innovation of DSC in optimizing performance and reducing risk is to ultimately satisfy the demand end of the supply chain (DSCI, 2017). Consumers, staff, and investors have more specific demands and this compels organizations to develop smart supply chains that are highly responsive and dependable. Adoption of technological innovations in supply chain management is needed to meet compelling customer demands in today's fast-paced world where flexibility, agility, and transparency are required in the production processes and across the supply network (Kleab, 2017; Pflaum, 2017; Schrauf & Berttram, 2016).

Digitalization, the use of digital innovations in a technical sense (Cichosz *et al.*, 2020), is of strategic importance for organizations because of its impact on the existing systems, models, and boundaries in the industry (Barrett *et al.*, 2015; Cichosz *et al.*, 2020). More organizations continue to invest in digital innovations that can potentially change communities, organizations, and the economic climate of countries (Cichosz *et al.*, 2020; Mikl *et al.*, 2021). Some companies like Amazon have stood at the forefront of digitalization of logistics and supply chain (L&SC), building digital products and services while wielding digitalization as a tool of change within and among organizations (Loebbecke & Picot, 2015).

Digitalization is not to be confused with automation. Automation is the use of advanced technology to achieve significant improvement in productivity. An example of automation is the use of robots to perform monotonous tasks with more speed and precision than humans can. Digitalization, on the other hand, involves transforming and refining value creation using digital technology. While the processes can remain the same, the use of technology will not only improve productivity but also ensure transparency. The end users can know exactly when to expect their product and get all information about its transit and storage on the supply chain (GSCI, 2018). Digitalization involves both connectivity (skilled usage of technologies to access the internet and share information digitally) and depth (how far-reaching digitalization is in the transformation of economies, business exchanges, and policies using interconnected and automated systems) (Cangul *et al.*, 2020).

Digital technology bridges the gap between companies and consumers by digitizing commerce (e-commerce), marketing, consumer experience, and social media. This evolution toward a digital ecosystem (the cloud, big data, the Internet of Things (IoT), 3D printing, augmented reality (AR), and so on) will aid the integration and transformation of various arms of the production process such as research and development (R&D), manufacturing, marketing, sales, supply chain and logistics, and other organizational units (Schrauf & Berttram, 2016). It is now possible to process, store, and transmit data on a large scale while spending negligible amounts.

Therefore, through digitalization, the transformation of almost any form of human labor (and lifestyle) directly or indirectly associated with data and cognitive non-routine processes is feasible. More advanced software promotes the mechanized interpretation of data. With this, decision-making can be almost autonomous and big data applications can be further integrated into value-creation activities (Cichosz *et al.*, 2020). However, traditional logistics and supply chain companies, especially those in the maritime industry, are still renowned for analog processes and this puts them at risk of missing out on digital innovations that revolutionize organizations and supply chains (O'Marah, 2017).

Digitalization is believed to enable supply chain integration. Integration in supply chain refers to the degree of strategic collaboration that occurs between supply chain inks (members) in the execution of processes within the organization and between organizations (Flynn *et al.*, 2010). Studies have established a positive relationship between supply chain integration and productivity (Frohlich & Westbrook, 2001; Zhao *et al.*, 2013). Digitalization can maximize organizational productivity by enhancing integration across the supply chain and aiding the attainment of organizational goals (Pui & Weisheng, 2021).

Adoption of a digital supply chain goes beyond investment in technologies and capacity building. It has to extend to human capacity management. Organizations have to find employees with the right skillset, manage organizational transformation, and build the right culture for operating a digital supply chain (Klötzer & Pflaum, 2017).

Global Overview of Maritime Supply Chain Digitalization

Digitalization has been the buzzword of the maritime industry for over a decade now and its impact and reach are on a steady rise (Manaadiar, 2020). According to projections by Pui and Weisheng (2021), the annual growth rate of digitalization in the supply chain market will be 8.5% from 2020 to 2027. In 2019, the market value of supply chain digitalization was reported to be $11.7 billion and it was estimated that the value would rise to $23.6 billion in 2020 (Pui & Weisheng, 2021). In 2016, the World Economic Forum projected that digitalization in logistics could rise to $1.5 trillion by 2025 (WEF, 2016). Digitalization in supply chain encompasses all processes from planning to execution and communication (Pui & Weisheng, 2021). As of 2016, almost 90% of companies were convinced about the potential competitive advantage that digitalization would give them in five years, although over 70% of them were unclear about what digitalization would signify for their organization (SupplyChainDigest, 2016).

Investment in the development of specialized digital supply chains is a phenomenon that cuts across industries, and it is even more very pronounced in the manufacturing sector. Recently, a PricewaterhouseCoopers (PwC) study of the rise of the fourth industrial revolution revealed that one-third of the over 2000 respondents reported fully digitalized supply chains in their companies. About 72% have expected digital transformation to have occurred in their organizations in five years. The motivation behind this investment is the expectation of significant economic returns. Highly digitalized supply chains can increase the operational efficiency of the companies that own them, yielding gains of 4.1% and a revenue boost of 2.9% annually (Pui & Weisheng, 2021).

The rate of digital supply chain adoption differs across industries. For example, in the field of electronics, manufacturers have prior experience in creating and managing digital supply chains. They have a track record of creating outsourced manufacturing networks. It is, however, different for the retail and fast-moving goods sector, which is still vulnerable to supply chain disruptions. But this sector is already making efforts to digitalize supply chains. More asset-intensive industries like chemicals are also doing the same (Schrauf & Berttram, 2016). However, digitalization has not been as widespread in logistics companies as it is in the media, telecommunications, banking, and retail sectors.

Logistics companies have had challenges in adopting technology and increasing innovation (Bellingkrodt & Wallenburg, 2013; Gunasekaran *et al.*, 2017; Riedl *et al.*, 2018). Lack of technological know-how, low level of education in the workforce, and difficulty in the diffusion of innovation among branches of organizations have been identified as factors contributing to the low rate of adoption of digitalization in the logistics sector (Cichosz *et al.*, 2020).

Organizations that do not evolve and embrace technological advancement stand the risk of becoming obsolete (Saxena, 2016) because supply chains are technical assets for a business. Their unique strength can provide a competitive advantage for organizations and are therefore fundamental to organizational success (Huo *et al.*, 2014; Min *et al.*, 2019). The evaluation of a supply chain is therefore based on effectiveness and efficiency (Huo *et al.*, 2014).

Emerging Technologies for Digital Supply Chain Networks

The traditional key processes of a supply chain include planning, sourcing, making, delivering, returning, and enabling (Schrauf & Berttram, 2016). With digitalization, these processes are refined around emerging technologies driven by the digital drivers of supply chain. According to Marmolejo-Saucedo and Hartmann (2020), the conceptual drivers of the digital supply chain are agility, integration of supply chain stakeholders, real-time performance and visibility, global web-based connectivity, scalability and flexibility, open flow of information, and smart processes (Figure 1).

The factors shown in Figure 1 are the drivers of digitalization in the supply chain and influence the core technologies of the digital supply chain.

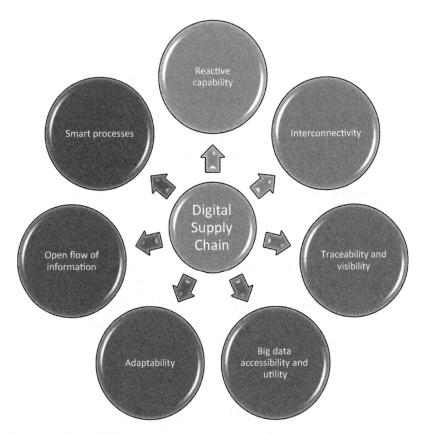

Figure 1. Drivers of digital supply chain.
Source: Marmolejo-Saucedo & Hartmann, 2020.

Agility refers to the ability to quickly predict and respond to opportunities and unforeseen challenges in the supply chain. Visibility and real-time performance refer to quick access to information needed for decision-making. With global web-based connectivity, companies adapt their supply chain to the internet and connect with partners to create supply chain networks with the aim of optimizing customer satisfaction.

Scalability and flexibility enable rapid responsiveness of companies to customer demands. With the open flow of information, as goods move along the supply chain, information is exchanged and this enhances responsiveness to customer demands (Schrauf & Berttram, 2016; Marmolejo-Saucedo & Hartmann, 2020). Smart processes provide opportunities for cost reduction and improved efficiency of the supply chain (Marmolejo-Saucedo & Hartmann, 2020).

Today, the adoption and implementation of digital technologies are major propellers of national economies (Veynberg *et al.*, 2020). Accelerated development of ICT and digital technologies has led to the emergence of digital supply networks of digital supply chains (Veynberg *et al.*, 2020). The joint deployment of emerging digital technologies and information systems results in greater supply chain efficiency (Arenkov *et al.*, 2020).

Grant Waterfall, head of PwC's cybersecurity unit, outlines "artificial intelligence, augmented reality, blockchain, internet of things, 3D printing/additive manufacturing, virtual reality, robotics and drones" as emerging technologies that will revolutionize many economic sectors, especially energy, healthcare, and logistics (Schrauf & Berttram, 2016). Although blockchain is a relatively young technology, it plays a critical role in the digital transformation of the supply chain. In 2017, blockchain has become one of the "eight most effective technologies" (Figure 2) that is capable of disrupting organizational business models (Veynberg *et al.*, 2020).

Digitalization has been found to be a viable means of managing risk in maritime supply chains. Although the rate of digitalization in maritime industry is slower than in other industries, its current applications and digital trends include cloud infrastructure, blockchain, artificial intelligence (AI), Internet of Things (IoT), and automation. Blockchain aims to secure and trace goods from door to door and also to run paperless maritime documentation. It is the most promising technology for the maritime industry (Cap *et al.*, 2021). There are a wide variety of innovative technologies that are

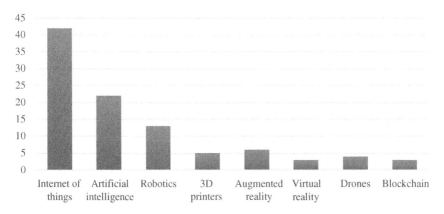

Figure 2.   Emerging technologies with a strong influence on enterprise business models.
Source: Veynberg *et al.*, 2020.

Table 1. Digital supply chain technologies and class distribution based on *Arenkov et al.* (2020).

Technologies	Data Analytics and Visualization	Process Automation and Asset Management	Data Sharing and Communication
Artificial intelligence	✓	✓	✓
Augmented reality		✓	
Blockchain			✓
Internet of things		✓	✓
3D/Additive manufacturing		✓	
Virtual reality		✓	
Robotics		✓	
Big data	✓		
Cloud infrastructure	✓	✓	✓
Social media			✓
E-Procurement	✓		✓
S & OP platforms	✓		✓
Smart warehouse	✓	✓	✓
Sensors	✓	✓	
Quantum computing	✓	✓	✓
APIs			✓

applicable in the digitalization of maritime supply network. Arenkov *et al.* (2020) classified these technologies into three broad groups: "data analytics and visualization, operation automation and asset management, and data sharing and communication." However, some technologies can belong to more than one class, as presented in Table 1.

For effective and efficient supply networks, the adoption of digital technologies is fundamental. These elements of the digital supply chain do not work independently. They are interrelated and work in collaboration with one another. To fully optimize the system, all the elements need proper attention. Organizations that can integrate them all and maintain transparency will have competitive advantages in customer service, flexibility, and efficient use of time and money. Those who are laggards in adopting this innovation will be left further behind (Schrauf & Berttram, 2016).

Blockchain Adoption in Supply Chain Management

Blockchain technology presents a novel way of exchanging information and value over the internet. Originally applied with bitcoin (Wagner & Wiśnicki, 2019), blockchain technology aids decentralization and immutability in the storage of verified data. In September 2015, blockchain became known publicly. It was supposed to be invented by Satoshi Nakamoto, one or more mystery-shrouded individuals. Nine financial powerhouses through collaborative effort created a new infrastructure for financial services that was based on blockchain technology. These financial powerhouses include Goldman Sachs, Barclays, J.P. Morgan, and others (Underwood, 2016).

At that time, blockchain was already a buzzword in fintech; it, however, took a while before the logistics and supply chain community realized the potential of blockchain adoption in supply chain management. Blockchain technology promises transparency (Tapscott & Tapscott, 2016), a vital and challenging feature in supply chain management (Abeyratne & Monfared, 2016). Hence, experts believe that blockchain is of enormous importance and is a "much-needed platform for economic renewal" (O'Marah, 2017) and market disruption (Dickson, 2016).

Blockchain technology has continued to garner attention across different industries with fintech at the forefront of these industries. The supply chain industry is gradually accepting the potential of blockchain technology as well. An online survey of logistics professionals revealed a generally optimistic attitude toward this new technology.

To garner more receptiveness toward blockchain technology, its unique benefits must be highlighted (Kersten *et al.*, 2017). The purpose of blockchain is to keep records of transactions and track them. It builds a chain one block at a time, and that is a ledger. Information stored in a ledger is visible to all the stakeholders. To rectify a mistake, a new block has to be built that relies on the block before it. For numerous transactions, several blocks can be created with several people and the progression of the process remains visible to all. This visibility/transparency of actions is advantageous to logistics, accounting, and risk management (Kapidani *et al.*, 2021).

The three most important features of a blockchain include decentralization, immutability, and verifiability. The network is run by its members and does not have a centralized authority or infrastructure. More transactions are added to the ledger using the blockchain's peer-to-peer network. Members own a copy of the ledger and add their signatures to verify transactions using public–private key cryptography before sharing them with the network. Therefore, only the owner of the private key can initiate the transactions. Members are able to retain anonymity because the keys are not connected to real-world identities. Its consensus algorithm makes it immutable. A block is made up of one or more transactions. Every member of the network can verify transactions in the block. If members are not able to agree to the validity of a new block, it is rejected. Also, if they agree to the validity of transactions in the block, it gets added to the chain. Each block of the chain has a cryptographic hash and holds records of its transactions as well as the cryptographic hash of the block before it. This way, the blocks are interdependent and they form a chain called a blockchain (Kersten *et al.*, 2017).

Blockchain appears to be predominantly promoted by technology providers, consultants, and journalists. A possible explanation for this is its novelty and lack of convincing use cases. However, supply chain management research on blockchain is still relatively new (Zhao *et al.*, 2016). The motivation behind the adoption of technological innovations in the maritime industry is to increase system/process efficiency. Blockchain technology offers increased speed of transactions, exchange, and potentially better integration in supply chain management (Wagner & Wiśnicki, 2019). Therefore, more attention should be given to possible applications (Kersten *et al.*, 2017).

Maritime Supply Chain in Difficult Times

The COVID-19 pandemic is the most severe global disaster since World War II. Aside from loss of life, it has caused unprecedented social and economic disruptions. In a bid to restrict the spread of COVID-19, countries went into a lockdown and took unprecedented and stringent measures. These alterations in social patterns affected mobility globally and disrupted economic activities. The maritime industry was not unaffected (Millefiori *et al.*, 2021).

According to statistics, the number of countries that imposed lockdowns between March and April 2020 is at least 90. This restriction led to constraints in the smooth functioning of the global supply chains, and consequently, global business and industrial activities. Disruption in the supply chain has consequently affected other economic sectors like manufacturing, retail, and construction. It was predicted that the electronics and automotive segments would experience the most severe impact because of the complex nature of their value and supply chains (PWC, 2020).

About 80% of global trade is by volume and 70% of this is carried out through the maritime industry. Therefore, the maritime industry acts as a good gauge of the global economic climate. In 2018, United Nations Conference on Trade and Development (UNCTAD) estimated total volumes in trade to have amounted to 11 billion tons, and a growth rate of 3.4% was projected for the period 2019–2024. However, with the advent of the pandemic, this rate needs to be revised. Globally, trade dropped by 3% in the first quarter of 2020; by then, UNCTAD forecasted an accelerated decline in the second quarter and a 20% decline for the whole year.

The United Nations Organization (UN) estimated a 15% decline in world trade in 2020 due to supply chain disruptions (PWC, 2020), and World Bank analysis showed a 10% decline in merchandise trade as of March 2020 and a 20% decline year after year. The trade decline triggered by COVID-19 has been declared to be more severe than the financial crisis of 2008–2009 (Mackenzie, 2020; UNCTAD, 2020a).

In the maritime industry, the effect of the pandemic was first and most severely felt in the tourism sector. There were reports of a coronavirus outbreak on cruise ships, notably from Yokohama, Corfu, and Sydney. These reports increased people's apprehension about traveling by sea (Depellegrin *et al.*, 2020; Moriarty *et al.*, 2020). Other measures taken to stop the spread of the virus included suspension of port operations and a ban on cruise traffic at terminals. By mid-March 2020, a sizable number of European cruise terminals had either completely or partially stopped operations. Governments enforced restrictions on maritime operations, leading to delayed port clearance. Some restrictions that were enforced impacted crew embarking and disembarking, cargo discharge and loading, quarantine, and finally, refusal of port entry and refueling. Other maritime sectors imposed other restrictions to ensure the safety of facilities and personnel (Millefiori *et al.*, 2021).

The pandemic has revealed the lapses in the world's food supply chains. According to World Food Programme (WFP) estimates, the number of people expected to be in acute hunger by the end of 2020 increased from 135 million to 265 million (PWC, 2020). The fishing and aquaculture sector also experienced containment measures that led to the suspension of voluntary fish farming, ultimately affecting the supply chain of fish food products

(European Commission, 2020). The restrictions on global maritime mobility, however, positively reduced sea pollution (Millefiori *et al.*, 2021).

A side-effect of the measures to restrict the spread of the pandemic is the creation of temporary "manufacturing deserts," a situation that occurs when a country's production drops so drastically that it becomes a dead zone for sourcing anything than essential items (Mackenzie, 2020). The emergence of the outbreak in China has affected the supply of products to countries that depend on China for finished and semi-finished products. In the last decade, China has been the world's largest exporter accounting for about 20% of the global intermediate products, with about $2.3 trillion worth of goods exported annually (WEF estimates). With the United States and Germany, these three major exporters control nearly 30% of total global exports. The effect of the lockdown on foreign manufacturers who depend on China for input has delayed production. For example, a year before the pandemic, more than 65% of India's imported active pharmaceutical ingredients (API) were supplied by China. With the emergence of the pandemic in China, India has had delayed supply and consequently delayed production and distribution of its pharmaceutical products. Medical items, for example, personal protective equipment (PPE), also had an increased demand globally and the disruptions experienced by the transport sector, a vital sector to the supply chain, have caused delayed supply (PWC, 2020).

It has taken a long time for organizations to develop efficient and effective supply chains. However, economic disruptions can affect an unprepared or unadaptable supply chain. Risk management and quick response to disasters are key aspects of an effective supply chain (Black & Glaser-segura, 2020).

Mattias Hedwall, Global Chair, International Commercial & Trade, Baker McKenzie, in a publication by the company, expressed the opinion that *Businesses need to focus on how to minimize supply chain disruption and to adjust rapidly to a changing landscape. This includes among others, infrastructure, tax and employment implications of changes and the option of quickly reversing changes if the situation stabilizes quickly.*

According to Anahita Thoms, Head of Trade (Germany), Baker McKenzie, to forge a way forward, *Export nations need to ensure that supply chains remain as intact as possible. This means that when and where credit insurers are withdrawing from covering international trade during this crisis, the government exceptionally steps in. Otherwise, there is a risk of a collapse of finely woven supply chains* (MacKenzie, 2020).

Current Trends in Maritime Supply Chain Digitalization: Where Does Africa Stand?

The maritime industry in Africa is vital to the economy of the continent. Maritime transport is the major means through which Africa connects to the global marketplace (UNCTAD, 2020b). The oceans, ports, and waterways are Africa's trade link to the rest of the world. International trade is needed to boost domestic commodity demands (Sackey *et al.*, 2021). This vital sector, however, hasn't always received adequate attention from governments and institutions (Baker, 2011).

Africa is home to 5 of 10 countries with the worst port performance (Sackey *et al.*, 2021). According to the CIA, in 2013, South Africa exported goods valued at about $91.05 billion and was ranked 42nd as an exporting country globally. In 2013 as well, South Africa's total importation was valued at about $99.55 billion and this earned the country the 34th position on the list of importing countries globally. South Africa mainly traded with China, Germany, Saudi Arabia, the United States, Japan, and India. Most of these trades were done through maritime vehicles and transit through one of the major seaports in Cape Town, Durban, Port Elizabeth, Richards Bay, and Saldanha Bay (Ramulifho, 2014).

Although Africa is only responsible for a small proportion of the global merchandise trade (2.5% of exports and 3% of imports in terms of volume as of 2020), UNCTAD estimates that Africa's contribution to global maritime trade is relatively larger. The volume of exports recorded by African ports in 2019 was 7% and the volume of imports unloaded was 4.6%. These shares are still much lower than that of Asian and American ports though. Africa accounted for 12% of developing countries' contribution to export and 7% of the contribution to imports in the global maritime industry as of 2019.

Therefore, unlike Asia, which has enjoyed greater integration in global manufacturing and trading networks, Africa contributes marginally to trade flows. Factors responsible for this low contribution to global trade include limited diversification and low trade concentration. Approximately 50% of merchandise exported by sea in 2019 was tanker trade, and about 67% of imports via sea were dry cargoes. Africa's maritime industry contributed 4% to global containerized trade volume, and this was mostly made up of imported manufactured goods. Strategic use of trade and industrial policy as well as integration initiatives like the African Continental Free Trade Agreement (AfCFTA) can aid containerized trade flows in Africa (UNCTAD, 2020b).

Africa owns a limited part of the world's shipping fleet. With a share of 0.31% in deadweight cargo as of 2020, only Nigeria is part of the top 35 owning nations. Liberia ranks high with a second position on the list of top flag states. Panama ranks first. Liberia also ranks third when graded based on deadweight capacity and value of the fleet. In 2020, Liberia's ship-carrying capacity was increased by 13% and this accounted for 13% of total deadweight globally. The topography of the African continent has a huge influence on the connectivity of its shipping countries. Countries located at the corners of the continent seem to enjoy better connectivity. Their international shipping routes connect to major ports like Morocco, Egypt, and South Africa. This is followed by countries like Djibouti, Togo, and Mauritius, which are subregional load centers. African ports are connected not necessarily because of intraregional connectivity, and connectivity boils down to factors such as plying similar overseas routes and transshipment services (UNCTAD, 2019).

The COVID impact on the maritime industry in Africa

COVID-19 has negatively impacted Africa. In Ghana, for instance, two notable regions were on lockdown (The Greater Accra and Ashanti regions). The location of the country's largest seaport Tema Port in the Greater Accra region negatively affected the maritime industry even though the remaining 14 regions remained operational with COVID restrictions in place. The effect of the pandemic escalated and caused serious economic, organizational, strategic, and psychological nightmares for citizens, businesses, nations, and travelers. This unprecedented disruption led to the collapse of businesses, loss of jobs, cancellation of contracts, and volatile supply and demand among other things (UNCTAD, 2020). Ships that were already berthed in the ports of Takoradi and Tema had to have restricted operations (Sackey *et al.*, 2021).

This development was not limited to Ghana; the situation was similar across the continent (Sackey *et al.*, 2021). Seaports were closed in Nigeria except for Lagos ports, the designated provider of "essential services." Vessels recorded to have visited COVID-19-affected countries from 1 February 2020 were denied entry into Nigerian ports from 30 March till 12 April 2020. By 20 April 2020, South Africa had restricted two of its eight seaports from catering to passenger traffic or disembarking crews. Import and export cargoes were, however, not restricted. Kenyan ports, instead of ceasing operations, allowed the importation and exportation of goods cargoes with reduced capacities (Oyenuga, 2021).

UNCTAD valued the reduction in Africa's export and import to be at –35% and –25%, respectively, in the second quarter of 2020. The values improved toward the beginning of the second half of the year to –21% for exports and –17% for imports, but this was still disconcerting. As of mid-2020, the number of ship calls in sub-Saharan Africa had dropped by –9.7% and container ship calls had dropped by –12.7%. Bulk shipping also declined, but it wasn't as significantly affected as the others. Port calls by dry bulk carriers had a 7.7% reduction and wet bulk carriers had a 1.4% decline.

The COVID effect on the connectivity of ports in Africa has been diverse. Although blank sailing has adversely affected the frequency of maritime services, some ports like Lagos, Durban, and TangierMed have fared better than other ports in their region. Cross-border crossings have hit a snag due to restrictions on inland transport. In some countries, on the other hand, the duration between when customs clear cargo and when it is transported changed from what it was in 2019. Due to COVID containment measures, it took longer durations for trucks to return to their departure points, causing a delay in the return of empty containers to the ports, which led to shipping lines incurring extra charges (UNCTAD, 2020b).

Blockchain Adoption in the African Maritime Industry: Current Challenges and Future Opportunities

In a survey of concerns regarding blockchain adoption in developing countries by Kapidani *et al.*, (2021), African experts express a positive attitude toward blockchain technology and acknowledge its potential in revolutionizing the maritime industry. They, however, highlighted some factors that affect blockchain adoption (Table 2). The factors were classified to be of social, technological, political, legal, economic, and environmental dimensions.

Awareness and knowledge of blockchain are considered to be most vital to blockchain adoption in the maritime industry, especially because knowledge is an asset that grows with exploitation. Infrastructure is a technological factor that influences blockchain adoption. Without it, blockchain adoption is impossible. Political and legal factors include favorable government and regulatory policies. The economic development of most developing countries

Table 2.   Selected factors affecting blockchain adoption in the African maritime industry based on Kapidani *et al.* (2021).

Challenges	Category	Factor Ranking
Awareness and knowledge	Social	1
Process complexity and observability	Tech	1
Supportive infrastructure	Tech	2
Government policies	Political	3
Industry regulatory framework	Legal	3
Social influence/change resistance	Social	3
Availability of skilled HR	Social	4
Standardization	Legal/Tech	4
Unwillingness to share info	Economic	5
Data privacy and security	Tech/Legal/Environment	5

is controlled by the government, case in point, Montenegro and South Africa. The fifth factor, which is of both economic and environmental dimensions, is the reluctance of parties involved to make operate a visible and transparent information sharing system. This is expected to reduce once blockchain adoption becomes mainstream. Respondents do not, however, believe that blockchain adoption will reduce opportunistic behavior. These regions have regularly experienced injustice and crisis and they do not believe that society has a say in the implementation and adoption of this technology. The transparency and complexity of blockchain, however, appear to be a suspicious paradox for most respondents (Kapidani *et al.*, 2021).

In Nigeria, for instance, the low rate of adoption of technological innovations continues to incapacitate the maritime industry's ability to drive tenable national development (Chidi *et al.*, 2020; Nsan-Awaji, 2019). Weak technological infrastructure is a major impediment to digitalization in African countries (Dahou & Chalfin, 2020). The refusal to adopt updated technologies in Nigeria's maritime industry has led to poor economic development and debilitated seaports (Ali & Odularu, 2020).

A study by Ikpogu (2021) established a lack of preparedness for transformation change, unwillingness to invest in the purchase and maintenance of technology, and lack of skilled human resources as barriers to digitalization in the maritime industry. Reports of factors such as gaps in the law, lack of fundamental facilities, and lack of clear leadership from the government by the respondents corroborate earlier reports by Wiafe *et al.* (2019) and Kapidani *et al.* (2021). Despite the potential of digitalization to revolutionize the African maritime sector, resident debilitating policy, institutional, regulatory, and legal frameworks impede the actualization of this potential (Ikpogu, 2021; Kapidani *et al.*, 2021).

Transitioning to digitalization is challenging. To manage this transition, proper positioning within a digitalization maturity model, a vision of a digitalized industry and a roadmap to attaining that vision are crucial (Pflaum, 2017). From a social construction perspective, stakeholders will be more prone to adopting digitalization only when they realize the opportunities and threats it presents. When stakeholders are aware of the possibility of being left behind with little or no stake in the control of opportunities and changes in digital technology, they might realize its implications on their credibility or, worse, their survival and be more receptive to adopting innovations (Herold *et al.*, 2021).

Notwithstanding, for a promising economy such as Africa, the early adoption of digital technologies such as blockchain maritime supply chain digitalization holds great potential. Yang (2019), in Bohemen (2020), posits a drastic reduction in kinds of delay associated with maritime services as one of the major promises of blockchain adoption. Other authors have cited an increase in the overall quantity of service (Helo & Hao, 2019), reduced redundancy and intermediaries (Jugović *et al.*, 2019), increased operational transparency (Norberg, 2019), reduction of fraudulent practices, and increased ease of doing business (Bohemen, 2020) as potential opportunities of blockchain adoption.

The evolution of conventional maritime operations to a smart and more digitalized one is a grossly underestimated goldmine for the global value chain. The Global Marine Technology Trends 2030 report, in a summary, presents three key pieces of information on the gains of digitalizing maritime section: *Firstly, strong opportunities for growth in the commercial shipping, ocean space, and naval sectors could be found in the future, if businesses could harness the scientific and industrial capabilities required to take advantage of the technologies and innovation. Secondly, the commercial shipping, ocean space, and naval sectors will undergo a rapid transformation as competition intensifies and technologies mature in other sectors. Thirdly, a stable, coherent framework of regulation and support is still essential to boost confidence to the private sector, to invest* (Papageorgiou, 2020).

Globally, the sustainability of technological innovation is an important agenda. To keep up with the trend, the African maritime industry needs to build capacity and align activities with sustainability goals and principles. Infrastructure, services, and operations need to be structured to build resilience (UNCTAD, 2020b). African countries like Morocco, Nigeria, and South Africa have particularly been recognized to be strategically located. The adoption and implementation of tenable technologies such as blockchain for maritime development are sure to yield great economic dividends at country and continental levels.

The African Card: Another Catch-up or A Leapfrog?

Africa is yet to thoroughly explore digitalization in its maritime industry. Port congestion is a major problem, particularly in South Africa, which is located on a busy international route. Digitalization presents a viable solution to this problem (Wiggett, 2020). West Africa has repeatedly experienced delays in the process of cargo clearance. The lack of integrated systems has been faulted for these mishaps that can be solved by the adoption of blockchain technology (Boison & Antwi-Boampong, 2020). The worst ranking countries in port performance are African countries. To get improved an performance, UNCTAD recommends improved infrastructure and reforms that equip ports to meet up to demand (UNCTAD, 2020b) There is a need to improve communication and management of information in ports, as this will aid in the eradication of delays in logistics and supply chain network in Africa. However, these problems continue to persist due to a lack of investment in technological innovation (Boison & Antwi-Boampong, 2020).

Some ports have made efforts to digitize their activities. The Durban port of South Africa, for example, has a fleet of drones that observe traffic and inspect operations without disrupting activities (Odoubourou, 2021). While there has been recognition of the merits of digitalization and some effort in some ports, it is yet to be backed by commensurate action. The rate of adoption and investment in infrastructure has been low (PMAESA, 2021).

Africa is known for being super late to the scene in terms of technology adoption. But in recent years, there has been rapid growth in interest and adoption of technology including blockchain in the finance sector. This interest has been triggered by development in IT infrastructure, economic growth, and technological leapfrogging, which has made emerging technologies such as Internet of Things (IoT) and Internet of Service (IoS) available to large firms, and a significant increase in IT skills and competences on the continent. More so, there is a growing number of studies investigating the adoption of various technologies in supply chain management in Africa (Agyei-Owusu *et al.*, 2021). The African approach to blockchain adoption in maritime supply chain digitalization should never be to play catch-up but to be part of the early adopters.

To achieve true success in this regard, a holistic stakeholder effort will be required. Even more so, a sound and consistent policy implementation by the government is needed if this potential is to be harnessed (Ikpogu, 2021).

Conclusions and Recommendations

Adoption of emerging digital technologies such as the blockchain has been recognized as a panacea to underdevelopment in Africa as well as a key to managing the economic crisis caused by the pandemic. It is therefore important to build capacity in this regard. However, there is a "readiness gap" in the maritime sector's automation and technology levels and this is a setback for Africa. This gap needs to be bridged. The peculiar problems facing the maritime industry, which include poor infrastructure quality, unfavorable regulations, poor governance, and lack of human resources, skills, and investment, also need to be addressed and resolved (UNCTAD, 2020b).

Smart technology promises an economic transformation to unprecedented proportions for Africa. To maximize this opportunity, efficient strategies need to be put in place (Siemens, 2019). Government and stakeholders need to fully understand what Africa stands to lose if they do not embrace innovation and consequently plan for change. Flexible and progressive policies that predict change and foster correct reactions should be put in place. All of these changes should be made bearing in mind the heterogeneity of the countries in the African continent and the differences in their stages of development, challenges, economic state, and needs (UNCTAD, 2019).

The continent requires improved infrastructure and the implementation of requisite port and trade facilitation reforms that can help ports in the region handle the ever-growing demand effectively (Sackey *et al.*, 2021). Africa needs to be proactive and take intentional steps toward being a contributor to technological advancement rather than just being a consumer continent. To achieve this, research and development should be adequately funded. Knowledge and capacity development are unarguably vital components in the innovation and adoption of new technologies. Therefore, in developing technological strategies, countries need to be committed and open to continual development, research, and experimentation, developing a system perspective, and proper integration of technology into industry operations (Ikpogu, 2021).

Future research direction

Future studies on supply chain and digital transformation in the African maritime industry may focus on analyzing stakeholders' influence on the adoption of digital technologies such as blockchain, premising the studies on different applicable theories of technology adoption including, but not limited to, the technology acceptance model (TAM), diffusion of innovation theory (DOI), theory of planned behavior (TPB), theory of reasoned action (TRA), and unified theory of acceptance and use of technology (UTAUT). While this chapter outlines major barriers and opportunities of blockchain technology in the maritime supply chain, further studies may seek to assess the overall readiness of the African maritime sector for technology adoption and digital transformation.

References

Abeyratne, S. A., & Monfared, R. P. (2016). Blockchain ready manufacturing supply chain using distributed ledger. *International Journal of Research in Engineering and Technology*, **5**(9), 1–10. https://doi.org/10.15623/ijret.2016.0509001.

Agyei-Owusu, B., Marfo, J. S., Quansah, E. K., & Kumi, C. A. (2021). The use of interorganizational information systems in digitalizing supply chains: A systematic literature review and research agenda for Africa. *27th Annual Americas Conference on Information Systems, AMCIS 2021*, 10.

Arenkov, I., Tsenzharik, M., & Vetrova, M. (2020). Digital technologies in supply chain management in production. *Atlantis Highlights in Computer Sciences*, **1**, 453–458. https://doi.org/10.1051/e3sconf/202015903006.

Arromba, I. F., *et al.*, (2020). Industry 4.0 in the product development process: Benefits, difficulties and its impact in marketing strategies and operations. *Journal of Business and Industrial Marketing*, **36**(3), 522–534.

Baker, M. (2011). Toward an African Maritime Economy: Empowering the African Union to Revolutionize the African Maritime Sector. *Naval War College Review*, **64**(2), 39.

Barrett, M., Davidson, E., Prabhu, J., & Vargo, S. L. (2015). Service innovation in the digital age: Key contributions and future directions. *MIS Quarterly: Management Information Systems*, **39**(1), 135–154. https://doi.org/10.25300/MISQ/2015/39:1.03.

Bellingkrodt, S., & Wallenburg, C. M. (2013). The role of external relationships for LSP innovativeness: A contingency approach. *Journal of Business Logistics*, **34**(3), 209–221. https://doi.org/10.1111/jbl.12020.

Black, S., & Glaser-segura, D. (2020). *Supply Chain Resilience in a Pandemic: The Need for Revised Contingency Planning*. Vol. 8, pp. 325–343. https://doi.org/10.2478/mdke-2020-0021.

Bohemen, J. Van. (2020). Blockchain technology and freight forwarder exploration of implications focused on practitioners in Shanghai. *World Maritime University Dissertations, 1594*.

Boison, D. K., & Antwi-Boampong, A. (2020). *View of Blockchain Ready Port Supply Chain Using Distributed Ledger NB!ICT(br)Innovation, Regulation, Multi Business Model Innovation and Technology*.

Cangul, M., Diouf, M. A., Esham, N., Gupta, P. K., Li, Y., Mitra, P., Miyajima, K., Ongley, K., Ouattara, F., Ouedraogo, R., Sharma, P., Simione, F. F., & Tapsoba, S. J. (2020). *Digitalization in Sub-Saharan Africa*. April, 33–49.

Cap, A., Wanis, A., Ahmed, C.-A., & Deanery, I. (2021). *Container Market Concentration in the Era of Digitalization: Evidence from North African Sea Ports*. June, 1–16.

Cichosz, M., Wallenburg, C. M., & Knemeyer, A. M. (2020). Digital transformation at logistics service providers: Barriers, success factors and leading practices. *International Journal of Logistics Management*, **31**(2), 209–238. https://doi.org/10.1108/IJLM-08-2019-0229.

Colbert, A., Yee, N., George, G. (2016). The digital workforce and the workplace of the future. *Academy of Management Journal*, **59**(3), 731–773.

Depellegrin, D., Bastianini, M., Fadini, A., & Menegon, S. (2020). The effects of COVID-19 induced lockdown measures on maritime settings of a coastal region. *Science of the Total Environment*, **740**, 140123. https://doi.org/10.1016/j.scitotenv.2020.140123.

DSCI. (2017). *Digital Supply Chain Transformation Guide: Essential Metrics — The Frontside Flip: Focusing on Customers and Revenue*. The Center for Global Enterprise and Digital Supply Chain Institute Project Partner.

European Commission. (2020). COVID-19 response: Fisheries and aquaculture. https://oceans-and-fisheries.ec.europa.eu/funding/covid-19-response-fisheries-and-aquaculture_en.

Flynn, B. B., Huo, B., & Zhao, X. (2010). The impact of supply chain integration on performance: A contingency and configuration approach. *Journal of Operations Management*, **28**(1), 58–71. https://doi.org/10.1016/j.jom.2009.06.001.

Frohlich, M. T., & Westbrook, R. (2001). Arcs of integration: An international study of supply chain strategies. *Journal of Operations Management,* **19**(2), 185–200. https://doi.org/10.1016/S0272-6963(00)00055-3.

GSCI (2018). *A Savvy Guide To the Digital Supply Chain How To Evaluate and Leverage Technology To Build a Supply Chain for the Digital Age.* April.

Gunasekaran, A., Subramanian, N., & Papadopoulos, T. (2017). Information technology for competitive advantage within logistics and supply chains: A review. *Transportation Research Part E: Logistics and Transportation Review,* **99**, 14–33. https://doi.org/10.1016/j.tre.2016.12.008.

Helo, P., & Hao, Y. (2019). Blockchains in operations and supply chains: A model and reference implementation. *Computers and Industrial Engineering,* **136**(July), 242–251. https://doi.org/10.1016/j.cie.2019.07.023.

Herold, D. M., Ćwiklicki, M., Pilch, K., & Mikl, J. (2021). The emergence and adoption of digitalization in the logistics and supply chain industry: An institutional perspective. *Journal of Enterprise Information Management,* **34**(6), 1917–1938. https://doi.org/10.1108/JEIM-09-2020-0382.

Huo, B., Zhao, X., & Lai, F. (2014). Supply chain quality integration: Antecedents and consequences. *IEEE Transactions on Engineering Management,* **61**(1), 38–51. https://doi.org/10.1109/TEM.2013.2278543.

Ikpogu, N. M. (2021). *Walden University.*

Jugović, A., Bukša, J., Dragoslavić, A., & Sopta, D. (2019). The possibilities of applying blockchain technology in shipping. *Pomorstvo,* **33**(2), 274–279. https://doi.org/10.31217/p.33.2.19.

Kapidani, N., Bauk, S., & Davidson, I. E. A. (2021). Developing countries' concerns regarding blockchain adoption in maritime. *Journal of Marine Science and Engineering,* **9**(12), 1326. https://doi.org/10.3390/jmse9121326.

Kersten, W., Blecker, T., & M., R. C. (2017). Digitalization in supply chain management and logistics. *Proceedings of the Hamburg International Conference of Logistics (HICL).* https://doi.org/10.15480/882.1442.

King Boison, D., & Antwi-Boampong, A. (2020). Blockchain ready port supply chain using distributed ledger. *Nordic and Baltic Journal of Information and Communications Technologies, January.* https://doi.org/10.13052/nbjict1902-097x.2020.001.

Kleab, K. (2017). Important of supply chain management. *International Journal of Scientific and Research Publications,* **7**(9), 397.

Klötzer, C., & Pflaum, A. (2017). Toward the development of a MM digitalization suppl.pdf. *Proceedings of the 50th Hawaii International Conference on System Sciences,* pp. 4210–4219.

Kohler, D., & Weisz, J.-D. (2018). Industry4.0, an industrial and societal revolution. *Futuribles,* **424**, 47–68.

Lambrou, M., Watanabe, D. & Iida, J. (2019). Shipping digitalization management: Conceptualization, typology and antecedents. *Journal of Shipping and Trade*, **4**, 11.

Lee, H. L., & Billington, C. (1992). Managing supply chain inventory pitfalls and opportunities. *Sloan Management Review*, **33**(3), 65–73.

Loebbecke, C., & Picot, A. (2015). Reflections on societal and business model transformation arising from digitization and big data analytics: A research agenda. *Journal of Strategic Information Systems* **24**(3), 149–157. https://doi.org/10.1016/j.jsis.2015.08.002.

Lu, Y., Morris, K. C., & Frechette, S. (2016). Current standards landscape for smart manufacturing systems. *National Institute of Standards and Technology, NISTIR*, 8107–8139.

Mackenzie, B. (2020). *Beyond COVID-19: Supply Chain Resilience Holds Key to Recovery*. Manaadiar, H. (2020)!" -34536738'0101. 00.

Marmolejo-Saucedo, J. A., & Hartmann, S. (2020). Trends in digitization of the supply chain: A brief literature review. *EAI Endorsed Transactions on Energy Web*, **7**(29), 1–7. https://doi.org/10.4108/EAI.13-7-2018.164113.

Mikl, J., Herold, D. M., Pilch, K., Ćwiklicki, M., & Kummer, S. (2021). Understanding disruptive technology transitions in the global logistics industry: The role of ecosystems. *Review of International Business and Strategy*, **31**(1), 62–79. https://doi.org/10.1108/RIBS-07-2020-0078.

Millefiori, L. M., Braca, P., Zissis, D., Spiliopoulos, G., Marano, S., Willett, P. K., & Carniel, S. (2021). Open COVID-19 impact on global maritime mobility. *Scientific Reports*, 1–16. https://doi.org/10.1038/s41598-021-97461-7.

Min, S., Zacharia, Z. G., & Smith, C. D. (2019). Defining supply chain management: In the past, present, and future. *Journal of Business Logistics*, **40**(1), 44–55. https://doi.org/10.1111/jbl.12201.

Moriarty, L. F., Plucinski, M., Marston, B., Kurbatova, E. V., Knust, B., Murray, E. L., Pesik, N., Rose, D., Fitter, D., Kobayashi, M., Toda, M., Canty, P. T., Scheuer, T., Halsey, E. S., Cohen, N. J., Stockman, L., Wadford, D. A., Medley, A. M., Green, G., … Team, S. C. C.-19. (2020). Public health responses to COVID-19 outbreaks on cruise ships — Worldwide, February–March 2020. In *MMWR. Morbidity and Mortality Weekly Report* (Vol. 69).

Norberg, H. C. (2019). The global supply chain. *SPP Briefing Paper*, **12**(9) (March). https://doi.org/10.2307/j.ctv23hcdqv.8.

O'Marah, K. (2017). Blockchain for supply chain: Enormous potential down the road. *Forbes*, 192–223.

Odoubourou, P. (2021). *African Ports, the Obligatory March Towards Digitalization — Maritimafrica*.

Oyenuga, A. (2021). Perspectives on the impact of the COVID-19 pandemic on the global and African maritime transport sectors, and the potential implications for Africa's maritime governance. *WMU Journal of Maritime Affairs*, **20**(2). https://Doi.org/10.1007/s13437-021-00233-3.

Papageorgiou, M. (2020). Digital transformation in the shipping industry is here. *NAFS Magazine, December 2020*, **138**. https://assets.kpmg/content/dam/kpmg/gr/pdf/2021/02/gr-digital-transformation-shipping-papageorgiou-nafs-magazine.pdf.

Pflaum, A. (2017). *Introduction to The Digital Supply Chain of the Future: Technologies, Applications and Business Models Minitrack The Digital Supply Chain of the Future: Technologies, Applications and Business Models Minitrack. January.* https://doi.org/10.24251/HICSS.2017.505.

Pilkington, M. (2016). Blockchain technology and applications. In F. X. Olleros and M. Zhegu (Ed.), *Research Handbook on Digital Transformations* (pp. 1–154). Edward Elgar. https://doi.org/10.4018/978-1-7998-3473-1.ch085.

PMAESA (2021). Report Calls for Accelerating Digitalization in the Ports & Maritime Sector. Port Management Association of Eastern & Southern Africa. https://www.pmaesa.org/news/report-calls-for-accelerating-digitalization-in-the-ports-maritime-sector/.

Pui, K., & Weisheng, L. (2021). Supply Chain 4.0: The impact of supply chain digitalization and integration on firm performance. *Asian Journal of Business Ethics*, **10**, 371–389. https://doi.org/10.1007/s13520-021-00137-8.

PWC (2020). Impact of COVID-19 on the Supply Chain Industry. PricewaterhouseCoopers Limited. https://www.pwc.com/ng/en/assets/pdf/impact-of-covid19-the-supply-chain-industry.pdf.

Ramulifho, A. E. (2014). Maritime spatial planning in South Africa: A nexus between legal, economic, social and environmental agendas. The Maritime Commons: Digital Repository of the World Maritime University Dissertations. https://commons.wmu.se/cgi/viewcontent.cgi?article=1453&context=all_dissertations.

Riedl, J., Jentzsch, A., Melcher, N. C., Gildemeister, J., Schellong, D., Höfer, C., & Wiederhoff, P. (2018). Why road freight needs to go digital — Fast. In *The Boston Consulting Group*. April (pp. 1–13).

Sackey, A. D., Tchouangeup, B., Lamptey, B. L., van der Merwe, B., Lee, R. O. D., Mensah, R., Fuseini, M. C., & Sackey, A. D. (2021). Outlining the challenges of Covid-19 health crises in Africa's maritime industry: The case of maritime operations in marine warranty surveying practice. *Maritime Studies*, **20**(2), 207–223. https://doi.org/10.1007/s40152-021-00220-7.

Schrauf, S., & Berttram, P. (2016). Industry 4.0: How digitization makes the supply chain more efficient, agile, and customer-focused. *Strategy&* (pp. 1–32). https://www.strategyand.pwc.com/gx/en/insights/2016/industry-4-digitization/industry40.pdf.

Siemens (2019). Dawn of Digitalization and its impact in Africa: Report. https://
assets.new.siemens.com/siemens/assets/api/uuid:4d4a6645-357a-48f3-a45c-
9a5e5a4352e3/dawn-of-digitalization.pdf.

SupplyChainDigest (2016). SCDigest Supply Chain Digitization Benchmark Survey
2016. JDA Software Group, Inc. https://www.scdigest.com/assets/reps/Supply_
Chain_Digitization_2016_ Survey_Data.pdf.

Tapscott, D., & Tapscott, A. (2018). *Blockchain Revolution: How the Technology
Behind Bitcoin Is Changing Money. Sage Publications, Inc.*, 384 pp.

UNCTAD (2019). Assessment of Potential Negative Impact of the System of Factors
on the Ship's Operational Condition During Transportation of Oversized and
Heavy Cargos. *Transactions on Maritime Science* **10**(1), 126–134. https://doi.
org/10.7225/toms.v10.n01.009.

UNCTAD (2020a). COVID-19 triggers marked decline in global trade: UNCTAD.
In *United Nations Conference on Trade and Development.*

UNCTAD (2020b). Review of Maritime Transport 2020: Highlights and figures on
Africa. Geneva, Switzerland. https://unctad.org/press-material/unctads-review-
maritime-transport-2020-highlights-and-figures-africa.

Veynberg, R., Koslova, M., Askarov, G., Bexultanov, A., & Yussupova, Z. (2020).
Digital technologies in supply chain management in production. *E3S Web of
Conferences*, **159**. https://doi.org/10.1051/e3sconf/202015903006.

Voorspuij J., & Becha H. (2021) Digitalisation in maritime regional and
global supply chains. In M. Lind, M. Michaelides, R. Ward, Watson R.
(Eds.) *Maritime Informatics*. Progress in IS. Springer, Cham. https://doi.
org/10.1007/978-3-030-50892-0_5.

Wagner, N., & Wiśnicki, B. (2019). Application of blockchain technology in
maritime logistics. *DIEM: Dubrovnik International Economic Meeting*, **4**(1),
155–164.

Ward R., & Bjørn-Andersen N. (2021) The origins of maritime informatics. In
M. Lind, M. Michaelides, R. Ward, Watson R. (Eds.) *Maritime Informatics*.
Progress in IS. Springer, Cham. https://doi.org/10.1007/978-3-030-50892-0_1.

WEF (2016). *World Economic Forum White Paper Digital Transformation of Industries:
In collaboration with Accenture Electricity Industry*, **4**(8).

Wellener, P., Dollar, B., Laaper, S., Ashton, H., & Beckoff, D. (2020). Accelerating
smart manufacturing. The value of an ecosystem approach. *Deloitte Development
LLC*, 24.

Wiggett, L. (2020). *Blockchain in Africa — Addressing Port Congestion Using DLT —
Trade Finance Global.*

Yang, C. S. (2019). Maritime shipping digitalization: Blockchain-based technology applications, future improvements, and intention to use. *Transportation*

Research Part E: Logistics and Transportation Review, **131**(September), 108–117. https://doi.org/10.1016/j.tre.2019.09.020.

Zhao, li, Huo, B., Sun, L., & Zhao, X. (2013). The impact of supply chain risk on supply chain integration and company performance: A global investigation. *Supply Chain Management: An International Journal*, **18**(2), 115–131. https://doi.org/10.1108/13598541311318773.

CHAPTER 7

Hospital Operations and Supply Chain Optimization: Combining Lean Management Tools with Process Mining, AI, and Digital Twin for Sterilization Processes

Karine Doan[*,‡] and Stefano Carrino[†,§]

*University of Applied Sciences and Arts Western Switzerland,
Haute école de gestion Arc, The Management Institute of Cities
and Regions, Switzerland
†University of Applied Sciences and Arts Western Switzerland,
Haute Ecole Arc Ingénierie, Data Analysis Group, Switzerland
‡karine.doan@he-arc.ch
§stefano.carrino@he-arc.ch

Abstract

To improve quality and safety and to contain costs, hospitals should optimize their processes. Therefore, they need to have a full understanding and visibility of their operations and supply chain flows. In this chapter, we combined a lean management approach using value stream mapping, with a data-driven approach using process mining applied to the surgery processes of a private hospital in Switzerland. As the sterilization process was identified as a major bottleneck, we developed a digital twin and artificial intelligence algorithms to optimize the hospital operations and supply chain management. As a result, the hospital increased the quality of its work environment, improved visibility in their processes, and developed a stronger communication channel with their teams. In addition, they could better plan schedules, which allowed the hospital to limit overtime of the operating room staff. Finally, they optimized costs and saved time in their overall sterilization process.

Keywords: Healthcare; Process mining; Artificial intelligence; Digital twin; Supply chain management.

Introduction

In Switzerland, the share of hospital care in the costs of the health system reached 35.3% in 2019, or 29.4 billion francs. Personnel costs account for the largest share of hospital expenditures, accounting for an average of 63% of the operating costs in 2017, compared with 8.1% for investment costs. On the revenue side, 85%, on average, was due to inpatient and care revenue. On average, 82.6% of the revenue came from acute care, 9.7% from psychiatry, and 7.7% from rehabilitation/geriatrics (Federal Statistical Office, 2019). According to the Federal Office of Public Health (FOPH), there were 281 hospitals in Switzerland in 2017, which several health system experts believe is far too many (FOPH, 2019). This high density of hospitals, which is less and less adapted to the shift from inpatient to outpatient care, leads to wasted resources, overcapacity in equipment, and deficits for many facilities, which do not handle enough cases to be profitable.

In order to contain the costs, the financing model revised in 2012 by the Swiss federal law on health insurance introduced an obligation of economy. Since 2012, Swiss hospitals have been paid for hospitalizations through flat rates, which means that a procedure requiring 2 hours of operating room (OR) and 4 days of hospitalization will be remunerated in almost the same way as the same procedure requiring 4 hours of OR and 10 days of hospitalization. In addition, the price list per service has recently been revised and some positions have lost almost 30% of their value. Thus, it is becoming imperative for hospitals to be as efficient as possible in order to cover their costs and, at the same time, invest in technology and new treatments.

The OR, the most important link in a hospital's value chain, is the scene of a multitude of processes. The surgeon transmits an operating order, a document that initiates a series of actions that will culminate in the patient being taken care of by a whole set of teams and service providers. Furthermore, the flow of material involves several actors, from the order to the reception and the setting up in the OR. The operation cannot take place without this crucial flow. The patients must be summoned and, of course, know where and how the operation will take place. Room, kitchen, and care must also be ready to receive them. The teams must be organized in such a way that they have the necessary qualified personnel to assist the surgeon. The surgeon and the anesthetists also have to be organized to be able to carry out the operation. To have the instruments ready for a surgery, the instruments need to be cleaned, sterilized, checked, and then properly stored.

This chapter presents optimization solutions based on the digitalization of the Hospital Information System (HIS) via a combined approach based on lean management and on process mining (PM) and artificial intelligence (AI) techniques in a private hospital in Switzerland. Missing data that are required to effectively apply PM and AI techniques are simulated creating a digital twin of the selected processes. The chapter is structured as follows: second section presents healthcare operations and supply chain management, the third section provides an overview on PM and AI applied in healthcare, the fourth section describes our methodology; our case study is described in the fifth section and finally sixth and seventh sections, respectively, present the discussion and the conclusion.

Healthcare Operations and Supply Chain Management

The healthcare operations and supply chain management (HOSCM) is defined as *the analysis, design, planning and control of all the steps required to provide a service to a patient* (Malik *et al.*, 2018, p. 4). The healthcare supply chain is a concept that goes beyond *the traditional input-output view of an operation to include all services for patients provided by various medical specialties and functions, within and across departments and also across organizations to include the suppliers* (Malik *et al.*, 2018, p. 4). Processes in healthcare represent a series of activities aimed at diagnosing, treating, and preventing all diseases in order to improve a patient's health. These processes are considered to be highly dynamic, complex, and multidisciplinary (Rojas *et al.*, 2016). In addition, the healthcare field faces many challenges — quality of information and data, duplication of key activities, lack of integration of information systems, lack of performance indicators, lack of skills and training, separation between purchasing, payers, and clinicians, and high variability in customer preferences and demand — that have a significant impact on its performance (Elmuti *et al.*, 2013). In this context, planning the capacity of ORs, the planning of staffing levels, the number of employees, and the scheduling of appointments, are major challenges in the daily management of operations within a hospital. To overcome these challenges, a supply chain must not only be able to handle a large number of events, both expected and unexpected (Liu *et al.*, 2007), but also become agile and smart. Agility demands *rapid strategic and operational adaptation to large-scale, unpredictable changes in the business environment focusing upon eliminating the barriers to quick response* (Elmuti *et al.*, 2013, p. 4). The concept of smart supply chain is defined as *the new interconnected business system, which extends from isolated, local, and single-company applications to supply chain wide systematic smart implementations* (Wu *et al.*, 2016, p. 3). A smart supply chain would utilize features such as the Internet of Things, smart machines, and smart infrastructure, thereby promoting interconnectivity and enabling real-time data collection and communication, smart decision-making, and efficient and responsive processes at all stages of the supply chain to better serve customers (Wu *et al.*, 2016). This definition suggests that smart supply chain management relies on advanced data analytics in which data are captured and analyzed throughout the value chain. To improve supply chain performance in healthcare, the extensive use of quantitative methods, such as process mining, enables improvements and generates cost reductions. This is especially important given the criticality of quality and safety in the healthcare industry. The potential benefits of using Big Data in analyzing HOSCM activities have been estimated to increase ROI, productivity, and competitiveness by 15–20% (Malik *et al.*, 2018).

Process Mining and Artificial Intelligence in Healthcare Process Optimization

Process mining focuses on extracting knowledge from data generated and stored in information system databases (i.e., process event logs). PM techniques can be categorized under three main activities: process discovery, compliance checking, and enhancement (van der Aalst, 2011). Automatic process discovery extracts process patterns from an event log. Compliance checking monitors deviations by comparing a given model with the event log and enhancement extends or improves an existing process model using information about the actual process recorded in the event log. The above three PM activities can be combined with AI and optimization techniques. The results can be used, for instance, to predict the future and recommend suitable actions.

PM techniques applied to healthcare have been the subject of an important international literature for the last ten years (Rojas *et al.*, 2016). Typically, any activity performed in a hospital by a physician, nurse, technician, or other hospital resource to provide patient care is stored in the hospital's HIS (database, systems, protocols, events, etc.). Activities are recorded in event logs for support, monitoring, and further analysis. Process models are created to specify the order in which different healthcare workers are expected to perform their activities within a given process, or to analyze the process design, or for resource management. In addition, process models are also used to support the development of the information system itself, for example, to understand how the information system is supposed to support process execution.

In addition to improving the management of medical centers, additional benefits can be achieved through the application of PM in healthcare. This can help identify and understand the actual behavior of resources; make suggestions for redesigning the process; analyze performance and reduce wait and service times. Furthermore, it allows gaining insights and improving peer collaboration; predicting patient behavior based on previous cases; adding information to activities such as patient data; and identifying activities that cause bottlenecks in the process.

PM has been used in healthcare process analysis to discover process models (Mans *et al.*, 2012; Zhou, 2009) and for compliance verification (Bose & van der Aalst, 2012; Kirchner *et al.*, 2013). Process models are created to specify the order in which different healthcare agents are expected to perform their activities within a given process to critically analyze the process design, for resource management, or are also used to support the development of the information system itself. A study demonstrates the applicability of PM using a real case of gynecological oncology processes in a Dutch hospital. The results show that PM can be used to provide new information to facilitate the improvement of existing care flows (Mans *et al.*, 2008). Rebuge and Ferreira (2012) introduce a methodology for applying process exploration techniques leading to the identification of regular behavior, process variants, and exceptional medical cases. This methodology is demonstrated in a case study conducted in a hospital emergency department in Portugal (Rebuge & Ferreira, 2012). On their part, Caron *et al.* (2014) developed a method of analysis of the clinical pathways with techniques of PM by creating a roadmap to unfold the process (Caron *et al.*, 2014). Another case study, applied in the urology department of a hospital in the Netherlands, shows how PM techniques can be used to link event data (Event Logs), reflecting clinical reality with clinical guidelines describing best practices in medicine (Rovani *et al.*, 2015).

One of the major challenges of the aforementioned studies lies in data capture (identifying and accessing data sources, integrating data from different sources, data quality, and creating a correct and complete event log) (Ghasemi & Amyot, 2016). Thus, most research has been limited to partial segments of the care delivery chain, limiting the use of data-driven approaches to designing the entire care chain (Malik *et al.*, 2018).

From an algorithmic point of view, the most commonly used techniques for PM are Heuristics Miner (Weijters *et al.*, 2006), Fuzzy Miner (Günther & van der Aalst, 2007), and Trace Clustering (Song *et al.*, 2009). Heuristics Miner is a discovery algorithm capable of generating process models. It is very robust against noise in event logs. Fuzzy Miner is a configurable discovery algorithm that allows, through its parameters, to generate multiple models at different levels of detail, which allows dealing with unstructured processes. The trace clustering technique allows the partitioning of event logs to generate simpler and more structured process models.

Three strategies are typically used to implement PM:

1. The first strategy is the direct implementation, which involves applying PM to a dataset collected directly from HIS sources for event logging. This is the most widely used strategy in the literature. This approach poses two main challenges: first, the extraction of data and construction of the correct event log; and second, the need to understand the tools, techniques, and algorithms available to perform the analysis.
2. The second strategy is semi-automated PM, in which the data extraction and event log creation are performed by custom development. These developments link one or more data sources and extract the data needed to create the event log using queries. However, knowledge of PM tools is still required to apply the available techniques to perform the right analysis. This strategy has the disadvantage of being defined in an ad hoc manner to extract data from specific tools and environments.
3. The third strategy is to implement an integrated processing suite in which the data sources are connected, the data extracted, the event log created, and the implemented PM techniques applied. This strategy is

applied in seven case studies and has the advantage that the person using the suite does not need detailed knowledge of how to connect to the data sources or how the PM techniques, algorithms, and tools work. The big disadvantage of this type of suite is that it has been developed for specific environments and its data sources do not provide a portable solution. In addition, it requires a significant investment in resources to complete the process of implementing the desired algorithms.

Often PM is intertwined with AI techniques to provide a set of complementary tools for optimizing the processes. Healthcare, having access to a considerable volume of data, is one of the main application fields for AI. AI has been most widely used for diagnosis, prognosis, or treatment planning. In particular, mining clinical pathways from historical data seems to generate a lot of attention from scientists (Ghasemi & Amyot, 2020; Malik *et al.*, 2018). Other applications of data analytics and predictive analytics used in healthcare include customer relationship management, fraud detection, and treatment effectiveness assessment (Malik *et al.*, 2018). For example, one study looked at the emergency department of an Australian hospital developing a simulation tool based on historical data. This data was used to understand patient treatment. AI was used to group patients by treatment similarity (Ceglowski *et al.*, 2007). Chi *et al.* (2008) proposed an algorithm to provide a personalized recommendation for hospital selection to help the patient maximize the probability of achieving the desired outcome (Chi *et al.*, 2008). Another study, also conducted in the United States, on the transfer of patients between departments, uses a traditional qualitative analysis based on field observations and interviews with various stakeholders (Abraham & Reddy, 2010). Swain (2016) applied data mining and AI techniques in a hospital in the United States to predict a profile of an adult population with predispositions to obesity (Swain, 2016). All studies planning a data analytics-based approach aim to reduce costs, be more competitive, and provide higher quality and more personalized care to patients (Malik *et al.*, 2018).

In most studies, the development of an ad hoc solution is required. To our knowledge, no portable solution has yet been developed that can be adapted to hospital processes different from those for which they were developed. In this case study, we confronted this problem, as we wanted to apply our solution, developed for a specific use case, to be general enough to be applied to similar processes in different hospitals with little adaptation.

Methodology

The purpose of this HOSCM project is to enable a private hospital "La Providence" to optimize its OR and supply chain processes. The hospital is located in Neuchâtel, Switzerland, and is part of the Swiss Medical Network, which holds 21 private hospitals and clinics and is one of the two main Swiss private hospital groups.

The hospital has 76 beds, 98 doctors, 222 collaborators, and performs about 4,387 operations on a yearly basis. In order to reach these objectives, we combined a lean management approach with PM techniques, artificial intelligence, and digital twin. In this way, we were able to develop a new methodology that meets the needs and requirements of the hospital and that can be replicated to other hospitals. We got the support from a team from Johnson & Johnson, a company active in consumer health care, medical devices, and pharmaceuticals, in conducting the project. We could benefit from their expertise in lean management and in the healthcare industry.

Due to the lockdown imposed by the COVID-19 pandemic, which touched Europe in March 2020 and the inherent constraints linked to this sanitary crisis, the work with the stakeholders was mainly done remotely. However, despite the limited availability of the interlocutors, the hospital team has always been able to provide the research team with the requested information.

The HOSCM project lasted 18 months, from June 2020 until December 2021, and has been organized in multiple phases as described below.

Phase 1: Goals and scope definition. The goals of the project were defined in partnership with the hospital team and divided into three categories, as listed in Table 1. The scope was limited to the OR processes and the activities with a direct impact on it, as these are the critical processes within a hospital.

Table 1.   Goals of the project.

Goals	Description of the Goals
Process time reduction	Time between each intervention: reduction from 50 minutes to 40 minutes
	Number of full time equivalents (FTEs) needed on assessed processes: –½ FTEs
	Input time on the HIS: –10%
Quality increase	Number of infections and number of repeated surgeries: 10–20% reduction
	Estimated increase in the number of surgical procedures: +2% per year
Cost reduction	Value of stock of surgical and non-surgical material: –10%
	Ratio of used material to material needed for an intervention: –10%
	Number of errors (use of material, …): –10%

Phase 2: Value Stream Mapping. In order to get a complete visibility of the OR processes, a value stream map (VSM) was created by performing a "Gemba walk." *The Gemba walk in health care is a direct observation of a patient's journey to gain an understanding of how the process works* (Lot *et al.*, 2018, p. 5). VSM is a fundamental tool of lean management to improve complex workflows by visualizing and quantifying process steps and eliminating or reducing unnecessary tasks considered as wastes (Lot *et al.*, 2018).

In addition, 11 semi-directive interviews of an hour were conducted with the staff of the OR. The analysis took place for over a week and all flows in the OR (patients, equipment, and sterilization) were analyzed for all the different types of operations.

All steps and times of the processes in the OR were captured and three VSM were created — the logistics, materials, and patient flows — using standard symbols (see fifth section). Those VSM allowed visualizing all the different steps of the OR and highlighted the main bottlenecks. The initial results identified the sterilization process as the main bottleneck impacting the entire process. The sterilization process plays a major and central role in the activities of the OR; without it, the entire process cannot function properly. Indeed, if the instruments are not sterilized, the surgical procedures cannot take place.

Phase 3: Database Collection. In parallel to phase 2, the HIS data of the surgical interventions, covering a period of 12 years (2008–2020), were collected to get a better understanding of the surgeries performed in the hospital (types of surgeries performed, average times of surgeries, availability of surgeons, surgical rooms used for which type of surgeries, etc.).

However, as most of the sterilization data were not recorded by the hospital in their HIS, they were manually collected in the field or estimated by the research team with the support of the hospital team.

Phase 4: Process Mining. In this project, the three kinds of PM have been realized (process discovery, conformance checking, and process enhancement). The main goal of process discovery was to identify the main processes linked to the OR process, the bottlenecks, and key activities. To complete this first step, PM required data extraction from HIS, cleaning, and pre-processing. Conformance checking was done by comparing the process models discovered with PM and the VSM models. This step aimed to assess and validate the quality of the automated process extraction.

A database describing the hospital processes in the last few years has been used for analyses. In particular, PM was applied to OR data from the beginning of 2019 to the end 2020, as data from the previous years were not reliable since the processes at the hospital had considerably evolved over time.

Finally, the process models derived from PM were analyzed in order to find recommendations and improve the existing processes.

Phase 5: Recommendations for Improvement. Based on the observations from the VSM and the analysis of the extracted data, recommendations for improvement were identified and prioritized according to the hospital's needs and their feasibility.

The sterilization process was clearly identified by all parties as being the highest priority in order to have a significant impact on the OR processes. In order to optimize this process, the project team analyzed all the information available extracted from the HIS. In addition, an in-depth analysis of the sterilization process was conducted to gather data not captured in the HIS. All other necessary information was estimated by the research and hospital team. Following the data retrieval, a digital twin of the sterilization processes was developed by the research team, as presented in the next phase.

Phase 6: Digital Twin and AI for Process Simulation and Optimization. When data are unavailable in an information system, PM reaches its inherent limitations. This is a common scenario in companies going toward digitalization but in which part of processes remain analogic. To overcome this hurdle, we investigated the feasibility of the realization of a digital twin of the process replacing missing data with observational data. In this project, the aim of a digital twin is twofold: generate reliable simulated data when real data is missing and evaluate different process optimization solutions in a simulated environment before the deployment in the actual process of the hospital. In fact, a digital representation of a process has the additional advantage of being easy to manipulate and allows for the use of AI algorithms for process optimization (e.g., finding the optimal sequences of actions and resource usage in the process).

Previous steps identified the sterilization process as critical. However, almost no data were available in the HIS for the application of PM techniques. For this reason, we created a digital twin of the sterilization process, that is, a tunable digital simulation of the sterilization process. This key phase of the project provided a better view of the sterilization steps and times, highlighting the obstacles that delay the sterilization processes. Furthermore, the digital twin is open to modification and scenario planning. It allows the hospital operating manager to optimize the sterilization flows, in terms of time or costs, by simulating various possible scenarios (e.g., varying the number of machines, employees' work schedule, etc.).

Formally, the sterilization process can be modeled as a *hybrid flow shop* (Ruiz & Vázquez-Rodríguez, 2010) in which multiple equivalent machines and resources are available for performing an action. The digital process representation should also consider the limited availability and the roles of the human resources (including lunch and break times). This kind of optimization problems belong to the category of NP-Hard problems, where the optimal solution is very time-consuming to compute also in a simulated digital environment. AI solutions and genetic algorithms are often used in the literature to optimize these kinds of problems in the search for a suboptimal (but good enough) solution (Rashidi *et al.*, 2010). In this project, the multiobjective fitness function used to measure the optimization performances is based on the pair time-cost. A sterilization process could be considered optimal if all the steps are performed in a short time with the least costs. Since these objective metrics could be competing (a shorter process time requires more resources at the expense of additional costs), the genetic algorithm solution aimed to find and iteratively update the Pareto front of the available solutions, that is, the set of individuals that are not dominated on both time and cost by any other individual (see fifth section). When the algorithm has run its course, the set of optimal solutions on the Pareto front are proposed to the process manager. The final decision is left to the hospital managers that will select the most suitable solution.

Genetic algorithms have been implemented using the DEAP framework (https://github.com/deap/deap). DEAP is an evolutionary computation framework for rapid prototyping and testing of genetic algorithms (and other evolutionary algorithms). The following hyperparameters have been used: Initial population — 30 individuals; Selection — Multiobjective optimization with NSGA-II; Mutation — 20% uniform probability (mutate an individual by replacing attributes); Crossover — 50% probability (two-points crossover); Stop criteria — two criteria have been implemented to stop the genetic algorithm iterations; a maximum timespan and a convergence criterion. In the first case, the simulator user can set the maximum amount of computation time; in the second case, if the Pareto front does not change for five generations, the computation is stopped, and the best configuration is selected.

Phase 7: Digital Twin Validation. To be of any use, a simulator has to be as close as possible to its real counterpart. The digital twin has been validated using a scenario replay approach qualitatively evaluated by the hospital staff. In practice, real workload observed over multiple days at the hospital was used as input for the digital twin. The objective was to observe the differences between the real processes and the simulated ones and evaluate if the simulation was close enough to the real behavior. In an iterative approach, if major differences were observed, the digital twin was fine-tuned in order to minimize them. Finally, when multiple scenarios were close enough to the real processes, the hospital team validated that the results provided by the simulator were compliant to reality.

After validation, the genetic optimization algorithm was executed providing process improvement suggestions.

Phase 8: Deployment and Assessment into a Real Environment. The last phase of the project consisted in the deployment and implementation of the optimization solutions in the hospital environment at "La Providence" and assessing their impact on the process performances.

Results

As described in the previous section, we followed a lean management approach, using VSM, in parallel of a data-driven approach (PM, AI, and digital twin) in order to optimize the efficiency of the hospital OR, targeting specifically the following objectives:

- Optimize the resources used in the operating room.
- Perform more operations in less time.
- Reduce waiting times.

The third section presents the main results of the application of the value stream mapping, process mining, and digital twin within the hospital OR.

Value stream mapping

At the beginning of the project in June 2020, initial maps ("as-is" situation) were created by our partner Johnson & Johnson (J&J) on the different activities related to the OR: logistic flows (material and instrument storage flows and areas), sterilization flows, patient flows, and IT flows. Several recommendations were made after this first assessment to improve the process steps, timing, and costs in the OR.

As illustrated in Figure 1, the sterilization process was identified as a bottleneck in the OR and therefore became the focus for the rest of the HOSCM project.

A second VSM (Figure 2) was performed in September 2021 after the deployment of the optimization solutions. The improvements were taken into account and the cycle times were recalculated, highlighting the progress from the initial map, resulting from the positive impact of the use of the digital twin (described in the next section) on a daily basis. This second VSM allowed the team as well to identify the future improvement paths (mentioned as "ideal state" on the VSM).

Process mining (operations process)

Based on HIS data, we used process discovery techniques in order to highlight critical steps in the operations. Figure 3 illustrates an example of the process steps as detected and recreated by the PM tools. In this particular representation (obtained using Disco 2.14.0 — https://fluxicon.com/disco), the main OR flow is represented. Arrows thickness and boxes color deepness are designed to highlight the relevance of the actions and transitions. The numbers in each case represent the occurrences of the action, while the numbers associated with the arrows represent the number of transitions from one action to another.

An additional outcome resulting from the analysis of such data-driven graphs is the discovery of process and data anomalies paving the way to deeper investigations. For instance, in the process illustrated in Figure 3, we detected 283 operations in which the action "operation end" precedes "start of anesthesia" highlighting abnormal data in the dataset.

Digital twin (sterilization process)

The results of the combination of the digital twin and the AI optimization are illustrated in Figure 4. The graph shows the realized web user interface suggesting several configurations to improve the sterilization process. Each point, the star-shaped dots and round dots, represents a different sterilization

144   *K. Doan & S. Carrino*

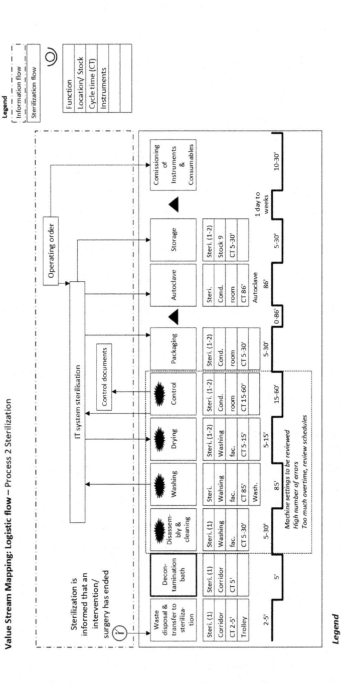

Figure 1. VSM with Bottlenecks Highlighted.

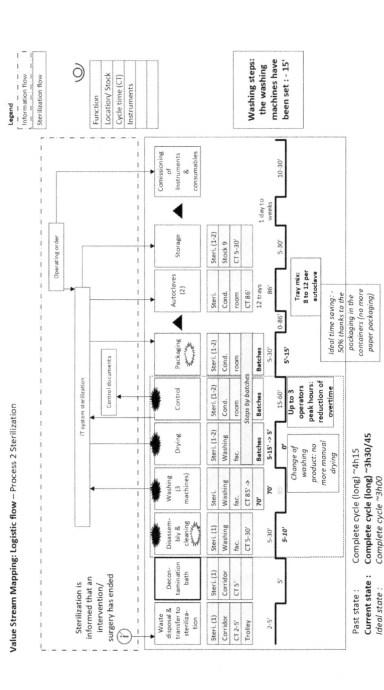

Figure 2. Second VSM (September 2021).

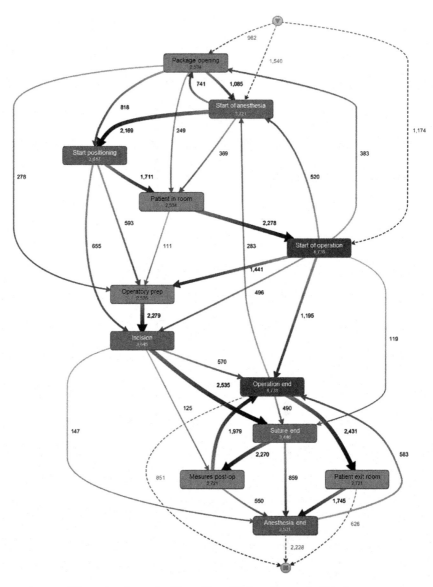

Figure 3.   Operating Room Flows Without Removal of Outliers.

process configuration. Green points are the optimal solutions balancing costs and process duration as computed by the genetic algorithm. For the specific scenario presented in Figure 4, the star-shaped dots on the top left of the graph corresponds to a sterilization process configuration that will allow for

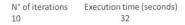

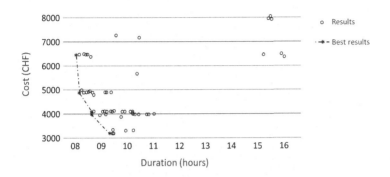

Figure 4. Genetic Algorithm Optimization Results.
Note: The star-shaped dots show the Pareto front with the best solutions. The round dots are suboptimal solutions explored by the optimization algorithm.

a fast execution (~8 h 20 m) but for a high cost (~6,500 CHF). Selecting the solution on the boom right on the Pareto front will halve the estimated costs (~3,100 CHF) for a process duration increased by one hour (~9 h 30 m).

For a given process configuration and the list of activities planned for a day (e.g., list of operations to be performed), the digital twin computes a set of key performance indicators (KPIs) estimating the usage of resources and the workload fluctuations over time of machines and employees.

Overall results

To summarize, the HOSCM project resulted in the following gains for the hospital "La Providence" (Table 2).

Due to the COVID-19 pandemic situation, many surgeries had to be rescheduled and therefore we were not able to achieve some of the initial goals described in Table 1. In addition, the research team mainly focused on the sterilization process, identified as critical, which limited the impact on the other processes.

Table 2.   HOSCM project gains.

Goals	Gains
Process time reduction	16 minutes saved on the washer cycle
	A 20% reduction in FTEs thanks to the optimization of the OR staff schedules
Quality increase	Better visibility on processes and easier communication to the teams
	A better quality of work and less stress for the OR staff
	Empowerment of the OR staff
Cost reduction	Cost avoidance. The hospital did not need to invest in a new autoclave as planned initially
	30% reduction in the number of instruments for abdominal surgery
Management	A dynamic dashboard with relevant KPIs for processes management
	A simulation tool, the digital twin, for optimizing the sterilization process

Limitation of This Research and Future Steps

The restricted scope of the intervention (OR and sterilization process), the size of the hospital and its type — private — can represent bias in the results. Furthermore, the data from HIS were captured before the pandemic of COVID-19 and therefore did not take into account this particular situation.

Understanding if this methodology can be replicated in a larger or public hospital is an important future research area. Furthermore, it would be interesting to develop a digital twin for an end-to-end process, capturing upstream and downstream value chain activities.

Finally, thanks to this research, we were able to demonstrate that combining a lean management approach with data-driven techniques is complementary. However, to fully use digital tools, the deployment of Internet of Objects would be imperative in order to collect all necessary data in the field. Though, it would be difficult to capture employees' perception.

Conclusion

Our case study focused on applying a methodology, which combined a lean management approach with PM techniques and digital twin to a private hospital in Switzerland in order to optimize their OR processes.

Patients are the primary beneficiaries of an efficient OR, where errors are reduced to a minimum. Simplification of processes increases safety and provides reproducible high-quality services. Surgeons also benefit from a stable and secure environment. Synchronization among the actors is essential to allow them to perform their surgeries with complete peace of mind. With clearly defined, optimized and well thought-out processes, surgeons will be surrounded by a well-prepared and organized team. The OR staff is empowered in their role and their procedures are perfectly clear. The serenity in which their interventions take place determines the serenity of the intervention itself.

This project demonstrates that a data-driven approach (PM, digital twin, and AI) combined with lean management tools (Gemba walk and VSM) allow understanding and piloting the flows in a proactive way. These two approaches have the same objectives — discovery of processes and highlighting of dysfunctions and bottlenecks — to foster optimization. However, the temporality and data requirements are not the same. PM techniques are dynamic since process representation is updated when new data are available, while VSM remains a static and resource-intensive method. Nevertheless, the VSM allows gathering information not captured in the HIS, necessary, in the context of this project, for the application of the PM and optimization techniques. For institutions and companies moving toward digitalization, the two approaches are therefore complementary and allow the identification of improvement potentials within complex processes.

Acknowledgments

This project was supported by Innosuisse, the Swiss Innovation Agency, Hospital La Providence, and Johnson & Johnson.

Special thanks to Romain Hugi and Pierre Bürki, assistants at the Haute Ecole Arc Ingénierie, HES-SO, for the development of the software integrating the process mining solution, the digital twin simulation, the genetic algorithm, and web user interface.

Our thanks go also to Stefanie Hasler, collaborator at the Haute école de gestion Arc, HES-SO, for her contribution in the VSM establishment, database creation, and KPI definition.

References

Abraham, J., & Reddy, M. C. (2010). Challenges to inter-departmental coordination of patient transfers: A workflow perspective. *International Journal of Medical Informatics*, **79**(2), 112–122.

Bose, R. P. J. C., & van der Aalst, W. M. P. (2012). Analysis of patient treatment procedures. In *Lecture Notes in Business Information Processing* (pp. 165–166).

Caron, F., Vanthienen, J., Vanhaecht, K., Van Limbergen, E., Deweerdt, J., & Baesens, B. (2014). A process mining-based investigation of adverse events in care processes. *Health Information Management Journal*, **43**(1), 16–25. https://doi.org/10.1177/183335831404300103.

Ceglowski, R., Churilov, L., & Wasserthiel, J. (2007). Combining Data Mining and Discrete Event Simulation for a value-added view of a hospital emergency department. *Journal of the Operational Research Society*, **58**(2), 246–254.

Chi, C.-L., Street, W. N., & Ward, M. M. (2008). Building a hospital referral expert system with a Prediction and Optimization-Based Decision Support System algorithm. *Journal of Biomedical Informatics*, **41**(2), 371–386. https://doi.org/10.1016/j.jbi.2007.10.002.

Elmuti, D., Khoury, G., Omran, O., & Abou-Zaid, A. S. (2013). Challenges and opportunities of health care supply chain management in the United States. *Health Marketing Quarterly*, **30**(2), 128–143.

Federal Office of Public Health (2019). Chiffres-clés des Hôpitaux suisses [Key numbers for Swiss hospitals]. Retrieved from https://spitalstatistik.bagapps.ch/data/download/kzp17_publikation.pdf?v=1566208444.

Ghasemi, M., & Amyot, D. (2016). Process mining in healthcare: A systematised literature review. *International Journal of Electronic Healthcare*, **9**(1), 60.

Ghasemi, M., & Amyot, D. (2020). From event logs to goals: a systematic literature review of goal-oriented process mining. *Requirements Engineering*, **25**(1), 67–93.

Günther, C. W., & van der Aalst, W. M. P. (2007). Fuzzy mining — Adaptive process simplification based on multi-perspective metrics. In *Lecture Notes in Computer Science (including subseries Lecture Notes in Artificial Intelligence and Lecture Notes in Bioinformatics)* (pp. 328–343).

Kirchner, K., Herzberg, N., Rogge-Solti, A., & Weske, M. (2013). Embedding conformance checking in a process intelligence system in hospital environments. In *Lecture Notes in Computer Science (including subseries Lecture Notes in Artificial Intelligence and Lecture Notes in Bioinformatics)* (pp. 126–139).

Liu, R., Kumar, A., & van der Aalst, W. M. P. (2007). A formal modeling approach for supply chain event management. *Decision Support Systems*, **43**(3), 761–778.

Lot, L. T., Sarantopoulos, A., Min, L. L., Perales, S. R., Boin, I. D. F. S. F., & Ataide, E. C. D. (2018). Using Lean tools to reduce patient waiting time. *Leadership in Health Services*, **31**(3), 343–351.

Malik, M. M., Abdallah, S., & Ala'raj, M. (2018). Data mining and predictive analytics applications for the delivery of healthcare services: A systematic literature review. *Annals of Operations Research*, **270**(1–2), 287–312.

Mans, R., Reijers, H., van Genuchten, M., & Wismeijer, D. (2012). Mining processes in dentistry. In *Proceedings of the 2nd ACM SIGHIT Symposium on International Health Informatics — IHI'12* (p. 379). ACM Press, New York, USA.

Mans, R. S., Schonenberg, M. H., Song, M., van der Aalst, W. M. P., & Bakker, P. J. M. (2008). Application of process mining in healthcare — A case study in a Dutch hospital. In *Communications in Computer and Information Science* (Vol. 25 CCIS, pp. 425–438).

Rashidi, E., Jahandar, M., & Zandieh, M. (2010). An improved hybrid multi-objective parallel genetic algorithm for hybrid flow shop scheduling with unrelated parallel machines. *The International Journal of Advanced Manufacturing Technology*, **49**(9), 1129–1139.

Rebuge, Á., & Ferreira, D. R. (2012). Business process analysis in healthcare environments: A methodology based on process mining. *Information Systems*, **37**(2), 99–116.

Rojas, E., Munoz-Gama, J., Sepúlveda, M., & Capurro, D. (2016). Process mining in healthcare: A literature review. *Journal of Biomedical Informatics*, **61**, 224–236.

Rovani, M., Maggi, F. M., de Leoni, M., & van der Aalst, W. M. P. (2015). Declarative process mining in healthcare. *Expert Systems with Applications*, **42**(23), 9236–9251.

Ruiz, R., & Vázquez-Rodríguez, J. A. (2010). The hybrid flow shop scheduling problem. *European Journal of Operational Research*, **205**(1), 1–18.

Song, M., Günther, C. W., & van der Aalst, W. M. P. (2009). Trace clustering in process mining. In D. Ardagna, M. Mecella, & J. Yang (Eds.), *Business Process Management Workshops*. BPM 2008. *Lecture Notes in Business Information Processing* (LNBIP, Vol. 17). Springer, Berlin, Heidelberg. https://doi.org/10.1007/978-3-642-00328-8_11.

Swain, A. K. (2016). Mining big data to support decision making in healthcare. *Journal of Information Technology Case and Application Research*, **18**(3), 141–154.

van der Aalst, W. M. P. (2011). *Process Mining* (Vol. 136). Springer, Berlin, Heidelberg. https://doi.org/10.1007/978-3-642-19345-3.

Weijters, A. J. M. M., van der Aalst, W. M. P., & de Medeiros, A. K. A. (2006). Process mining with the HeuristicsMiner algorithm. *Beta Working Papers*, **166**, 1–34. Retrieved from https://pdfs.semanticscholar.org/1cc3/d62e27365b8d7ed6ce9 3b41c193d0559d086.pdf.

Wu, L., Yue, X., Jin, A., & Yen, D. C. (2016). Smart supply chain management: A review and implications for future research. *The International Journal of Logistics Management*, **27**(2), 395–417.

Zhou, W. (2009). *Process Mining: Acquiring Objective Process Information for Healthcare Process Management with the CRISP-DM Framework*. Eindhoven University of Technology. Retrieved from http://alexandria.tue.nl/extra2/ afstversl/tm/Zhou2009.pdf.

https://doi.org/10.1142/9789811286636_0008

CHAPTER 8

Autonomous Mobile Robots for Warehousing and Distribution Industry: A Step Toward Intralogistics 4.0

Abhay K. Grover[*,‡] and Muhammad H. Ashraf[†,§]

*Robert H. Smith School of Business, University of Maryland, MD, USA
†College of Business, California State University Long Beach, CA, USA
‡akgrover@umd.edu
§hasan.ashraf@csulb.edu

Abstract

This chapter enriches readers' understanding regarding the significance of Autonomous Mobile Robots (AMRs) within the context of the warehousing and distribution industry. It offers insights into the evolving growth trends of AMRs, the current state of academic research on this technology, and real-world applications of AMRs in the logistics sector. Additionally, the chapter thoroughly discusses the challenges associated with AMR adoption and proposes a mid-range theory to facilitate their integration within the facilities. In sum, this chapter provides valuable insights for academics and practitioners alike who are eager to explore the adoption of AMRs within the warehousing and distribution industry.

Keywords: Autonomous mobile robots; Warehouse; Intralogistics 4.0; Logistics.

Introduction to Autonomous Mobile Robots (AMRs)

The challenges of modern-day supply chain managers are much complex. They are dealing with increased interdependencies and vulnerabilities along with heightened consumer expectations. The so called "next gen supply chains" are expected to be flexible, efficient, resilient, and sustainable. These expectations have challenged the warehousing and distribution industry to manage and move products at record speeds (Ashraf *et al.*, 2022). As a result, the industry has turned their much-needed attention to the digital supply chain phenomenon of intralogistics 4.0, that is, the application of the Internet of Things (IoT) and advanced robotics to the physical flow of materials within the walls of the facility (Winkelhaus *et al.*, 2021; Fragapane *et al.*, 2021). And one such promising intralogistics 4.0 technology is autonomous mobile robots (AMRs) (Fragapane *et al.*, 2021, 2022).

Although the commercial application of AMRs started just recently, the first AMR patent was published in 1987 (Mattaboni, 1987). Unlike traditional automated guided vehicles (AGV), a fleet of AMRs can autonomously manage the physical flow of material in the warehouses. AMRs can comprehend and move through complex physical environments such as warehouses and distribution facilities without any assistance from operators or fixed predetermined paths. Through wireless communication protocols, they interconnect all active agents (people, processes, goods, other AMRs, and facilities) to de-centrally coordinate information, make real-time optimal decisions, and execute consequential actions (Kirks *et al.*, 2018). In general, they host an array of advanced sensors such as laser scanners, 3D visions cameras, and proximity sensors, along with artificial intelligence (AI)-enabled processors to navigate their environment. Some of the AMRs can operate on an average 13–14 hours on a single charge at speeds of up to 3–4 meters/second and carry payloads of up to 1,500 kg while complying with industrial safety standards such as ISO 13849 and EN1525.

With substantial navigational flexibility, AMRs have opened exceptional prospects for autonomizing intralogistics operations. However, despite a promising future, AMRs have not received much attention from both the academicians and practitioners. The objective of this chapter is to help readers understand the significance of AMRs and bring more academic attention to the cause of advancing the application of AMRs among warehouses and distribution facilities. We believe that AMRs can help unlock enormous operational efficiencies for such facilities.

Our chapter is structured in the following way: second section provides an overview of the growth trends in AMRs. The third section provides a brief impression of the literature and direction of current academic research on AMRs. The fourth section provides an outline of several theories that can be used to advance the knowledge of intralogistics 4.0 adoption among warehouses and distribution facilities. We then propose an example of a midrange theory for intralogistics 4.0 adoption. The fifth section provides operational benefits of AMRs and the sixth section helps understand the challenges facing AMR adoption in logistics and warehousing. The seventh section outlines how to measure the performance of AMRs and the eighth section presents some real-world case applications of AMRs for logistics, warehousing, and distribution.

The growth trends of AMRs

The demand for AMRs has increased due to rising e-commerce activity around the world. Major industries that are adopting the technology range from automotive, electronic, fast-moving consumer goods, logistics, healthcare, and education sectors (Report Linker, 2022). According to Statista, "the global market for autonomous mobile robots (AMR) was sized about 2.4 billion U.S. dollars in 2021. The market is expected to grow at a compound annual growth rate (CAGR) of around 23 percent ... by 2028" (Statista, 2022). Industries are increasingly working with technology firms and automation solution providers to transform their material-handling operations.

Europe has mostly dominated the AMR market in 2021 with a revenue share of over 30%, whereas the Asia Pacific is anticipated to witness a significant growth over the next few years. The growing e-commerce industry in emerging and developed economies is promoting the deployment of AMRs for inventory management. The adoption of AMRs is also trending traction due to intense competition within the logistics sector to achieve the advantages through reduced delivery times. Firms are deploying AMRs in their warehouses to automate intralogistics tasks, including picking, packing, sorting, traveling, (un)loading, and palletizing.

For instance, in September 2021, Shenzhen-based Hai Robotics raised $200 million to strengthen its AMRs with advancements, helping them to reach the global market (Crowe, 2021). Similarly, firms such as 6 River Systems and inVia Robotics, one of the larger service providers of AMRs, saw a more than three times increase in their sales in 2019 (Banker, 2018). 6 River Systems also established a multiyear global deal with GXO Logistics, Inc., to address their AMR needs in logistics operations (Wessling, 2022b). Another major logistics firm, DHL, signed an agreement with Locus Robotics in 2021 to add 2000 AMRs to its distribution network (Magill, 2022). Similarly, Amazon increased the number of AMRs in its fulfillment centers from 200,000 to more than 500,000 within three years. The company's recent addition of AMR is called Proteus, deployed in outbound handling areas for GoCarts (Garland, 2022).

Overall, the growth trend of AMR looks very promising. The next two decades of technological innovation coupled with increased consumer expectations can help drive the adoption of AMRs among warehouses and distribution facilities.

Recent Literature Overview

Table 1 summarizes some recent studies on AMR assimilation. Most of the studies in the literature have researched how to improve the operational performance of AMRs once they are adopted (e.g., Fragapane *et al.*, 2021; Kousi *et al.*, 2019; Lamballais *et al.*, 2017). Other studies use systematic literature review to understand the current state of research in AMR and logistics 4.0 (e.g., Winkelhaus & Grosse, 2020; Dong *et al.*, 2021; Dolgui *et al.*, 2022; Winkelhaus *et al.*, 2021). A few other studies investigate the design of AMR systems for specific applications, such as Liaqat *et al.* (2019) and Morenza-Cinos *et al.* (2019).

Further, existing research identifies several factors affecting the adoption of AMRs. For example, Fragapane *et al.* (2021), Kousi *et al.* (2019), Lamballais *et al.* (2017), Wang *et al.* (2020), Dolgui *et al.* (2022), and Winkelhaus *et al.* (2021) suggest that factors such as path planning, utilization rate, facility layout, and material flows significantly impact the operational performance of AMRs. Whereas studies such as Fragapane *et al.* (2022), Winkelhaus and Grosse (2020), Morenza-Cinos *et al.* (2019), Dong *et al.* (2021), and Dolgui *et al.* (2022) look at pre-adoption factors such as

Table 1. Overview of recent literature.

Author	Research Method	Objective of Study	Contributions
Fragapane et al. (2021)	Systematic literature review of 108 articles	"Identify and classify research related to the planning and control of AMRs" (p. 405).	"AMR planning and control framework to guide managers" (p. 405).
Fragapane et al. (2022)	Analytical model	"Investigate conditions under which it is advantageous to implement the AMR-driven flexible production networks" (p. 127).	"Promote a deeper understanding of the role of AMRs in Industry 4.0-based production networks" (p. 125).
Kousi et al. (2019)	Discrete event simulation	Propose a service-oriented architecture "to eliminate the stoppages of assembly lines due to lack of consumables" (p. 812).	Design a "service-based control system responsible for material supply operations planning and coordination in assembly lines" (p. 801).
Lamballais et al. (2017)	Analytical model	"Understand how order cycle time and robot utilization is influenced by ware-house layout and operating policies" (p. 976).	"Develops several models for estimating performance and robot utilization in Robotic Mobile Fulfillment System (RMFS)" (p. 976).
Liaqat et al. (2019)	Observation based simulation	"Development of a Highway Code for AMRs, development of simulation models for an ideal AMR … and physical testing of real AMR … " (p. 4617).	Facilitate "implementation of AMRs through identification of adverse behaviors" (p. 4617).
Winkelhaus & Grosse (2020)	Literature review of 114 articles on Logistics 4.0	"Unify diverse approaches in research to a Logistics 4.0 framework to generate a new picture of the state of logistics research" (p. 18).	Framework "to identify future strategies and technologies to fulfill certain logistics tasks" (p. 18).

(Continued)

Table 1. (*Continued*)

Author	Research Method	Objective of Study	Contributions
Morenza-Cinos *et al.* (2019)	Design science research methodology	"Propose an autonomous robot system [AMR] that can perform stock-taking using RFID for item-level identification" (p. 1020).	An autonomous robot system [AMR] solution for stock-taking is proposed.
Dong *et al.* (2021)	Systematic literature review	Identify "the impact of emerging and disruptive technologies on freight transportation" (p. 386).	"Provides a novel approach to select emerging and disruptive technologies" (p. 386).
Wang *et al.* (2020)	Analytical model and simulation	"Investigates the operation cycle of the rack-moving machine [AMRs] for storage and retrieval" (p. 4367).	"Presents guidelines for configuration of the rack-moving mobile robot system layout" (p. 4367).
Dolgui *et al.* (2022)	Systematic literature review	Understand the current state of the art in production and warehouse assembly systems (AS) 4.0 field.	Identify research challenges for different technologies including AMRs for material management and preparation.
Winkelhaus *et al.* (2021)	Systematic literature review and qualitative, explorative methodology	"Examine the influences of the transition toward Intralogistics 4.0 on work characteristics of intralogistics employees" (p. 343).	Framework toward "Intralogistics 4.0-implemented workplaces" (p. 343).

costs of AMRs, managerial decision-making, human skills, and selection tools for AMRs.

Overall, there is a considerable gap in the recent literature, especially when it comes to AMR adoption, assimilation, and performance management. There is lack of empirical research to establish the validity of some of the proposed benefits of AMRs for warehouse and distribution centers. Beyond systematic literature review and analytical modeling, there is scope for researchers to conduct qualitative research and develop grounded theory to help understand the adoption process of AMRs. There is also an opportunity to use case study methodologies to develop a deeper understanding of the managerial decision-making process of AMR adoption. It is also important to understand the dos and don'ts of AMR adoption. At the same time, there is a significant opportunity for making theoretical contributions.

Theory Toolbox for AMR Research

Winkelhaus and Grosse (2020) presented the conceptual framework of logistics 4.0 and inductively refined it using a systematic literature review. The conceptual framework was adopted from the technology, organization, and environment (TOE) framework, originally developed for technology adoption (Tornatzky *et al.*, 1990). With the conceptual framework of logistics 4.0, Winkelhaus and Grosse's (2020) goal was to present a unified approach to theoretically explain the adoption of logistics 4.0 and provide a holistic understanding of the state of logistics 4.0 research. They identified several firm-level contextual aspects that influence the process of technology adoption and implementation. However, their conceptual model had a broader focus on logistics 4.0 and did not expand on the domain of AMRs and similar intralogistics technologies. Use of other theories such as the technology adoption framework (Hanna *et al.*, 1995) and dynamic capability theory can help expand logistics 4.0 framework and extend it to understand the adoption of AMRs and similar intralogistics 4.0 technologies.

Conceptual Framework of Logistics 4.0: Winkelhaus and Grosse (2020) identified three contextual dimensions that influence the process of technology adoption and implementation for logistics 4.0. The first dimension being the external changes in the environment which are controlled by the external stakeholders and their characteristics. For example, customer demand of customized and high-quality products has changed the competitive landscape.

Other issues such as globalization, sustainability, and the immediate political environment affect how firms adopt and implement technology as well. The external environment acts as pull force for industry 4.0 systems such as AMRs.

The second dimension is the technological building blocks. It consists of the latest developments in the technology within a focused domain which drives the paradigm shifts. Technologies such as AMRs, additive manufacturing, cloud computing, and blockchain are disruptive advancements, which are becoming more affordable. These technology building blocks act as a push force for industry 4.0 adoption and implementation. The third dimension emphasizes on logistics and its three aspects, that is, tasks, domains, and human factors. Logistics tasks are all activities centered on logistics that help make it more successful. These tasks could be strategic activities at the management level or more tactical activities at the execution level. Winkelhaus and Grosse (2020) separated these activities into four domains based on material flow, that is, supply logistics, intralogistics, distribution logistics, and reverse logistics. Also, they introduced human factors to the model. They argued that the ability of technology to be accepted and implemented successfully depends on the cognitive capabilities of humans. Human factors such as their physical limits, social interactions, and bounded rationality influence their decision-making and in-turn the quality and efficiency of logistics 4.0. Ultimately, logistics 4.0 adoption and implementation are the outcome of the interaction of these three dimensions.

Technology Adoption Framework: Hanna *et al.* (1995) describe a simple model for technology adoption. The idea behind the technology adoption framework is to methodologically define all the activities a firm undertakes when adopting a particular technology. These activities include researching for new technology, assessing various technology alternatives, negotiating technology acquisition, procuring the technology, physically installing the technology, integrating, and adapting to the technology. Furthermore, they categorized these activities into four broad stages: information stage, analysis stage, acquisition stage, and utilization stage.

Hanna *et al.* (1995) define the information stage as the first stage of the adoption process where in a firm collects essential information to make an educated choice. The critical success factors of this stage relate to the quality and quantity of information, the efficiency of the infrastructure that provides the available. They define the analysis stage as the second stage in the adoption process wherein the firm processes and analyzes the information collected. At this stage, the critical success factors are internal technical capability, understanding of information needs, and communication within the organization. They define the acquisition stage as the technology adoption process stage, where a firm gathers the necessary resources to acquire or develop a technology system. Availability of adequate financial resources is one of the critical success factors at this stage. The last stage is the utilization stage, which is defined as the technology adoption process stage, where a firm works on actual implementation and employment of the technology. This stage's critical success factor includes managerial support, internal technical capabilities, and steep learning curves.

Dynamic Capability Theory: Dynamic capability concept as defined by Teece *et al.* (1997) is the ability of a firm to strategically adapt its resources by integrating, building, realigning, or reconfiguring its internal and external competencies to capitalize on the ever-changing environment. These capabilities help the firms to create sustainable competitive advantages over their rivals. The ability to react and adapt to changing environment is multidimensional. These different dimensions of capabilities include scanning, absorption, innovation, adaptation, relation building, and system integration capabilities (Falcone *et al.*, 2019).

Dynamic capabilities perspective has been used to identify how firm-level dynamic capabilities affect the adoption and implementation of Industry 4.0. Bag *et al.* (2020) introduced the dynamic capabilities perspective by testing the TOE capabilities on logistics 4.0 capabilities and firm performance. Demeter *et al.* (2020) used the dynamic capabilities theory to "examine the resource alteration underlying the digital manufacturing transformation" (p. 820). Further, the study by Gupta *et al.* (2020) looked at how firms orient themselves when using Industry 4.0 and digital supply chains. This study uses the dynamic capability framework to extend the logistics 4.0 framework and suggest that a firm's ability to respond to its external environment affects the adoption and implementation of technologies, including intralogistics 4.0.

Overall, there is an opportunity to contextualize these frameworks for intralogistics 4.0 technologies such as AMRs. As an example, we propose the integrated framework of intralogistics 4.0.

Integrated Framework of Intralogistics 4.0: We use the conceptual framework of logistics 4.0 as proposed by Winkelhaus and Grosse (2020) and extend it by

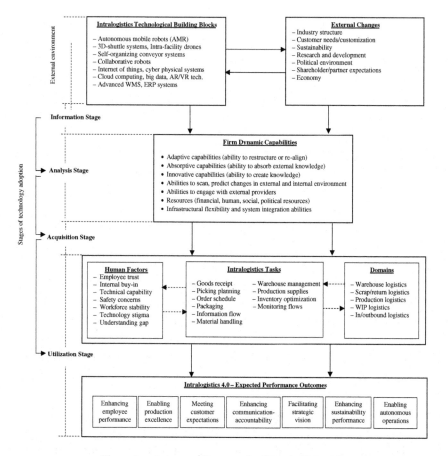

Figure 1.   Integrated Framework of Intralogistics 4.0.

using the dynamic capability theory and the technology adoption framework by Hanna *et al.* (1995). Our proposed integrated framework of Intralogistics 4.0 is presented in Figure 1. We used the dynamics capability framework to introduce the fourth dimension of firm-level dynamic capabilities. The changes in external environment along with the technological developments create the pull and push force for Intralogistics 4.0 adoption, respectively. We also suggest that a firm's interaction with its external environment shapes the information stage of technology adoption. The effect of the push and pull is realized depending upon a firm's dynamic capabilities, which define how responsive the firm is to its external environment. The dynamic capabilities of a firm such as adaptive, assimilative, and absorptive capabilities shape the analysis stage of the firm's technology adoption. These firm-level dynamic capabilities affect the intralogistics and its three aspects, that is, tasks, domains, and human factors. The interaction of firm's dynamic capabilities, human factors, and intralogistics tasks shape the acquisition stage of technology adoption. For example, a firm's thorough understanding of intralogistics 4.0 technologies and resource availability along with employee-level knowledge and capabilities to manage the technologies determine whether a particular technology will be acquired or not. Finally human factors, intralogistics tasks, and domains affect the utilization stage of intralogistics 4.0.

Operational Benefits of AMRs

AMRs have primarily impacted the effectiveness of automated and manual workflows in warehouse operations, pressing apprehensions about the impact of the ongoing labor crisis and the boost in e-commerce volume. With considerable navigational flexibility, AMRs are versatile machines and can provide numerous operational benefits. Below, we briefly discuss operational benefits within the context of the warehousing and distribution industry.

Increased Flexibility: AMRs differ from AGVs because they are not fixed to specific route. Instead, they can operate anywhere within a pre-defined area (Fragapane *et al.*, 2022). Conventionally, an AGV functions with a central hierarchical structure, whereas AMRs work autonomously, involving decentralized decisions, such as real-time routing and scheduling (Fragapane *et al.*, 2022). There is no requirement to place tracks and magnetic strips, set up dedicated routes, or even confine equipment such as forklifts, dollies, pallet jacks, etc., and warehouse workers from operating in zones where the robots are deployed (Dunakin, 2021). AMRs are smaller and more agile than AGVs, therefore, they have greater facility access and increased operational flexibility (Mosallaeipour *et al.*, 2018). For instance, Mobile Industrial Robots' (MIR) MiR250 robot can transport items of up to 250 kg and can drive at 7.2 km/h. Moreover, it has a compact design (800 mm × 300 mm), allowing it to navigate the confined spaces.[1]

---

[1]Mobile Industrial Robots: https://www.mobile-industrial-robots.com/solutions/robots/mir250/.

Ability to Scale: AMRs can be added to warehouse operations as needed. The number of robots and hours of work per day can be effortlessly attuned to meet fluctuations in warehouse volume, even if there is an unanticipated peak or off-peak season (Wieciek, 2020). This helps warehouses avoid the operational challenges associated with finding workers and the time associated with hiring and training new staff. Adding individual units over time is also more affordable than the instant, considerable expenditure of modifying or swapping fixed systems (Konopacki, 2022). Complementing this scalability feature is Robot as a Service, commonly abbreviated as Raas, which offers the ability to scale robot usage as needed (Anandan, 2018). For instance, InVia Robotics, a RaaS vendor, provides warehouses with the option to increase their AMR usage by sending more robots to the facility during peak times (Demaitre, 2021). This modular deployment also allows warehouses to avoid high initial investment of acquiring AMRs all at once, thereby freeing up capital that can be spent on other capital-intensive expenditures (Romaine, 2019).

Easy Integration: AMRs can seamlessly interface with already installed systems such as, warehouse management systems (WMS), to improve overall warehouse efficiency.[2] AMR service providers, such as Process Equipment & Control (PEC), provide turnkey solutions that integrate seamlessly with existing warehouse systems.[3] Integrating WMS and ERP with the AMRs lets a warehouse aggregate data across numerous zones and allows collaborative actions, such as picking or sorting, for quicker fulfillment (Dunakin, 2021). The system identifies the best next move for each worker and AMR based on their real-time position, existing tasks, and job priority. Since the integrated system is dynamic and intelligent, the critical orders can take priority over standard orders in the picking queue and promptly inform the combined human and AMR workforce.[2] The system identifies the nearest available worker and the AMR to fulfill the order in the most efficient way possible.

Enhanced Agility: Warehouse operations are agile since they quickly have to pivot the direction of their operations and respond to changing internal and external signals. Legacy material-handling equipment, like AGVs and

---

[2]AMR integration capability: https://fetchrobotics.com/fully-integrated/.
[3]Process Equipment & Control: https://processequipmentandcontrols.com/what-we-do/automated-warehouse-systems/.

conveyors, need fixed routes and infrastructure changes prior to deployment. This can mean a substantial upfront cost and a postponement in deployment (Fragapane *et al.*, 2022). AMRs can be up and running without any infrastructure modifications. They can quickly acclimate to the new warehouse floor layouts or process changes without extensive setup costs (Flexqube, 2022). This also means that AMRs can be swapped to execute new tasks quickly and move between facilities relatively without difficulty. For example, Waypoint's Vector AMR can be deployed within 15 minutes after unboxing.[4] AMRs' ability to contribute to fast-paced warehouse operations reduces the lead time for fulfilling bulk orders in large warehouses and the traveling times of operators within the facility (Flexqube, 2022).

Improved Safety: A recurrent cause of warehouse injuries is restricted or obstructed visibility (Kane Logistics, 2022). Built-in sensors, Light Detection And Ranging (LiDAR) scanners, mapping, and universal fleet management guarantee that AMRs can spot and react to humans and other objects in their pathway, reducing the likelihood of injuries and accidents (Schlechtriem, 2021). According to the Occupational Safety and Health Administration (OSHA), there are more than 100,000 accidents each year involving forklift safety and approximately 95,000 injuries related to forklift accidents (Bragatto *et al.*, 2014). With AMRs taking on material-handling roles, the number of forklifts or other machinery-related accidents can be minimized. In addition to injuries due to heavy machinery, worker injuries attributed to lifting or lowering objects are a significant concern for warehouse operations (Grosse *et al.*, 2015). Using AMRs can reduce injuries brought on by repetitive lifting and lowering jobs while also minimizing accident and efficiency risks. Lastly, AMRs can reduce pointless contact between employees, which is important considering the growing demand for workplace safety amid COVID-19 (Cardona *et al.*, 2020).

Add-on Capability: AMRs use customizable top modules which can be attuned to the shape and form of the payloads. For instance, Nord-Modules' QM180 module is compatible with more than 100 different AMR models and can transport up to 485 lb (220 kg) per load (Price, 2020). The QM180

---

[4]Waypoint's Vector: https://waypointrobotics.com/wp-content/uploads/2020/05/Waypoint Robotics_Brochure2020_Vector_Website_Pages-1.pdf.

also has a raising/lowering mechanism to transport items and offload them to different height stations. Similarly, articulated robotic arms can be added to an AMR that facilitates picking, sorting, packing, and various other applications within warehouse operations (McNulty, 2022). Paired with other technologies, these arms can dramatically reduce labor needs. Another add-on capability is the stacker-bots add-on that can retrieve inventory from the floor, shelf, or conveyor level and feed sorters, automated storage and retrieval, work cells, and other equipment.[5] Other add-ons include stereo vision systems, shuttle-based storage systems, under-ride carts, telescopic forks, etc., mounted on AMRs, making them suitable to operate in various set-ups (Azadeh *et al.*, 2019; Ben-Tzvi & Xu, 2010).

Operational Efficiency: AMRs add efficiency to several operations related to material-handling. As the warehouse's product volume grows, AMR deployment can grow concurrently with little additional expense. It permits to automate low-value operations such as pushing carts, cleaning floors etc., allowing the workers to concentrate on higher-value activities (Kickham, 2022). AMRs can help transport materials without any disruptions, which can help the warehouse run smoothly (Kickham, 2022). These robots can carry carts, flow racks, or pallets of goods to a work cell without human support or changes to the facility. In addition, AMRs, such as Omron's LD Series robot, are accompanied by digital displays providing information, such as product features and where to locate them, thereby reducing errors and customer frustration due to erroneous deliveries.[6] Also, since AMRs are not operated by humans, accidents due to human error are minimized (Santagate, 2020). In addition, AMRs can be programmed for multiple pickups and delivery points and can increase the storage capacity of warehouses as they can navigate through narrower paths (Fragapane *et al.*, 2021).

Challenges Facing AMR Adoption in Logistics and Warehousing

Despite their potential, warehouses still struggle to integrate AMRs successfully into their operations. As *Robotic Business Review*[7] puts it, ... *implementa-*

---

[5]Stacker-bots developed by Conveyco: https://www.materialhandling247.com/product/flow_rack_autonomous_mobile_robot_replenisher/agvs.

[6]Omron LD Series: https://automation.omron.com/en/us/products/family/ld.

[7]Challenges of AMRs: https://www.roboticsbusinessreview.com/rbr-webinars/autonomous-mobile-robotics-week-focuses-on-amr-adoption-opportunities-challenges/.

tion of AMR solutions can be difficult and fraught with uncertainty. Mistakes can be costly, but inaction will all but guarantee suboptimal industrial performance. .... These AMR adoption challenges range from selection criteria and safety standards to facility layouts, performance management, and scaling (Fragapane *et al.*, 2021). As such, we classify the adoption challenges into three broad categories: (i) challenges before adopting AMRs, (ii) challenges at the time of acquiring AMRs, and (iii) challenges after adopting AMRs.

Challenges before adopting AMRs

Safety Concerns: AMR safety is often one of the first questions asked by potential adopters. Even though modern-day AMRs are equipped with state-of-art sensors and cameras to maintain a safe distance from workers inside the facility, it does not fully address the safety concerns for warehouse management. Salvini *et al.* (2022) intensify this doubt, arguing that the AMRs are still not fully equipped with "sensing and control capabilities to be fully aware of their environment and to react adequately" (p. 442). This lack of sensing capability becomes a major concern for warehouses, especially in emergency evacuation situations. AMRs can cause problems as they might still be operating while workers are trying to evacuate. Therefore, regardless of the diligence of AMR manufacturers to apply safety precautions that go above and beyond safety standards set by ANSI and ISO, AMRs still suffer from safety challenges.

Interface Concerns: Most warehouses in the western world are already equipped with automated or semi-automated systems such as mechanized storage and retrieval systems, WMS, and automated pallet stacking systems (Azadeh *et al.*, 2019). These technologies are also referred to as legacy systems. Though these technologies have proven reliable and supportive for the warehouse industry, they are rigid and somewhat challenging to integrate with smart technologies, such as AMRs. Most of these systems are siloed systems, posing a challenge to integrate them successfully with modern technology (Akhtar, 2022). Integrating a legacy system requires defining "interfaces for each subsystem" and building an "object wrapper", which might be time-consuming, labor-intensive, and costly (Akhtar, 2022). Therefore, warehouses are particularly concerned about the interface complexity of the AMRs with the already installed systems, making the decision to adopt AMRs complicated and fraught with uncertainty (Akhtar, 2022).

Facility Modification: Despite its plug and play image, AMR implementation requires the modification of warehouse facilities. For instance, additional paths must be defined inside the facility for the AMRs to allow clearance for workers to reach exit doors in case of emergency (Dittmar, 2020). Similarly, LED lights and visual and audio indicators have to be installed in the facility to provide a visual indication to workers regarding AMR's movement. Also, safety fencing needs to be placed to designate areas as robot-only, which may reduce the warehouse's storage capacity. Additionally, the surface on which AMR travels impacts its balance and ability to stop safely; therefore, surface irregularities such as potholes and irregular slopes need to be revamped (Dittmar, 2020). Preparing the facility for AMRs may also include installing the latest Wi-Fi equipment or other signal integration for effective machine-to-machine and machine-to-human communication (Dittmar, 2020).

Dependence on Service Providers: The selection of an appropriate AMR service provider can also be a significant challenge for warehouses. Because of the intricate nature of AMR technology, warehouses are significantly dependent on external service providers to help them successfully adopt AMRs. Service providers often have a technical knowledge edge over their potential customers (in this case, warehouses), which may place the latter in an unfavorable position to accurately analyze and assess the capabilities of AMRs that may or may not benefit them (Handley *et al.*, 2019). Therefore, increased dependence on the service provider increases the warehouse's perception of being exposed to opportunistic holdups. Also, without enough qualified workers, warehouses are not able to garner the full benefits of the technology and, therefore, are not willing to acquire the technology (Hughes *et al.*, 2019).

Challenges at the time of acquiring AMRs

Upfront Costs: On average, a single unit of AMR may cost between $30,000 and $100,000 depending on the size of the warehouse and the payload requirements (Bechtsis *et al.*, 2018). In addition to purchasing costs, customers also have to incur high setup and configuration costs, deployment costs, training costs, and reconfigurations costs. Moreover, costs related to facility modification, hiring experts, developing feasibility studies, and establishing maintenance centers are also included in the initial investment. Such huge investment followed by high setup and maintenance costs make warehouses, especially the small and medium-sized, skeptical about investing in the technology.

AMR Accessory Costs: The eventual cost of implementing AMRs is influenced by the type of AMR and the number of accessories acquired (Romaine, 2019). Accessories such as a horizontal linear camera for visuals, auto-iris feature for light condition adaptations, charging stations for electrical power supply, automatic charging units, and loading docks (e.g., Fragapane *et al.*, 2021) are not part of the basic AMR module and must be purchased separately. For instance, one unit of the base Omron LD series AMR costs around $42,400. However, Omron offers various added features such as HD cameras costing up to $700 per unit, photoelectric sensors costing around $500 per unit, bar code scanners costing around $1,300 per unit, thermal transfer label printers costing around $800 per unit, conveyor beds costing up to $1,500 per unit, and robotic arm costing up to $45,000.[8] Such added features not only make the process of acquisition complex for warehouses but also add to the base unit cost of the AMRs.

Challenges after adopting AMRs

Operational Issues: Once the AMRs are deployed, warehouses may experience numerous operational challenges, especially during the initial phases of deployment. For instance, in warehouses, the environment is continuously changing due to the movement of items and shifting walls of boxes and pallets, which makes it difficult for AMRs to distinguish their surroundings to properly operate and adapt. Similarly, in warehouses such as bulk warehouses, items are often haphazardly placed, along with new SKUs arriving at all times in various shapes and sizes, making it difficult for AMRs to learn and adapt to the new variables. Additionally, warehouses usually have large loading/unloading bay doors that allow sunlight to enter the warehouse. In such cases, an AMR can mistake light from a reflection for a physical object, thereby disrupting its path. Also, AMRs are well suited for tight spaces with a lot of features for them to navigate through. However, in larger warehouses, with big-open spaces, it can be difficult to link the AMR path to a map.[9] Last, since the warehouses lack the technical expertise in AMRs, any maintenance-related activity is dependent on the AMR service provider's availability. Therefore, if

---

[8]Accessory costs: https://www.kingbarcode.com/.
[9]Overcoming the Challenges of Robotics in the Warehouse: https://inviarobotics.com/blog/overcoming-challenges-robotics-warehouse/?cn-reloaded=1.

there are frequent AMR breakdowns, it may lead to significant disruptions in warehouse operations, leading to major financial and service losses.

Vendor Disagreements: Warehouses that lack a basic understanding of AMR applications may implement it for the primary reason of contesting with their competitors or for the prime reason of gaining acceptability in the market (Copeland & Shapiro, 2010). In such cases, warehouse operatives are highly dependent on AMR service providers. However, with the lack of knowledge, they often fail to understand the basic applications of the AMRs leading to disagreements with the service providers. Such disagreements are especially intensified when there are inconsistencies between the service provider and the standard set by the warehouse operatives. Disagreement with vendors is a major concern for the warehouses and impacts their willingness to pursue the AMRs into the exploitation stage.

Employee Resistance: In the United States, about 1.5 million workers are associated with the warehouse industry, whereas 1.8 million workers are employed in the UK, and millions more work in warehouses globally (Lui *et al.*, 2022). According to Stornelli *et al.* (2021), one of the biggest challenges for warehouses to successfully deploy AMRs is overcoming employee resistance. According to a survey by *Harvard Business Review*, 42% of employees had a negative sentiment about technology adoption (Liu *et al.*, 2022). Employee resistance mainly emerges due to workers' perceived established competencies (Sjödin *et al.*, 2018) and fear of job losses (Borges & Tan, 2017). Perhaps the major reason for this is the fear of the unknown. Warehouse workers are the backbone of the industry and the deployment of AMRs may bring in new challenges and uncertainties for them.

Measuring the Performance of AMRs

Measuring the performance of AMRs in dealing with complex and changing environments is extremely important for the warehouse to authenticate its decision to implement the technology. Even though there are no set performance metrics to measure AMR performance, literature in this domain suggests various approaches that could serve the purpose. In any case, the performance of AMRs is reliant on the type of industry, and the jobs it is deployed for. Table 2 provides an overview of the metrics provided in the literature.

Table 2. AMR performance metrics.

Performance Metric	Applicability in the Context of Warehouse	Adapted Potential Measures
Navigation	The AMR needs to be aware of the surroundings in which it is working.	Physical observation.
Obstacle encounter	The AMR needs to successfully avoid any obstacles in the warehouse.	Efficiency: (i) The time needed for obstacle extraction, (ii) the number of operator interventions per unit, and (iii) the ratio of operator time to robot time.
Perception	Interpreting sensor data which includes identification and judgment of motion.	Percent detected.
Judgment of extent measures	The accuracy of quantitative judgments about the surroundings.	Absolute and/or relative judgments of distance, size, or length.
Judgment of motion	Accuracy with which the ego-motion or movement of objects in the environment is judged.	Absolute estimates of robot velocity.
Management	How many robots can be effectively controlled by a human.	Response time.
Contact error	The number of unintentional collisions between the robot and surrounding objects.	Frequency of contact errors.
Security	The security of robot motion, considering the distance between the robot and obstacles in its path.	Distance between the vehicle and the obstacles throughout the task.
Repeatability	How accurately can the AMR arrive at the same position repeatedly?	Number of inaccurate positions.
Processor usage	Does AMR work well with the available processing and memory resources?	Number of rejected/denied commands.

Source: Adapted from Steinfeld *et al.*, 2006; Ceballos *et al.*, 2010.

Real-World Case Application of AMRs for Logistics, Warehousing, and Distribution

Ford Motor Company: One of Ford's major car assembly facilities outside of United States of America is in Almussafes-Valencia, Spain. It produces about 450,000 vehicles per year, including some of the more popular models such as Kuga, Transit Connect, and S-Max. One of the challenges faced by the 300,000 square-meter facility was the delivery of industrial and welding materials from the production warehouse to the assembly line (Sonya, 2019). It was a repetitive, non-value-added, and a time-consuming task for the employees. Ford production engineers were actively looking to automate the process without adding any external beacons, magnets, or tapes on the floor or walls. They onboarded three successive Mobile Industrial Robots (MiR) AMRs between 2018 and 2019 (Weinberg, 2019). Their AMRs are equipped with automatic shelving systems with more than a dozen slots to hold parts of various shapes and sizes. A single AMR can carry up to 220 pounds (100 kg) of materials. Their robots can safely navigate the complex plant floor autonomously between the production warehouse and assembly line. According to maintenance control engineers at Ford (as cited in Weinberg, 2019), *the robot had to avoid unforeseen obstacles, modify its route or stop when necessary and work safely alongside people and other vehicles in the plant, such as forklifts…. We programmed it to learn the entire plant and this, together with the sensors with which it is equipped, means that it does not need any external help to circulate safely.* According to their estimates it helped them free up 40 manhours per day, allowing their employees to focus on more value-added tasks. One of their key learning was that it is important to identify the business needs and specific use cases for AMR deployment. It is also important to think about the robot's integration with other business processes early in the process (Weinberg, 2019).

Saddle Creek Logistics Services: Saddle Creek is one of the top 100 third-party logistics providers in the United States. They are based out of Lakeland, Florida and provide services in warehousing, e-Commerce distribution, and fleet management. They serve industries like consumer-packaged goods, fashion and medical apparel, and miscellaneous medical supplies. Some of their key customers include Lowe's, Sam's, and Del Monte (Transport Topics, 2021). During COVID-19 pandemic, the company faced three times its normal order volume, especially from the medical apparel and supply clients. At the same time, they were facing challenges from worker shortages in the tight labor market due to COVID-19. The firm onboarded a fleet of 20 Locus AMRs at one of their fulfillment centers in Fort Worth, Texas in 2020. The robots were integrated with their WMS. When an order is placed, AMRs with empty bins are dispatched to respective pickup locations with instructions on their digital display. An associate helps pick and scan the items and then the robots head to the pack out area. AMRs helped reduce the non-value-added walking time for associates so that they can focus more on picking and sorting actual orders. Saddle Creek was able to increase their productivity by three times and accommodate about 30–40% volume spikes. According to Saddle Creek's director, *The robots give us the ability to scale. If the client has a big sales day, we're able to get that volume out the next day.* Saddle Creek has expanded their operations to 37 AMRs since then and have been able to meet their service level agreements (SLA) (sclogostics.com, 2022).

Bergler Industrieservices: Bergler Industrieservices is a small medium enterprise based out of Germany. They provide third-party logistics services along with fulfillment and packaging services. They have over 300 customers across four locations. They recently inaugurated an 11,000 squared meter facility in Erlensee, Germany for sorting, packing, and distributing orders for customers of several different e-commerce operator clients (Wessling, 2022a). One of their biggest challenges is that their employees spend a lot of non-value-added time moving between the pickup, packing, and shipping location around the warehouse. Bergler recently invested in Geek +'s P-800 picking AMR along with their WMS. The AMR can slide under the part racks and can move them between the warehouse and operator station while optimizing the route, location, and speed autonomously. The robots use AI-driven vision sensors along with QR codes to complete their tasks. They can fully charge in about 10 minutes and run for three hours on single charge. Per Bergler, Geek +'s good-to-person AMR solution increased their facility productivity by two to three times by speeding their pickup operations and helping operators focus on value-added tasks. In fact, AMRs have helped Bergler improve storage density as the AMRs can navigate through narrow aisles while maintaining a low profile. According to Bergler's CEO, autonomizing picking operations has allowed them to expand their facility and services (Wessling, 2022a).

FM Logistics: FM Logistics is a supply chain management, warehousing and handling, and transportation firm based out of Lorraine, France. It has about 28,600 employees across fourteen countries and three continents with about €1.5 billion in annual revenue. The company has over 4 million square meters of warehouse space across all its locations (FM Logistics, 2022). They serve the consumer products, retail, beauty and cosmetics, industrial manufacturing, and healthcare sectors. One of its key clients is IKEA. One of their challenges was handling of materials leftover process in the warehouse. They were facing labor shortages, often forcing them to operate with fewer employees. In this tight labor market, they had dedicated employees helping remove the trash to recycle and waste collection areas. This trash was being generated from the product returns and the packing processes. They recently implemented a MiR 500 AMR in one of their warehouses in Jarosty, Poland to move used packaging 24 × 7 and six days a week (Oitzman, 2022a). The robot transports a load of up to 500 kg, improving worker safety and optimizing warehouse costs. As per the process manager at FM Logistics, this is a joint effort between FM Logistics and IKEA and "Mobile Industrial Robots' [AMR] technology is much cheaper in use than the competing concept of AGV [Auto Guided Vehicles] trucks. In this particular case, it is a solution more than two times cheaper than an AGV."

UPS Supply Chain Solutions: UPS Supply Chain Solutions is one of the largest firms providing end-to-end supply chain management and global trade compliance support. UPS Supply Chain Solutions operates a 38,000 square-meter warehouse facility for its two large e-commerce clients in Louisville, Kentucky. The warehouse is designed to provide end-to-end fulfillment workflows for these clients. One of the challenges faced by UPS was hiring and retaining warehouse operators. It was struggling to fill open job positions and at the same time keep the cost of operations down as the cost of labor was going up. As a result, UPS onboarded a fleet of Locus AMRs or Locusbots to help autonomize the workflow in warehouses. Locus provided these robots under Robot as a Service (RaaS) business model where in UPS paid a subscription fee for pre-agreed service delivery levels. Locus was able to interface their fleet management solution with UPS's WMS. As a result, the productivity of the operators doubled to 80–90 lines per hour (LPH) against an initial target of 74 LPH. According to Oitzman (2022b), *The bots are loaded with 12 different languages, which enable workers to operate with the bots in their native language. Generally, it takes 15–30 minutes of training to get a new worker up to speed. Managers also use the Locus dashboards on smart phones and laptops to monitor productivity trends. This enables supervisors to modify the workflow from a zone pick to a cluster pick workflow to optimize the warehouse throughput.* In addition, these robots have also increased the morale of the existing workforce as the bots have led to gamification of the process.

Conclusions and Future Directions

AMRs are unlike traditional AGVs and can autonomously manage the workflows of material in the warehouses. They can help support with several warehouse operational tasks such as receiving, unloading, picking, packing, and shipping. They provide significant navigational flexibility and have the potential to unleash unique opportunities for autonomizing intralogistics operations. Unlike existing technologies, AMRs can understand and navigate through a complex physical environment. Through wireless communication protocols, they interconnect all active agents (people, processes, goods, other AMRs, and facilities). One of the biggest challenges with supply chain digitization is converting physical information to digital data points and AMRs can provide the necessary medium to help connect this cyber-physical space. There are several opportunities for researchers, managers, and policymakers to help unlock the potential of AMRs.

Our literature review suggests that the research in the field of adoption and management of AMRs is in a nascent stage. There is an opportunity for researchers to significantly contribute toward theory building in terms of AMR adoption. Scholars can help identify business requirements and critical success factors that can help all stakeholders understand theoretical motivations and drivers of AMR adoption among firms. Empirical researchers can help identify themes and subthemes to theoretically motivate the development of variables and latent constructs whereas the analytical researchers can help define model constraints, corner conditions, or identify competing factors and trade-offs. There is a need and opportunity for scholars to develop comprehensive case studies to understand the human and behavioral factors required for the successful implementation of AMRs systems in warehouse operations. We hope our chapter motivates future qualitative, empirical, and analytical research in operations management focused on management of AMRs for success.

Furthermore, as promising the AMR technology sounds, the biggest question is "are we ready yet?" — ready from the perspective of infrastructure, policy, and skills. There are several gaps that we need to address from policy standpoint to help unlock the potential of technologies such as AMRs, for example:

(a) While the urban and suburban areas in the United States are expecting the rollout of 5G internet speeds, some of the rural areas are still struggling with internets speeds as low as 3.7 Mbps (Mendoza, 2019). According to an estimate, about 20% of small operations are in rural areas of the United States (*Inc*, 2020).

(b) The gap between estimated employer demand of technically skilled labor force and the estimated labor supply is widening year on year. According to EMSI, 2020, the gap between the skill demand and supply for expertise such as controls engineering, programmable logic controllers, agile software development, user experience design, and maintenance systems is more than 50% nationally. So, the skilled talent required to program, implement, and maintain advanced technologies such as AMR systems is limited.

(c) According to United States Census Bureau (2019), approximately 10,000 baby boomers, that is, employees born between 1946 and 1964, retire every day. Manufacturers are greatly concerned about the loss of the "specific company knowledge" and are strongly considering technology as a part of their succession planning. But baby boomers are the first generation undertaking the job of passing on their skills to machines with limited understanding of computer systems using advanced algorithms. Managers are facing a humongous task of extracting business knowledge from baby boomers and translating it into technology expectations (Dam, 2019).

(d) Modern factories are more vulnerable to cybercrimes than ever before because an interconnected digital ecosystem can provide hackers with a central access point to the entire system. More the number of IoT devices, higher the risk. Most manufacturers lack the required experience to prevent cyber threats; this area demands more research (Kumar *et al.*, 2018).

Further, for managers on the journey of AMR acceptance, adoption, implementation, and management, having an in-depth understanding of the key business requirements, critical success factors, and management challenges can help to select, plan, model, design, and organize these AMR systems for performance. The technology management literature suggests that focusing on the critical success factors at the early stages of technology adoption, that is, the information gathering and analysis stage can help managers avoid a wide variety of issues during the utilization stage (Argote & Hora, 2017).

To fully leverage the unique system features of the AMRs, managers need to understand their business motivations, baseline performance, business vision, project scope, project team, resource constraints, and limitations. Often a lack of information on technological possibilities and lack of realistic and quantifiable expectations leads to several issues in management and organization. Per Winkler and Zinsmeister (2019), higher investment of resources in the early project stages (planning, modeling, feasibility studies) reduces vulnerabilities and improves the quality of the technology implementation and management.

References

Akhtar, A. (2022). Top challenges in building integration with legacy applications & legacy middleware. *Royal Cyber*. Retrieved from https://www.royalcyber.com/blog/integrations/integration-with-legacy-systems/.

Anandan, T. (2018). Robots for rent — Why RaaS works. *Association for Advancing Automation*. Retrieved from https://www.automate.org/industry-insights/robots-for-rent-why-raas-works.

Argote, L., & Hora, M. (2017). Organizational learning and management of technology. *Production and Operations Management*, **26**(4), 579–590.

Ashraf, M. H., Chen Y., & Yalcin, M. G. (2022). Minding Braess Paradox amid third-party logistics hub capacity expansion triggered by demand surge. *International Journal of Production Economics*, **248**, 108454.

Azadeh, K., De Koster, R., & Roy, D. (2019). Robotized and automated warehouse systems: Review and recent developments. *Transportation Science*, **53**(4), 917–945.

Bag, S., Gupta, S., & Luo, Z. (2020). Examining the role of logistics 4.0 enabled dynamic capabilities on firm performance. *The International Journal of Logistics Management*, **31**(3), 607–628.

Banker, S. (2018). Collaborative robots used in e-commerce fulfillment. *Forbes*. Retrieved from https://www.forbes.com/sites/stevebanker/2018/06/16/collaborative-robots-used-in-ecommerce-fulfillment/?sh=2504edac5e02.

Bechtsis, D., Tsolakis, N., Vlachos, D., & Srai, J. S. (2018). Intelligent autonomous vehicles in digital supply chains: A framework for integrating innovations towards sustainable value networks. *Journal of Cleaner Production*, **181**, 60–71.

Ben-Tzvi, P., & Xu, X. (2010). An embedded feature-based stereo vision system for autonomous mobile robots. *2010 IEEE International Workshop on Robotic and Sensors Environments*, pp. 1–6.

Borges, L. A., & Tan, K. H. (2017). Incorporating human factors into the AAMT selection: A framework and process. *International Journal of Production Research*, **55**(5), 1459–1470.

Bragatto, P. A., Pirone, A., & Gnoni, M. G. (2014). Application of RFID technology for supporting effective risk management in chemical warehouses. *Safety, Reliability, and Risk Analysis: Beyond the Horizon*. Taylor & Francis Group, London, UK.

Cardona, M., Cortez, F., Palacios, A., & Cerros, K. (2020). Mobile robots application against Covid-19 pandemic. *Proceedings of the 2020 IEEE ANDESCON* (pp. 1–5).

Ceballos, N. D., Valencia, J. A., Ospina, N. L., & Barrera, A. (2010). *Quantitative Performance Metrics for Mobile Robots Navigation*. INTECH Open Access Publisher, London, UK.

Copeland, A. M., & Shapiro, A. H. (2010). *The Impact of Competition on Technology Adoption: An Apples-to-PCs Analysis*. Federal Reserve Bank of New York, New York.

Crowe, S. (2021). Hai Robotics raises $200M for autonomous case handling robots. *The Robot Report*. Retrieved from https://www.therobotreport.com/hai-robotics-raises-200m-autonomous-case-handling-robots/.

Dam, A. V. (2019). Baby boomers are retiring in droves. Here are three big reasons for concern. Retrieved from https://www.chicagotribune.com/business/success/ct-biz-baby-boomers-retire-dollarsense-20190301-story.html.

Demaitre, E. (2021). InVia robotics offers RaaS to optimize both people and robots in warehouses. *Robotics 247*. Retrieved from https://www.robotics247.com/article/invia_robotics_offers_raas_to_optimize_both_people_and_robots_in_warehouses.

Demeter, K., Losonci, D., & Nagy, J. (2020). Road to digital manufacturing–a longitudinal case-based analysis. *Journal of Manufacturing Technology Management*, **32**(3), 820–839.

Dittmar, H. (2020). 8 steps to implement autonomous mobile robots. *Collaborative Robotics Trends*. Retrieved from https://www.cobottrends.com/8-steps-implement-autonomous-mobile-robots/.

Dolgui, A., Sgarbossa, F., & Simonetto, M. (2022). Design and management of assembly systems 4.0: Systematic literature review and research agenda. *International Journal of Production Research*, **60**(1), 184–210.

Dong, C., Akram, A., Andersson, D., Arnäs, P. O., & Stefansson, G. (2021). The impact of emerging and disruptive technologies on freight transportation in the digital era: Current state and future trends. *The International Journal of Logistics Management*, **32**(2), 386–412.

Dunakin, C. (2021). 5 ways autonomous mobile robots are transforming warehouses. *River Systems*. Retrieved from https://6river.com/how-autonomous-mobile-robots-are-transforming-warehouses/.

Falcone, E., Kent, J., & Fugate, B. (2019). Supply chain technologies, interorganizational network and firm performance: A case study of Alibaba Group and Cainiao. *International Journal of Physical Distribution & Logistics Management*, **50**(3), 333–354.

Flexqube (2022). Optimize warehouse logistics with AMRs. *Plant Engineering*. Retrieved from https://www.plantengineering.com/articles/optimize-warehouse-logistics-with-amrs/.

FM Logistics (2022). Overview. Retrieved from https://www.fmlogistic.com/about-us/overview-fm-logistic/.

Fragapane, G., de Koster, R., Sgarbossa, F., & Strandhagen, J. O. (2021). Planning and control of autonomous mobile robots for intralogistics: Literature review and research agenda. *European Journal of Operational Research*, **294**(2), 405–426.

Fragapane, G., Ivanov, D., Peron, M., Sgarbossa, F., & Strandhagen, J. O. (2022). Increasing flexibility and productivity in Industry 4.0 production networks with autonomous mobile robots and smart intralogistics. *Annals of Operations Research*, **308**(1), 125–143.

Garland, M. (2022). Amazon unveils first fully autonomous mobile robot. *Supply Chain Drive*. Retrieved from https://www.supplychaindive.com/news/amazon-unveils-first-fully-autonomous-mobile-robot-proteus-warehouse/626164/.

Grosse, E. H., Glock, C. H., Jaber, M. Y., & Neumann, W. P. (2015). Incorporating human factors in order picking planning models: Framework and research opportunities. *International Journal of Production Research*, **53**(3), 695–717.

Gupta, S., Modgil, S., Gunasekaran, A., & Bag, S. (2020). Dynamic capabilities and institutional theories for Industry 4.0 and digital supply chain. *Supply Chain Forum: An International Journal*, **21**(3), 139–157.

Handley, S. M., de Jong, J., & Benton Jr., W. C. (2019). How service provider dependence perceptions moderate the power–opportunism relationship with professional services. *Production and Operations Management*, **28**(7), 1692–1715.

Hanna, N., Guy, K., & Arnold, E. (1995). The diffusion of information technology: Experience of industrial countries and lessons for developing countries. *The World Bank Discussion Papers*.

Hughes, L., Dwivedi, Y. K., Misra, S. K., Rana, N. P., Raghavan, V., & Akella, V. (2019). Blockchain research, practice and policy: Applications, benefits, limitations, emerging research themes and research agenda. *International Journal of Information Management*, **49**, 114–129.

Inc. Editorial (2020). Rural businesses. Retrieved from https://www.inc.com/encyclopedia/rural-businesses.html#:~:text=No%20data%20breaking%20down%20businesses,rural%20areas%2C%20including%20small%20towns.

Kane Logistics (2022). Top causes of warehouse accidents. *ID Logistics*. Retrieved from https://www.kanelogistics.com/blog/top-causes-of-warehouse-accidents.

Kickham, V. (2022). Making way for automation. *DC Velocity*. Retrieved from https://www.dcvelocity.com/articles/53851-making-way-for-automation.

Kirks, T., Jost, J., Uhlott, T., & Jakobs, M. (2018). Towards complex adaptive control systems for human-robot-interaction in intralogistics. *IEEE 21st International Conference on Intelligent Transportation Systems (ITSC)*, pp. 2968–2973.

Konopacki, C. (2022). The cost advantages of autonomous mobile robots (AMRs). *MUL Technologies*. Retrieved from https://www.multechnologies.com/blog/cost-advantages-of-autonomous-mobile-robots.

Kousi, N., Koukas, S., Michalos, G., & Makris, S. (2019). Scheduling of smart intra–factory material supply operations using mobile robots. *International Journal of Production Research*, **57**(3), 801–814.

Kumar, S., Mookerjee, V., & Shubham, A. (2018). Research in operations management and information systems interface. *Production and Operations Management*, **27**(11), 1893–1905.

Lamballais, T., Roy, D., & De Koster, M. B. M. (2017). Estimating performance in a robotic mobile fulfillment system. *European Journal of Operational Research*, **256**(3), 976–990.

Liaqat, A., Hutabarat, W., Tiwari, D., Tinkler, L., Harra, D., Morgan, B., Taylor, A., Lu, T., & Tiwari, A. (2019). Autonomous mobile robots in manufacturing: Highway code development, simulation, and testing. *The International Journal of Advanced Manufacturing Technology*, **104**(9), 4617–4628.

Lui, J., Narsalay, R., Afzal, R., Sharma, I. N., & Light, D. (2022). Research: How do warehouse workers feel about automation? *Harvard Business Review*. Retrieved from https://hbr.org/2022/02/research-how-do-warehouse-workers-feel-about-automation.

Magill, K. (2022). DHL supply chain deepens robotics partnership ahead of peak season. *Supply Chain Drive*. Retrieved from https://www.supplychaindive.com/news/dhl-locus-robotics-partnership-fulfillment-carhartt/632760/.

Mattaboni, P. J. (1987). U.S. Patent No. 4,638,445. U.S. Patent and Trademark Office, Washington, DC.

McNulty, D., Hennessy, A., Li, M., Armstrong, E., & Ryan, K. M. (2022). A review of Li-ion batteries for autonomous mobile robots: Perspectives and outlook for the future. *Journal of Power Sources*, **545**, 231943.

Mendoza, N. F. (2019). Many US rural areas still suffer slow internet speeds. Retrieved from https://www.techrepublic.com/article/many-us-rural-areas-still-suffer-slow-internet-speeds/#:~:text=Rural%20areas%20lag%2C%20 not%20only,speed%20is%20only%2039.01%20Mbps.

Morenza-Cinos, M., Casamayor-Pujol, V., & Pous, R. (2019). Stock visibility for retail using an RFID robot. *International Journal of Physical Distribution & Logistics Management*, **49**(10), 1020–1042.

Mosallaeipour, S., Nejad, M. G., Shavarani, S. M., & Nazerian, R. (2018). Mobile robot scheduling for cycle time optimization in flow-shop cells, a case study. *Production Engineering*, **12**(1), 83–94.

Oitzman, M. (2022a). IKEA deploys MiR robots to help clean up warehouse. *Mobile Robots Guide*. Retrieved from https://mobilerobotguide.com/2022/07/22/ ikea-deploys-mir-robots-to-help-clean-up-warehouse/.

Oitzman, M. (2022b). UPS doubles productivity with Locus robotics. *Mobile Robot Guide*. Retrieved from https://mobilerobotguide.com/2022/07/29/ ups-doubles-productivity-with-locus-robotics/.

Price, S. (2020). Nord modules releases Quick Mover 180 autonomous mobile robot. *Control Automation*. Retrieved from https://control.com/news/nord-modules-releases-the-quick-move-180/.

Report Linker (2022). Giving intelligence teams an AI-powered advantage. https:// www.reportlinker.com/.

Romaine, E. (2019). Cost factors & justification for autonomous mobile robots. Retrieved from https://www.conveyco.com/warehouse-robots-cost/ (accessed March 25, 2022).

Salvini, P., Paez-Granados, D., & Billard, A. (2022). A safety concerns emerging from robots navigating in crowded pedestrian areas. *International Journal of Social Robotics*, **14**, 441–462.

Santagate, J. (2020). 5 ways to improve warehouse operations with autonomous mobile robots. *ASCM Insights*. Retrieved from https://www.ascm.org/ascm-insights/5-ways-to-improve-warehouse-operations-with-autonomous-mobile-robots/#:~:text=Because%20autonomous%20mobile%20robots%20 are,to%20changes%20in%20real%20time.

Schlechtriem, M. (2021). 4 reasons why mobile robots are the solution to operational safety. *MEILI Robots*. Retrieved from https://www.meilirobots.com/ resources-list/operational-safety.

Sclogistics.com (2022). Autonomous mobile robots case study: Fulfillment. Retrieved form https://www.sclogistics.com/resource-center/case-studies/autonomous-mobile-robots-case-study-fulfillment/.

Sjödin, D. R., Parida, V., Leksell, M., & Petrovic, A. (2018). Smart factory implementation and process innovation. *Research-Technology Management*, **61**(5), 22–31.

Sonya, D. (2019). Ford completes 2.3-billion-euro investment in Spanish car plant. *Reuters.* Retrieved from https://www.reuters.com/article/us-ford-spain/ford-completes-2-3-billion-euro-investment-in-spanish-car-plant-idUSKBN-0L925B20150205.

Statista (2022). Size of the global market for autonomous mobile robots (AMR) from 2016 to 2021, with a forecast through 2028. *Statista.* Retrieved from Autonomous mobile robotics market size worldwide 2016–2028 | Statista.

Steinfeld, A., Fong, T., Kaber, D., Lewis, M., Scholtz, J., Schultz, A., & Goodrich, M. (2006). Common metrics for human-robot interaction. *Proceedings of 2006 ACM Conference on Human–Robot Interaction* (pp. 33–40). ACM, Salt Lake City, UT.

Stornelli, A., Sercan, O., & Simms, C. (2021). Advanced manufacturing technology adoption and innovation: A systematic literature review on barriers, enablers, and innovation types. *Research Policy,* **50**(6), 104229.

Teece, D. J., Pisano, G., & Shuen, A. (1997). Dynamic capabilities and strategic management. *Strategic Management Journal,* **18**(7), 509–533.

Tornatzky, L. G., Fleischer, M., & Chakrabarti, A. K. (1990). *Processes of Technological Innovation.* Lexington Books, Lexington, MA.

Transport Topics (2021). Top100 logistics. Retrieved from https://www.ttnews.com/logistics/companies/saddle/2022.

United States Census Bureau (2019). 2020 census will help policymakers prepare for the incoming wave of aging boomers.

Wang, K., Yang, Y., & Li, R. (2020). Travel time models for the rack-moving mobile robot system. *International Journal of Production Research,* **58**(14), 4367–4385.

Weinberg, N. (2019). Case study: Why Ford deployed AMRs to automate Spanish factory. *Robotic Business Review.* Retrieved from https://www.roboticsbusinessreview.com/case_studies/case-study-why-ford-deployed-amrs-to-automate-spanish-factory/.

Wessling, B. (2022a). Bergler automates picking operations with Geek+ AMRs. *Mobile Robot Guide.* Retrieved from https://mobilerobotguide.com/2022/07/15/bergler-automates-picking-operations-with-geek-amrs/.

Wessling, B. (2022b). GXO to implement 6 River Systems' Chuck globally. *The Robot Report.* Retrieved from https://www.therobotreport.com/gxo-to-implement-6-river-systems-chuck-globally/.

Wieciek, J. (2020). 5 lessons learnt in scaling autonomous mobile robots from 10 to 10K. *aiTechPark.* Retrieved from https://ai-techpark.com/5-lessons-learnt-in-scaling-autonomous-mobile-robots-from-10-to-10k/.

Winkelhaus, S., & Grosse, E. H. (2020). Logistics 4.0: A systematic review towards a new logistics system. *International Journal of Production Research,* **58**(1), 18–43.

Winkelhaus, S., Grosse, E. H., & Glock, C. H. (2021). Job satisfaction: An explorative study on work characteristics changes of employees in Intralogistics 4.0. *Journal of Business Logistics*, **43**(2), 343–367.

Winkler, H., & Zinsmeister, L. (2019). Trends in digitalization of intralogistics and the critical success factors of its implementation. *Brazilian Journal of Operations & Production Management*, **16**(3), 537–549.

Index

Printed in the United States
by Baker & Taylor Publisher Services